Forgiveness and Retribution
Responding to Wrongdoing

Forgiveness and Retribution: Responding to Wrongdoing argues that, ultimately, forgiveness is always the appropriate response to wrongdoing. In recent decades, many philosophers have claimed that unless certain conditions are met, we should resent those who have wronged us personally and that criminal offenders deserve to be punished. Conversely, Margaret R. Holmgren posits that we should forgive those who have ill-treated us, but in many cases, only after working through a process of addressing the wrong. Holmgren then reflects on the kinds of laws and social practices a properly forgiving society would adopt.

Margaret R. Holmgren is associate professor of philosophy at Iowa State University. She co-edited *Ethical Theory: A Concise Anthology* (2000) with Heimir Giersson.

"Margaret Holmgren's book is a daring attempt to defend a new paradigm of forgiveness that would radically reorient our attitudes toward those who wrong us and our way of thinking about punishment and criminal law. No doubt the discussion it provokes will be intense."
　　　　　– George W. Harris, author of *Reason's Grief: An Essay on Tragedy and Value*

"Moral, political, and legal philosophers who prize theoretical unity and comprehensiveness will appreciate Margaret Holmgren's new book, which begins with a foundational virtue ethic and from it systematically derives conclusions about how individuals and institutions should respond to wrongdoers. Holmgren's work is probably the most thoughtful and thorough defense of an unconditional forgiveness approach to wrongdoers, one that critically responds to work by contemporary retributivists and that should give them pause. Of particular interest is the fact that Holmgren argues that principles such as respect for offenders and for victims, to which retributivists standardly appeal, are best interpreted in ways that support anti-retributivist conclusions, such as the restitutional approach to punishment for which Holmgren is rightly well-known."
　　　　　– Thaddeus Metz, Humanities Research Professor, University of Johannesburg

"Margaret Holmgren has written a very stimulating book on forgiveness... An additional virtue of her book is a discussion of forgiveness in the context of criminal punishment – a discussion in which she makes creative suggestions concerning the social and legal institutions that a truly forgiving society would adopt. I recommend that all those interested in a serious discussion of forgiveness read this book and ponder its many insights."
　　　　　– Jeffrie G. Murphy, Arizona State University, author of the book *Getting Even: Forgiveness and Its Limits*

Forgiveness and Retribution

Responding to Wrongdoing

MARGARET R. HOLMGREN

Iowa State University

CAMBRIDGE
UNIVERSITY PRESS

CAMBRIDGE UNIVERSITY PRESS
Cambridge, New York, Melbourne, Madrid, Cape Town,
Singapore, São Paulo, Delhi, Mexico City

Cambridge University Press
32 Avenue of the Americas, New York, NY 10013-2473, USA

www.cambridge.org
Information on this title: www.cambridge.org/9781107017962

First published 2012

Printed in the United States of America

A catalog record for this publication is available from the British Library.

Library of Congress Cataloging in Publication data
Holmgren, Margaret R. (Margaret Reed), 1951–
Forgiveness and retribution : responding to wrongdoing / Margaret R. Holmgren.
p. cm.
Includes bibliographical references and index.
ISBN 978-1-107-01796-2 (hardback)
1. Forgiveness. 2. Conduct of life. 3. Retribution. 4. Criminal
justice, Administration of. I. Title.
BJ1476.H65 2012
155.9′2–dc23 2011032288

ISBN 978-1-107-01796-2 Hardback

For my sister, Janet W. Holmgren
In memory of my mother, Jean Dunn Robb, and of Campbell

Contents

Preface

Human history is full of turning points. Although we may prefer not to think about it, the one we face now is arguably the most momentous of all that have occurred up to this point in time. If we do not learn to work together as a global community within the next decade or two, we may well cause irreparable damage to the planet that results in seriously diminished life prospects for all who inhabit it in the future. In fact, irreversible damage is already occurring, and our goal now must be to minimize it.

I believe that if we are to rise to the occasion and meet the critical challenge that our generation has been handed, each of us must establish within ourselves a predominant attitude of real goodwill toward all beings. This task is different from attempting to work out policies that maximize preference-satisfaction globally, or from attempting to articulate a hierarchy of universal human rights. Both of these latter aims are important, but not as important as learning to care on a deep and abiding level about every being there is.[1] If we could learn to do this one thing, I think our policies would fall into place and we would be able to do what we need to do to create a good future for all. This book on forgiveness is my small contribution toward this vision that I pray we will all have the wisdom to adopt.

This book, then, is intended for anyone who has a serious interest in forgiveness. Although it addresses the philosophical literature on forgiveness, I have tried to make it accessible to those in other disciplines

---

[1] The term "care," as I use it here, should be understood to entail respect. The concept of respect will be discussed in Chapter 2.

and also to a lay audience. A lay friend very generously offered to read the entire manuscript for me, and she reported that she was able to follow the reasoning throughout, with interest. I hope that other readers who are not professional philosophers will have the same experience.

I have one important caveat to issue about this book. It seems to me that true moral growth is not simply a matter of constructing a moral theory that performs better than its competitors in achieving reflective equilibrium, and then using will power to adhere to the results. Although it is well motivated, this "white-knuckle virtue," as I call it, does not reflect a true change in our attitudes. Instead, it amounts to a suppression of the attitudes we actually hold. A more meaningful kind of moral growth comes with a deep change in attitudes – a change in what we see as most salient in the various situations we encounter in our lives, in how we feel about these situations, and in how we are motivated to behave. Changes of this sort generally do not occur overnight. Instead, they require a good deal of contemplation over time and, among other things, an honest exploration of the various nuances of our current feelings and attitudes.

When we realize that we have been seriously wronged by others or have seriously wronged them, we are likely to go through an initial period of pain and confusion in which our thoughts and feelings are not what we would ideally like them to be. Although this book will provide a strong defense of unconditional genuine forgiveness, I ask the reader to bear in mind that this state is generally achieved through the type of process just described. It is therefore important that we not condemn ourselves or others for experiencing negative emotions as we respond to wrongdoing.[2] To do so is not only unfair, it is also counterproductive in that it is likely to obstruct the path to lasting moral transformation.

Finally, Sharon Lamb has suggested that persons who write about forgiveness are often deeply influenced by their religious beliefs, and that some authors may be engaged in the task of promoting them.[3] It would therefore be helpful for those of us who write on forgiveness to be explicit about these matters at the outset. I was raised as an Episcopalian, although I never developed a high level of religious devotion in my early years. From the age of fifteen until the fall of 1999, I had no religious affiliation. In the fall of 1999 I was exposed to Tibetan Buddhism, and

---

[2] It goes without saying that engaging in negative behavior is another matter. Here, clearly, suppression is a good thing.

[3] Sharon Lamb, *Before Forgiving*, p. 10.

I have been practicing and studying in this tradition since that time. While Tibetan Buddhism has deeply influenced my belief system in the past decade, my thinking about response to wrongdoing has remained quite consistent over the past twenty-five years. I believe that part of my attraction to Tibetan Buddhism is its harmony with the deepest values I have held over time. In any case, it is not my intention here to advocate for Tibetan Buddhism. To do so would be antithetical not only to the spirit of philosophical inquiry but also to the spirit of Tibetan Buddhism itself, which eschews proselytizing and supports individuals in pursuing whatever path of moral or spiritual growth is most productive for them. Tibetan Buddhism also harmonizes nicely with Western philosophy in that it invites individuals to subject every idea to rigorous critical scrutiny.

My work on forgiveness began with a conversation over dinner with Joseph Kupfer and Lu Klatt, and they have each offered me important insights from the disciplines of philosophy and psychology, respectively. From a broader standpoint, I owe a great debt of gratitude to the late Edmund L. Pincoffs. He and I talked extensively about punishment, desert, and virtue-oriented approaches to ethics. Robert Enright contacted me after the publication of my first article on forgiveness. Although we had been working in different disciplines, we found that we had arrived independently at remarkably similar views of forgiveness. I have profited from discussions with him, as well as from discussions on this topic with Jeffrie Murphy. In my judgment, Jeffrie Murphy has done more to stimulate the philosophical discussion of forgiveness than any other author. The spirited interdisciplinary discussion of forgiveness that has emerged in the two-and-a-half decades following the publication of Murphy and Hampton's *Forgiveness and Mercy* has been very fruitful.

Special thanks go to my friend Kay Knifer of Lyons, Colorado, who read the entire manuscript from a lay perspective and offered me much-needed support and encouragement. I also owe a large debt of gratitude to many other individuals who have helped me to refine my thinking and complete this work. Specifically, I would like to acknowledge Kevin deLaplante, Carla Fehr, George Harris, Ned Hettinger, Janet Krengel, Sharon Lamb, Thomas Magnell, Kate Padgett Walsh, Bill Robinson, Tony Smith, and Christianna White. In the spring of 1998, Iowa State University provided me with a faculty development leave that was beneficial in the very early stages of my research. I also owe a great deal to Robert Dreesen, my editor at Cambridge University Press, to three anonymous readers for Cambridge who read carefully through the manuscript and made many valuable suggestions, and to the Cambridge editorial staff (especially Abigail Zorbaugh). Special thanks go as well to my manuscript editor, Ronald Cohen, who played a significant role in shaping the text, which I consider very much improved as a result of his work, and who patiently coached me through the process of creating the index. Finally, I would like to acknowledge my mother, the late Jean Dunn Robb, and my sister, Janet Warner Holmgren, for the tremendous support they have given me throughout this project.

Portions of the material in this book have been published previously. I would like to thank the publishers for kindly granting me permission to use their materials.

An earlier version of much of Chapter 3 was published as "Forgiveness and the Intrinsic Value of Persons," in *American Philosophical Quarterly* 30/4 (October 1993): 341–352. Reprinted with permission.

An earlier version of much of Chapter 4 was published as "Self-Forgiveness and Responsible Moral Agency," in *The Journal of Value Inquiry* 32 (1998): 75–91. Copyright Kluwer Academic Publishers. Reprinted with kind permission of Springer Science + Business Media B.V.

Portions of Chapters 3 and 4 were published in "Forgiveness and Self-Forgiveness in Psychotherapy," in *Before Forgiving: Cautionary Views of Forgiveness in Psychotherapy,* edited by Sharon Lamb and Jeffrie G. Murphy (New York: Oxford University Press, 2002): 112–135. By permission of Oxford University Press, Inc.

A small portion of Chapter 4 was published as a portion of "Strength of Character," in *The Journal of Value Inquiry* 38 (2004): 393–409. Copyright Kluwer Academic Pulishers. Reprinted with kind permission of Springer Science + Business Media B.V.

An early version of part of Chapter 7 was published as "Punishment as Restitution: The Rights of the Community," in *Criminal Justice Ethics* 2/1 (Winter/Spring 1983): 36–49 (Copyright 1983, The Institute for Criminal Justice Ethics). Material reprinted by permission of the publisher (Taylor & Francis Ltd., http:www.tandf.co.uk/journals) and the Institute for Criminal Justice Ethics, John Jay College of Criminal Justice, 444 West 56th Street, New York, NY 10019.

I

Introduction and Overview

My purpose in this book is to develop and defend a broadly coherent position on response to wrongdoing. The response I wish to defend is the response of forgiveness, or more specifically, unconditional genuine forgiveness – a concept I define in some detail in the next two chapters.

My approach to the question of how we ought to respond to wrong-doing diverges from the traditional approach to this question. For a long time, philosophers addressing this topic have focused primarily on crime and punishment. Their central concern has been to articulate the legal practices we ought to adopt to respond to serious wrongdoing. Much has been written about whether the state is justified in punishing criminal offenders, and if so, on what grounds, how severely, and under what circumstances.

Very recently, the discussion of response to wrongdoing has turned to what P.F. Strawson calls the "reactive attitudes" of forgiveness and resentment.[1] I believe that this new focus is potentially very fruitful. I also believe that an examination of basic attitudes is the best place to start if we wish to formulate a broadly coherent position on response to wrongdoing, for two primary reasons. First, as an immediate practical matter, we are each faced with concerns about forgiveness and resentment in our personal lives. Human wrongdoing is ubiquitous, and sooner or later each of us struggles to adjust to the fact that someone has wronged us or that we have wronged someone else. Further, the way in which we respond to wrongdoing has a significant effect on the quality of our lives. From the personal level to the international level, the quality

[1] P.F. Strawson, "Freedom and Resentment."

1

of our relationships with one another is at least partially defined by our attitudes toward forgiveness. And our attitudes toward self-forgiveness play a significant role in forming our conceptions of ourselves, and consequently in determining our ability to function well in various aspects of our lives. It is therefore important to each of us to be as clear as possible about the moral status of the attitudes of forgiveness and resentment and their self-referential counterparts. Any position on response to wrongdoing that fails to address these attitudes is seriously incomplete.

Second, from a more theoretical point of view, I think the basic attitudes of forgiveness and resentment are much more central than we have recognized to a more comprehensive account of response to wrongdoing, as I will argue here. In the past four decades, the predominant methodological approach in practical ethics has been to address social issues using some version of wide reflective equilibrium. On this approach, we construct moral theories that perform well in explaining our considered moral judgments and that cohere well with relevant background theories. We then apply these theories to moral issues, hoping they will give us approximately the results we want. Finally, we work back and forth, making adjustments in our beliefs at various levels in an attempt to develop an overall package of beliefs that is more or less coherent. (I will say more about this methodology at the end of this chapter.) While this approach is good as far as it goes, it seems that in applying it we have missed a deeper and more fundamental level of moral thought. In his classic article, "The Schizophrenia of Modern Ethical Theories," Michael Stocker points out that "one mark of a good life is harmony between one's motives and one's reasons, values, justifications. Not to be moved by what one values – what one believes good, nice, right, beautiful, and so on – bespeaks a malady of the spirit. Not to value what moves one also bespeaks a malady of the spirit."[2] Stocker goes on to argue that the reasons for action articulated in our most prominent moral theories (respecting rights, maximizing utility, being able to will the maxims of our actions as universal law, etc.) fail to coincide with appropriate motives for action.

I believe that we will be able to avoid the kind of malady of the spirit that Stocker identifies, and construct more compelling and holistic moral theories if we begin by examining our basic attitudes and the motivations they incorporate. If we carefully examine our motives and attitudes to ensure that they are worthy, then every other aspect of our

---

[2] Michael Stocker, "The Schizophrenia of Modern Ethical Theories," p. 453.

moral lives should fall into place – the actions we take as individuals, the moral theories we construct, and the social practices we institute. His Holiness the Fourteenth Dalai Lama makes this point in *Ethics for a New Millennium*. He says, "In Tibetan, the term for what is considered to be of the greatest significance in determining the ethical value of a given action is the individual's *kun long*... When this is wholesome, it follows that our actions themselves will be wholesome."[3] He tells us that the Tibetan term *kun long* is generally translated as "motivation," but this translation does not capture its full meaning. A more complete translation would be "overall state of heart and mind." It includes cognitive awareness, affective response, and motivation, all of which are inseparable components of the same psychological state. For convenience, I will refer to this state as an attitude (a more detailed discussion of attitudes will be found at the beginning of Chapter 2).

This book begins, then, with an examination of the basic attitudes of forgiveness and resentment, and proceeds from this examination to questions about moral theory and social practices. I argue that the attitudes of unconditional genuine forgiveness and genuine self-forgiveness incorporate the attitudes of respect, compassion, and real goodwill for persons. Further, I argue that the attitudes of unconditional genuine forgiveness and genuine self-forgiveness are always appropriate and desirable from a moral point of view in response to wrongdoing. I then argue that if we extend the basic attitudes of respect, compassion, and real goodwill to all persons equally, we will be led to adopt a justice-based moral theory that enjoins us to secure for each person the most fundamental interests in life compatible with like benefits for all. Finally, I argue that from these basic moral attitudes and the moral theory that emerges from them, we will be led to endorse a specific set of social practices as a public response to wrongdoing. My hope is that by proceeding in this manner, we will be able to generate a broadly coherent account of response to wrongdoing that is both philosophically rigorous and holistically compelling. An account of this sort should bring our motives and reasons for action into harmony with one another, and allow us to function as whole and healthy moral agents.

By structuring my account of response to wrongdoing in this way, I am aligning myself directly with virtue ethicists. If my extended argument is successful, it should help to counter a long-standing objection to virtue ethics: that virtue ethics may tell us who we should be, but it

[3] His Holiness the Fourteenth Dalai Lama, *Ethics for a New Millenium*, p. 30.

fails to give us sufficient guidance as to what we should do. The defense of the attitude of unconditional genuine forgiveness that follows has a multitude of specific implications for our actions and social practices, as we shall see.

More specifically, this book constitutes an extended development and defense of what I will call the "paradigm of forgiveness." There are two senses of the word "paradigm" that should be distinguished at this point. First, we may use the word to refer to a particularly clear, typical, or unproblematic example of whatever it is that we want to address. This is not the sense of paradigm that I am using in this book. The second sense of paradigm, which is what I intend here, is, broadly speaking, a philosophical or theoretical framework. My goal is to develop a relatively comprehensive theoretical framework in reference to which we can think about response to wrongdoing.

To elaborate further, our initial examination of the attitudes of forgiveness and self-forgiveness will reveal that these attitudes express a particular moral orientation toward persons. In the context of this orientation, certain features of persons are regarded as salient – our capacity to experience happiness and misery; our basic desire for happiness; our capacity for moral choice, growth, and awareness; our status as autonomous beings who can lead meaningful lives only as the authors of our own choices and attitudes; and our status as limited beings who are vulnerable to error. Further, certain responses to these salient features of persons are regarded as morally appropriate. These responses are, broadly speaking, respect, compassion, and real goodwill.[4] Clearly this moral orientation toward persons rests on a set of philosophical presuppositions about the nature of persons, which I attempt to make explicit. I argue that if we endorse the basic attitudes of forgiveness and self-forgiveness, the moral orientation toward persons that they express, and the philosophical presuppositions about the nature of persons on which they rest, then, as noted, we will be led to adopt a justice-based moral theory and a particular set of social and legal practices as a public response to wrongdoing. I refer to the unified position that emerges from this examination as the paradigm of forgiveness and I defend it on moral and philosophical grounds. (It is important to note, however, that my development of the paradigm of forgiveness in this book is not complete. In particular, the completion of this project would require a

---

[4] The general account of virtue that I draw on here is John McDowell's, developed in his "Virtue and Reason."

well-developed position on both self- and other-defense, which I do not undertake here.[5])

At the same time, I am centrally concerned in this book to compare the paradigm of forgiveness with retributivist positions on response to wrongdoing. There have been a number of different attempts to defend retributive reactive attitudes and retributive theories of punishment, so we lack a single, unified paradigm of retribution. Nevertheless, retributivists systematically endorse a set of conclusions that are opposed to those that emerge in the paradigm of forgiveness. Those who defend retributive reactive attitudes (whom I will refer to as "attitudinal retributivists") hold that enduring attitudes of resentment and self-condemnation are morally appropriate under certain circumstances, while the paradigm of forgiveness endorses attitudes of forgiveness and self-forgiveness in these circumstances instead. And those who endorse retributive theories of punishment argue that punishment is an intrinsically appropriate response to crime, whereas the paradigm of forgiveness holds that punishment can be justified only if it provides fundamental benefits for all citizens.

To arrive at their conclusions, retributivists generally start from three very plausible moral claims – claims that are also endorsed in the paradigm of forgiveness. These claims are that we must respect the offender as a moral agent, that we must respect the requirements of morality, and that we must respect the victims of wrongdoing. In spite of the agreement on these basic moral tenets, however, retributivist analyses of response to wrongdoing differ from the analysis that emerges in the paradigm of forgiveness in important ways. In addition to the divergent conclusions cited earlier, retributive positions often differ from the paradigm of forgiveness in that they express a different moral orientation toward persons, rest on different philosophical presuppositions about the nature of persons, lead to moral theories with a fundamentally different structure, and result in different implications for our social and legal practices. Throughout the book, I explicate these differences, and in each case I argue that in spite of the plausibility of some of their central moral tenets, retributivist analyses are seriously problematic on both moral and philosophical grounds.

Retributivism has been enjoying a resurgence of popularity recently, and for good reason. The defects of the utilitarian approach to responding

---

[5] I thank an anonymous reader from Cambridge University Press for drawing this important point to my attention.

to wrongdoing have by now been well explored in the literature. Initially, when the discussion of wrongdoing centered primarily on crime and punishment, critics of the utilitarian position focused on the troubling possibility that it might sanction punishment of the innocent, severe punishment for lesser crimes, and the abolition of some well-established excuses in the criminal law. Some authors attempted to correct for these problems either by adopting rule utilitarianism or by introducing principles of fairness to govern the distribution of punishment.[6] Rules or principles designed to guarantee the fairness of punishment were thought to be the only aspect of retributivism worth preserving.

However, in R.A. Duff's words, "a striking feature of penal theorizing during the last three decades of the twentieth century was a revival of positive retributivism – of the idea that the positive justification of punishment is to be found in its intrinsic character as a deserved response to crime."[7] I think this phenomenon can be attributed to two objections to the utilitarian position that go beyond the concerns about unfair punishment. The first is the simple fact that utilitarianism does not seem to account for our deep-seated moral intuitions about response to wrongdoing. As Andrew Oldenquist has observed, "The universal insistence upon retribution for grievous crimes is deeply felt, intractable, and largely independent of utilitarian considerations."[8] Several authors have made the same point about retributive reactive attitudes – for example, Jeffrie Murphy, Peter French, and Robert Solomon.[9] Both retributive reactive attitudes and retributive intuitions about punishment seem to be deeply engrained in the human psyche. Any adequate account of response to wrongdoing must either endorse these intuitions or offer a persuasive explanation of why they are mistaken.

Second, philosophers have argued that the utilitarian analysis of response to wrongdoing is problematic in that it fails to respect offenders as autonomous moral agents. Strawson's distinction between reactive participant attitudes and what he calls the "objective" attitude sheds light on this problem. Strawson's reactive attitudes – resentment, forgiveness,

---

[6] For the former strategy, see, for example, John Rawls, "Two Concepts of Rules," or Richard Brandt, *Ethical Theory*. For the latter, see H.L.A. Hart, *Punishment and Responsibility*.

[7] R.A. Duff, "Legal Punishment," p. 10.

[8] Andrew Oldenquist, "An Explanation of Retribution, p. 464.

[9] See Jeffrie G. Murphy, *Getting Even*; Peter A. French, *The Virtues of Vengeance*; Susan Jacoby, *Wild Justice: The Evolution of Revenge*; and Robert Solomon, "Justice v. Vengeance – On Law and the Satisfaction of Emotion."

love, gratitude, and so on – are the attitudes we hold toward one another in the context of engaged interpersonal relationships. We hold these attitudes toward those with whom we hope to relate as equals, with a status comparable to our own, and regarding whom we therefore have certain hopes and expectations. In contrast, Strawson defines the objective attitude as follows: "To adopt the objective attitude toward another human being is to see him, perhaps, as an object of social policy; as a subject for what, in a wide range of senses, might be called treatment; as something certainly to be taken account of, perhaps precautionary account, of; to be managed or handled or cured or trained; perhaps simply to be avoided."[10] The utilitarian analysis of response to wrongdoing seems to embody the objective attitude that Strawson describes. Offenders seem to be in some sense "objectified" as we try to manage their attitudes, beliefs, and behaviors in the attempt to maximize good consequences. They do not seem to be addressed in a straightforward manner as persons who are our equals, or as autonomous moral agents.

In contrast, retributive reactive attitudes seem to be rooted directly in respect for persons as autonomous moral agents. Retributive reactive attitudes are clearly inappropriate toward beings that lack the capacity for moral agency. My golden retriever, Campbell, repeatedly digs holes in the backyard as she hunts for small animals. Although this activity damages the lawn and creates extra work for me, I do not resent her for it. I do not judge her to be selfish, arrogant, bad, or evil. Nor do I withhold my goodwill from her until she repents and does her best to fill in the holes. Instead, I try to think of ways to manage her behavior. In short, I adopt Strawson's objective attitude toward her, and here the objective attitude seems appropriate. On the other hand, if one of my colleagues were to engage in the same behavior, I would fail to respect him as an autonomous moral agent if I tried to manage his behavior by pepper spray or by taking him to obedience school.

It is important to recognize that I do not adopt an objective attitude toward Campbell because I cannot have a relationship with her. In fact we have a wonderful relationship characterized by a variety of other reactive attitudes (love, affection, gratitude, etc.). Unlike some of our other reactive attitudes, however, retributive reactive attitudes require the possibility of relationship between *moral agents*. It seems, then, that to hold an attitude of resentment toward an individual who has engaged in wrongdoing is to acknowledge that individual as an autonomous

---

[10] Strawson, "Freedom and Resentment," p. 9.

moral agent who is capable of full participation in the moral community. Conversely, to adopt an objective attitude toward a moral agent is to fail to regard the individual in this manner. Thus, retributivism seems to incorporate a ground-level respect for the offender's autonomy and capacity for moral agency.

For retributivists, however, the capacity for moral agency is a double-edged sword in that it carries with it both rights and responsibilities. On the one hand, our capacity for moral agency imposes obligations on others to respect our autonomy, to regard us as equals, and to refrain from managing or manipulating us for their own ends. On the other hand, our capacity for moral agency also renders us subject to the requirements of morality and makes us accountable for the extent to which we abide by them. As moral agents, we are responsible for recognizing the overriding importance of moral requirements and for recognizing the value of the beings or objects that these requirements protect. At this point we can see that in addition to embodying a ground-level respect for persons as moral agents, retributive reactive attitudes seem to embody a fundamental respect for both the requirements of morality and the victims of immoral behavior.

These three forms of respect are closely entwined in our retributive reactive attitudes. When an individual violates a moral requirement and harms someone as a result, we tend to respond with resentment or moral anger. In part, this anger reflects the extent to which we care about the person harmed. For example, if we respond with pleasure, indifference, or amusement when someone is murdered, we clearly lack sufficient concern and respect for that person. But moral anger reflects more than our concern and respect for the person harmed. If one of our loved ones is killed in a tornado, we would feel profound grief rather than moral anger. Resentment and moral anger respond not only to the value of the one who has been harmed, but at the same time to the fact that the harm was inflicted wrongfully by a moral agent who could have and should have done otherwise. Again, if we were to respond to a moral offense with indifference or amusement, our response would show that we do not take the requirements of morality seriously and that we do not take the offender seriously as a moral agent. Retributivism, then, seems to embody these three fundamental forms of respect in a very coherent, direct, and plausible manner. In doing so, it seems to avoid the central problems that arise in utilitarian analyses of response to wrongdoing and also to be strongly grounded in our best deontological moral theories.

As plausible as this position may seem, I believe that it is seriously mistaken. Here I take it as a given that any plausible position on response to wrongdoing will embody the three forms of respect just described: respect for the offender as a moral agent, respect for the requirements of morality, and respect for the victims of immoral behavior. Nevertheless, while granting the validity of these central moral tenets, I argue that the paradigm of forgiveness actually expresses these three forms of respect much more fully and adequately than retributive positions. Further, although retributivists succeed in avoiding Strawson's version of the objective attitude, they commit another more subtle form of objectification of persons that makes their positions very difficult to defend on both moral and philosophical grounds. The paradigm of forgiveness, on the other hand, avoids both Strawson's objective attitude and this latter form of objectification, and as a result is more philosophically and morally defensible.

Briefly, my argument progresses through the chapters as follows. Chapter 2 creates the framework for the discussion in the remainder of the book. I first present an analysis of attitudes in general, and suggest that they are the central elements of character traits. Attitudes are described as having three components: a cognitive component, an affective component, and a motivational component. I go on to identify three types of attitudes: integrated, conflicted, and fragmented. I argue that a virtue is a morally worthy integrated attitude that has been sufficiently ingrained to constitute a fairly regular response to a given type of recurring situation. Therefore, in the context of the virtue-ethical analysis of response to wrongdoing that I will develop here, the central task is to determine which of the attitudes that we might adopt in response to wrongdoing is the most appropriate and desirable from a moral point of view. To aid us in this task, I introduce the concept of a genuine attitude, which will be important in both Chapters 3 and 4.[11]

I then provide a conceptual analysis of the attitude of resentment by articulating the three components it incorporates. In the same manner, I provide an analysis of forgiveness, which may be construed as a corrective attitude that replaces an initial attitude of resentment that we have found to be unworthy. Finally, in order to avoid confusion in the discussion that follows, I address several of the controversies in recent literature about the nature of forgiveness, including the especially contentious

---

[11] I am especially grateful to an anonymous reader from Cambridge University Press for pointing out the need to clarify this concept early in the manuscript.

questions of who can forgive, whether there are restrictions on the motive for forgiving, whether forgiveness is best construed as an internal change of heart or as a speech act, and whether groups can forgive or be forgiven.

Geoffrey Scarre has argued that we have good reason to approach the moral analysis of forgiveness from a utilitarian perspective rather than from the perspectives of duty or virtue.[12] Chapter 3 begins with a critical analysis of this claim, in which I suggest instead that we have good reason to set aside the perspectives of duty and utility and to adopt the perspective of virtue. I respond here to some central objections that Scarre and others raise to a virtue-ethical approach to the analysis of forgiveness.

From a virtue-ethical perspective, forgiving is a process that may take some work. Premature forgiveness may well be incompatible with the victim's self-respect, and therefore morally inappropriate. It may also amount to condoning the wrong, deceiving oneself, or evading difficult tasks, rather than truly forgiving the offender. I outline the process that victims of wrongdoing must often complete in order to respect themselves and reach a state of genuine forgiveness. Both retributivists and advocates of the paradigm of forgiveness can endorse this process. Further, both types of theorists can agree that the victim of wrongdoing who has not sufficiently completed the process of addressing the wrong may legitimately hold an attitude of resentment toward the offender.

Retributivists and advocates of the paradigm of forgiveness will part company, however, on the question of whether someone who has completed this process (or who has no need to do so) should forgive the offender or continue to resent him. In developing the paradigm of forgiveness, I argue that an attitude of unconditional genuine forgiveness is always appropriate and desirable from a moral point of view, regardless of whether the offender repents and regardless of what he has done or suffered. On the other hand, retributivists argue that forgiveness is morally *inappropriate* under certain circumstances. Most commonly, they hold that an attitude of resentment is called for when the offender fails to repent or when he has done something especially heinous.

In order to defend my claim that an attitude of unconditional genuine forgiveness is always appropriate and desirable from a moral point of view, I argue that this attitude fully incorporates the attitudes of self-respect, respect for morality, and respect for the offender as a moral

[12] Geoffrey Scarre, *After Evil*, Chapter 3.

agent. Further, I argue that an attitude of resentment, when it is adopted by a person who has completed the process of addressing the wrong, fails to do so. Here I respond to a number of authors who have argued to the contrary, including critics of my earlier statement of this position (for example, Murphy, Hieronymi, Griswold, Scarre, and Allais). Further, I offer a critique of alternative defenses of forgiveness proposed by Garrard and McNaughten, Benjabit and Heyd, and Allais.

I am particularly concerned in this chapter to articulate the way in which attitudinal retributivism commits a second form of objectification of persons as they attempt to avoid Strawson's objective attitude. Specifically, retributivists conflate the offender in various ways with his actions and attitudes, and as a result, adopt a perspective of judgment toward the conglomerate of the offender and his wrongful actions and attitudes. They thereby fail to respect the offender both as a sentient being and as a moral agent who retains his basic moral capacities in spite of his wrongdoing. In this chapter I articulate some of the *moral* problems involved in this kind of error, and suggest that by avoiding this error, we can liberate the deontological analysis of response to wrongdoing from the self-righteousness, judgment, and drama that often emerge in retributive analyses. In Chapter 5 I examine some of the *philosophical* problems that retributivists encounter by objectifying offenders in this manner.

Chapter 4 takes up the moral analysis of self-condemnation and self-forgiveness. (This chapter is important in laying the groundwork for the critique of prominent communicative and expressive theories of punishment addressed in Chapter 7.) I begin with a brief conceptual analysis of the attitudes of self-condemnation and self-forgiveness, again delineating the cognitive, affective, and motivational components of each attitude. I then describe the process of addressing the wrong that all persons who are guilty of moral wrongdoing must undertake. Self-forgiveness is not morally appropriate before this process is sufficiently complete, in that it will be incompatible with respect for the victim of wrongdoing, respect for the requirements of morality, and respect for oneself as a moral agent. Further, if we attempt to forgive ourselves before this process is complete, our self-forgiveness will be defective in that it will amount to self-deception, evasion of the tasks involved in addressing the wrong, or condoning the wrong rather than truly forgiving ourselves for having committed it.

I then argue that for the person who has sufficiently completed the process of addressing the wrong, self-forgiveness is always appropriate and desirable from a moral point of view, regardless of what he has done, regardless of whether he has been able to make adequate amends for the wrong, and regardless of whether the victim is willing or able to forgive him. Attitudinal retributivists argue that self-forgiveness is appropriate only under certain circumstances, and that an attitude of self-condemnation is otherwise required. Again, I defend the attitude of genuine self-forgiveness by arguing that it is fully compatible with, and in fact required by, respect for the victim, respect for the requirements of morality, and respect for oneself as a moral agent. Further, an attitude of self-condemnation is ultimately incompatible with these three forms of respect. As before, I am particularly concerned to establish in Chapter 4 that after the process of addressing the wrong is sufficiently complete, an attitude of self-condemnation involves a morally problematic objectification of oneself.

In Chapter 5 I complete the defense of the basic attitudes that ground the paradigm of forgiveness by examining the philosophical underpinnings of the attitudes of forgiveness and resentment. Three topics are addressed: the equality of human worth and moral status, personal identity, and moral responsibility. In defending the attitudes of forgiveness and self-forgiveness in Chapters 3 and 4, I simply assume that all persons have equal intrinsic worth and moral status. However, a growing number of retributivists reject this position and endorse instead the claim that human worth is based on moral merit. Here I defend my egalitarian position against a classic meritarian argument to the contrary: that there is strong empirical evidence to show that persons vary significantly with regard to all qualities that could reasonably be considered morally significant. I argue that, like the retributive positions I have been considering, this argument is constructed from the perspective of judgment, in which we conflate persons with their actions, attitudes, and characteristics, and then sit in judgment of the conglomerate. Drawing on the work of Bernard Williams, I argue that the features of persons that are regarded as salient in the context of the paradigm of forgiveness lead us to a perspective of identification rather than to a perspective of judgment. A perspective of identification based on these salient features of persons supports an egalitarian position on human worth and moral status. In this section I also address the claim that the actuality of a goodwill, rather than the mere capacity for a goodwill, should ground recognition respect for persons, and I refute the objections to an egalitarian position on response to wrongdoing developed by John Kekes in *Facing Evil*.

It is important for any substantive moral position to be compatible with a plausible analysis of personal identity. Drawing on the work of Derek Parfit and Christine Korsgaard, I argue that my defense of the attitudes of forgiveness and self-forgiveness is fully compatible with a reductionist analysis of the self. George Sher has argued that claims of desert, on which many attitudinal retributivists rely, presuppose a conception of thickly constituted selves whose identity is at least partially constituted by their abilities and preferences. Sher also asserts that such a conception is compatible with a plausible reductionist analysis of the self. Because my defense of unconditional genuine forgiveness requires that we separate the offender from his preferences (or more specifically, from his past and current actions and attitudes), I examine Sher's argument in some depth. I argue that if we adopt a conception of thickly constituted selves whose identity is partially constituted by our preferences, we will not be able to provide a coherent account of moral choice, moral deliberation, moral agency, or moral responsibility. Therefore the type of analysis of the self that Sher proposes must be rejected by retributivists, and it remains unclear whether retributivists can defend their position in a manner that is compatible with a plausible position on personal identity.

In this book I do not directly address the debate on freedom, determinism, and moral responsibility. However, I do address a common objection to the paradigm of forgiveness: that it fails to incorporate a robust notion of personal responsibility. Retributivism is often thought to hold moral agents more fully responsible for their transgressions than a position that endorses an attitude of unconditional genuine forgiveness. I argue, to the contrary, that the paradigm of forgiveness does in fact incorporate a robust conception of personal responsibility. Further, I identify two special difficulties that retributivists will encounter in this regard – difficulties that go beyond the general challenges that have been raised in the debate on freedom, determinism, and moral responsibility. First, drawing on my discussion of Sher's work, I construct a dilemma for the retributivist. The retributivist must either assert or deny that the offender is in some way constituted by his preferences, actions, or attitudes. If she takes the first horn of the dilemma, then, as I have argued, she will be left without a coherent account of moral choice, moral deliberation, moral agency, and moral responsibility. If she takes the second horn of the dilemma, I argue that her position on response to wrongdoing will be very difficult to defend on moral grounds. Second, as Erin

Kelly has pointed out, retributivist positions that rely on desert claims require a highly developed account of the extent of the responsibility that we bear for each of our misdeeds, and it is not clear that we are generally epistemically situated in such a way as to be able to make reliable judgments of this sort.[13]

I then turn to the task of developing a response to wrongdoing in the public domain. Given the paradigm of forgiveness as I have developed it so far, what would a properly forgiving society look like?[14] In Chapter 6, I explain the connection between basic moral attitudes and moral theories that can be used to justify laws, social policies, and social institutions. Specifically, I argue that the basic moral attitudes of respect, compassion, and real goodwill that are incorporated in an attitude of forgiveness, when extended to all persons equally, lead to at least the broad outlines of a moral theory structured in terms of a central principle of justice: that all persons ought to be secured the most fundamental interests in life compatible with like interests for all, and that no individual ought to be required to sacrifice an important interest so that others can benefit in less important ways. It is important to recognize that the kind of moral theory that emerges in the paradigm of forgiveness does not constitute a departure from the virtue-ethical approach to response to wrongdoing developed in this book, and I explain why this is the case.

Retributivists generally believe that the appropriate public response to wrongdoing is legal punishment. Whether or not they believe that a desert-based moral theory emerges from retributive reactive attitudes, many retributivists believe that the moral justification for a practice of legal punishment rests, at least in part, on the claim that the offender *deserves* the punishment in view of the nature of his offense. For these retributivists, then, desert is a fundamental moral concept, and an adequate moral theory will be structured, at least in part, in terms of desert. Advocates of the paradigm of forgiveness and these retributivists will therefore be centrally divided on the question of whether we ought to adopt a justice-based moral theory or a desert-based moral theory.

I argue here that desert-based moral theories will encounter significant structural problems when we attempt to justify desert claims, to determine how much of a given burden or benefit is deserved, and to balance considerations of desert against other moral considerations such as needs or rights. Further, I attempt to show that these structural

[13] Erin Kelly, "Doing Without Desert."
[14] I owe this formulation to an anonymous reader for Cambridge University Press.

problems can largely be avoided if we adopt the kind of justice-based moral theory that emerges in the paradigm of forgiveness. However, as Samuel Scheffler and others have argued, a theory of justice that fails to accord desert a fundamental or preinstitutional role may conflict significantly with our considered moral judgments.[15] It seems, therefore, that we have a choice between endorsing a structurally flawed desert-based moral theory or a justice-based moral theory that fails to accord with the significant moral intuitions that we generally express in terms of desert. I suggest in Chapter 6 that this is a false dilemma. The justice-based moral theory that emerges in the paradigm of forgiveness is capable of explaining many of the considered moral judgments that we express in terms of desert. In Chapter 6 I begin to defend this claim by showing briefly how this theory can explain the moral convictions that we express in terms of desert in the domain of distributive justice. In Chapter 7 I complete the defense of this claim by explaining in much more detail how our justice-based moral theory accounts for many of our central moral convictions expressed in terms of desert in the domain of retributive justice, or public response to wrongdoing.

At this point we are in a position to consider the implications of the paradigm of forgiveness for the laws and social policies we ought to adopt as a public response to wrongdoing in a properly forgiving society. In Chapter 7 I argue that the basic attitudes that ground the paradigm of forgiveness, and the kind of justice-based moral theory that they entail, lead to a public response to wrongdoing that has three central components: prevention of wrongdoing, restitution for primary harm wrongfully inflicted on the immediate victim(s) of an offense, and restitution for secondary harm wrongfully inflicted on the members of the community. In addition to articulating and defending these three components of the public response to wrongdoing, I am concerned throughout Chapter 7 to defend two additional claims. First, I argue that the paradigm of forgiveness explains many of the central moral convictions that we often express in terms of desert in the domain of retributive justice (thus completing my defense of the justice-based moral theory outlined in Chapter 6). Second, I respond to John Kekes' claim that "choice-morality" embodies a soft reaction to evil and fails to protect innocent persons sufficiently from undeserved harm.[16] Although the

---

[15] Samuel Scheffler, "Responsibility, Reactive Attitudes, and Liberalism in Philosophy and Politics."

[16] John Kekes makes the case for this claim throughout *Facing Evil*.

paradigm of forgiveness is a species of choice-morality, I argue that the three components of the public response to wrongdoing taken together provide a strong defense against unnecessary harm, and that the paradigm of forgiveness can be expected to perform at least as well as (if not better than) retributive positions in this regard.

Turning to the three components of the public response to wrongdoing that emerge in the paradigm of forgiveness, I begin by arguing that advocates of this paradigm will be fundamentally concerned to prevent unnecessary harm for all persons – victims and offenders alike. They will therefore place a strong emphasis on nonpunitive techniques for preventing wrongdoing from occurring in the first place. A variety of such techniques may be used, and I discuss them in some detail.

I then argue that the basic attitudes that ground the paradigm of forgiveness and the moral theory that emerges from them will lead to a systematic practice of requiring offenders to make restitution for the primary harm they have wrongfully inflicted on their immediate victims, within reasonable limits of sacrifice.

The most controversial aspect of the public response to wrongdoing has been the practice of legal punishment. Most authors now recognize that there is a public aspect to criminal wrongdoing, and retributivists argue that legal punishment is an intrinsically appropriate response to those who commit criminal violations. Positive or strong retributivism holds that criminal wrongdoing is not only a necessary condition but also a sufficient condition for the moral legitimacy of legal punishment. Three types of strongly retributive theories are examined here: those based on the fundamental notion of desert, those based on claims of reciprocity or unfair advantage, and those based on the moral imperatives of communication or expression. I argue that although these theories contain some important insights, they are all seriously flawed.

Drawing again on the basic attitudes that ground the paradigm of forgiveness and the type of moral theory that emerges from them, I go on to argue that the morally appropriate response to criminal wrongdoing is to require criminal offenders to make restitution for the secondary harm they wrongfully inflict on the members of the community. There are different methods by which criminal offenders can make restitution for wrongfully inflicted secondary harm, and in any given set of circumstances, we must select the one that provides the most effective restitution to the members of the community within the limits of sacrifice that can legitimately be required of the offender. I argue that in some circumstances, a practice of legal punishment may constitute the preferred means by which criminal offenders can make restitution to the members of the community, and I work out some of the implications of my analysis for how this practice ought to be articulated. Finally, I defend this third component of the public response to wrongdoing against objections that are likely to be raised by retributivists, and I also explain how it incorporates some of their central insights.

A discussion of the paradigm of forgiveness would not be complete without addressing the restorative justice movement, and the eighth and final chapter addresses this topic. The restorative justice movement has received substantial attention in recent literature and it is also making inroads into the practices of criminal justice in many jurisdictions around the world. I make no attempt to canvas the different versions of restorative justice here. Instead, I explain how the paradigm of forgiveness incorporates five of the central tenets of this movement, although in some cases with certain qualifications. In fact, the paradigm of forgiveness and the restorative justice movement are based on very similar moral ideals. Therefore the paradigm of forgiveness may be conceived as a possible theoretical framework to ground the restorative justice movement.[17]

A discussion of these matters also provides an opportunity to consider in more detail how the public response to wrongdoing ought to be implemented in the context of the paradigm of forgiveness, and what a properly forgiving society would look like. The refinements of the public response to wrongdoing suggested here are derived in part from the processes of addressing the wrong described in Chapters 3 and 4, and in part from the basic attitudes that ground the paradigm of forgiveness. In particular I am concerned to establish that the kind of face-to-face meetings between offenders and victims envisioned in the restorative justice movement (whether they take place in lieu of a criminal trial or after a criminal trial has been completed and a requirement set for the offender) can greatly facilitate the process of addressing the wrong for both offenders and victims.

Before we begin, let us consider briefly the methodology that will be employed in the extended discussion that follows. As I have noted, the predominant methodological approach in normative ethics in the past four decades has been to adopt some version of wide reflective equilibrium. This is the methodology that I will adopt here, although, as I have indicated, I will attempt to employ it in such a way that we achieve a

---

[17] Again, I owe this point to an anonymous reader for Cambridge University Press.

holistic level of understanding that allows our reasons and motives to be in harmony with one another. The method of wide reflective equilibrium requires us to attempt to develop moral theories or principles that explain a significant range of our moral intuitions (or considered moral judgments). It also requires that we attempt to make these theories or principles coherent with relevant background theories – moral or nonmoral theories that seem to bear on the plausibility of the moral theories we are attempting to construct. In the process of performing these tasks, we work back and forth between our considered moral judgments, moral theories, and relevant background theories, making revisions at each level as warranted until we achieve an overall package of beliefs that is more or less coherent. Beliefs that are part of a broadly coherent and plausible package of beliefs are then considered to be justified, or at least strongly supported.

It is important to recognize that not all theorists will endorse this methodology, or employ it in the same manner. Disagreements abound among philosophers about the nature and status of moral judgments and about the proper approach to the study of ethics. Unfortunately I cannot address these issues in any detail here, as the philosophical debate on these matters is so complex and extended that an adequate discussion of them would require a book in itself. Nevertheless, it will be instructive to consider briefly a basic division between theorists on the question of how we ought to approach the questions of normative ethics.

In his well-known article "Is There a Single True Morality?" Gilbert Harman articulates this division as follows: "One side says that we must concentrate on finding the place of value and obligation in the world of facts as revealed by science. The other side says we must ignore that problem and concentrate on ethics proper."[18] Employing a somewhat broader conception of reflective equilibrium than I have described, Harman goes on to say that "both sides agree that we must begin at the beginning with our initial beliefs, both moral and nonmoral, and consider possible modifications that will make these beliefs more coherent with each other and plausible generalizations and other explanatory principles," in an attempt to reach reflective equilibrium.[19] However, in the process of doing so, the two groups of theorists come to very different conclusions.

---

[18] Gilbert Harman, "Is There a Single True Morality?" p. 29.
[19] *Ibid.*

One group of theorists (naturalists) concludes that we will achieve the most coherent and plausible package of beliefs overall "by supposing that everything true must fit into a scientific account of the world and by supposing that the central question about morality is how, if at all, morality fits into such a scientific account."[20] For the naturalist, then, as Harman points out elsewhere, there are no clear boundaries between science and philosophy, or more specifically, between science and ethics.[21] Although philosophers may work at an abstract theoretical level, they are (or should be) contributing to a scientific account of our experience, and ethicists, in particular, should be constructing a scientific account of our moral experience. For example, ethicists may draw on psychology, sociology, evolutionary biology, or some other branch of science to explain the occurrence of certain sets of our considered moral judgments. In this case, they will tend to be relativists, skeptics, or projectivists, all of whom believe that there is no objective truth of the matter about ethics. Or in a more objective vein, they may attempt to correlate our moral beliefs with a particular set of scientific facts – for example, facts about human flourishing. (The problem with this latter approach lies in arguing that we *ought* to adopt the specific correlation that the theorist has identified, especially when other correlations are possible.)

On the other hand, the second group of theorists (ethical autonomists) comes to a very different conclusion. These theorists note that we tend to have strongly held initial beliefs that certain actions and attitudes actually are morally defensible, whereas others actually are not. In working through a process of seeking reflective equilibrium, we must assign an initial credibility to our most strongly held beliefs. We can of course revise these beliefs, but *only if* we have an adequate reason to do so. In the absence of such a reason, we must take these beliefs at face value and incorporate them into our theories as we seek reflective equilibrium. The ethical autonomist holds that we do not have sufficient reason to abandon our strongly held initial beliefs that certain actions and attitudes actually are morally defensible whereas others are not. Therefore we should assign initial credibility to these beliefs, set aside the question of how if at all our moral experience fits into a scientific account of the

---

[20] *Ibid.*, p. 47.
[21] See, for example, Gilbert Harman, "Three Trends in Moral and Political Philosophy," p. 421. Harman makes this point in several other places as well.

world, and, to use Harman's phrase, "concentrate on ethics proper." In other words, our approach to normative ethics should be to pursue ethics autonomously, taking our considered moral judgments at face value and constructing moral theories in a serious attempt to determine what is actually right and wrong.

Although I cannot argue the point here, it seems to me that the autonomous approach to ethics is correct. The problem with naturalism is nicely summarized by Geoff Sayre McCord as follows: "Despite its advantages, naturalism has difficulty capturing well what people take to be the true nature of morality. In saying something is good or right or virtuous we seem to be saying something more than, or at least different from, what we would be saying by describing it as having certain natural features. Correspondingly, no amount of empirical investigation seems by itself, without some moral assumptions in play, sufficient to settle a moral question."[22] If, as Sayre-McCord suggests, naturalists systematically fail to capture a significant component of our strongly held initial moral beliefs, then I think their approach to ethics must be rejected. Our initial beliefs should certainly be subject to revision, but it is important to note that we cannot revise them at will, nor can we revise or discard them merely to attain a simpler or more coherent theoretical perspective. Although the analogy is imperfect, we can see this point in reference to scientific theory. If we had simply revised or discarded our observations of the orbit of Mercury because they conflicted with Newton's highly coherent and plausible theory, the theory of general relativity might not have developed, or might have developed differently. Our strongly held initial beliefs constitute one of the major bases we have for progressing in our pursuit of knowledge, and it seems that we ought then to take them at face value until we have sufficient reason to believe that they are mistaken.

The naturalist will of course have responses to these objections, and we lack the space here to adjudicate adequately between the two positions. Suffice it to say that in this book I will adopt the perspective of the autonomous ethicist and assign initial credibility to our considered moral judgments. In other words, I will assume that these judgments are in some sense objective. Not only do I believe that this position is correct, I also believe that there are two strategic reasons to adopt this position in this context. First, forgiveness and resentment are responses to wrongdoing that have their natural home in the context of a belief

---

[22] Geoff Sayre-McCord, "Metaethics," p. 5–6.

system that holds that certain actions actually are wrong. And, second, a defense of unconditional genuine forgiveness will be strongest if we make this assumption. To show that it is appropriate to forgive actions that actually are wrong is presumably more challenging than to show that it is appropriate to forgive actions that may be wrong in some subjective sense. I will leave it to readers of other metaethical persuasions to adapt what is said here to their own positions, if they wish to do so.

It is important to recognize that although the ethical autonomist regards ethics as a discipline that is distinct from science, she will hold that the empirical sciences have an indispensable role to play in the study of ethics. Although the empirical sciences will not supply the nomological (or more abstract) premises in moral arguments, they will supply critical factual premises that allow us to reach more particular moral conclusions.[23] As the discussion progresses, I will flag for the reader some of the points at which the empirical sciences have an important role to play in developing the paradigm of forgiveness.

Finally, let me call to the reader's attention a basic assumption that I will make throughout the book. I will assume that in the absence of specific encumbering conditions, we actually are autonomous moral agents

---

[23] The explanation of wide reflective equilibrium that I have presented so far, and that is commonly seen in the literature on this topic, leaves open the sense in which nonmoral background theories might bear on the plausibility of our moral theories. I have explored this topic in my article "The Wide and Narrow of Reflective Equilibrium." I argue there that attempts to deduce moral theories from nonmoral background theories have been unsuccessful. Further, if we could succeed in deducing a moral theory from a reliable nonmoral background theory, we should abandon the methodology of wide reflective equilibrium and simply adopt the moral theory that we have successfully derived in this manner. Some theorists seem to imply that a nonmoral background theory can bear on the plausibility of a moral theory in a looser sense. For example, John Rawls suggests in *A Theory of Justice* (p. 28) that utilitarianism is plausible only if one assumes that a group of persons is like a single person, or forgets that it is not. However, for any given nonmoral claim or fact, there will always be different ways in which we can respond to that fact. (For example, we can respond to the fact that cats experience pain when tortured by torturing cats, by not torturing cats, by ignoring cats, etc.). What we would like to know is which of the many possible responses we *ought* to adopt. It seems, then, that when we suggest that a fact or nonmoral theory makes a moral principle more plausible, we are implicitly appealing to a more abstract moral principle that is often left unexpressed. For example, to return to Rawls's claim, we may hold that it is important for beings that can have good experiences to have good experiences. Then, because individuals rather than groups have the capacity to have good experiences, we conclude that a justice-based moral theory that focuses on the experiences of individuals is more plausible than utilitarianism, which focuses on some kind of maximization of good experiences within a group. If my reasoning here is correct, then nonmoral theories will provide subsumptive premises in moral arguments rather than nomological premises.

who are capable of deliberating about moral issues and making meaningful choices about which actions we will perform and which attitudes we will adopt. This is an assumption that is shared by the retributivist. There has been a great deal of philosophical discussion both about the truth of this claim and about what kinds of considerations could call this claim into question. For our purposes here, I will assume that it is true, and acknowledge that if scientists or philosophers succeed in showing that we have sufficient reason to reject it, then the account of response to wrongdoing that I develop here will have to be revised (as will retributivist accounts of response to wrongdoing). Let us now turn to an examination of the attitudes of forgiveness and resentment.

2

The Nature of Forgiveness and Resentment

In this chapter I define the basic attitudes of resentment and forgiveness. It is important to have a clear understanding of these attitudes at the outset, given that we will start from these attitudes in developing the paradigm of forgiveness and defending it against various forms of retributivism. Further, an understanding of the virtue-oriented approach to response to wrongdoing that I will develop here requires a clear understanding of the nature of moral attitudes and their relationship to character traits. This chapter begins with a brief explanation of attitudes and character traits. I then define the attitudes of resentment and forgiveness. Finally, in order to avoid unnecessary confusion in the moral analysis that follows, I address some recent controversies about the nature of forgiveness.

ATTITUDES AND CHARACTER TRAITS

Let us begin with a brief discussion of attitudes. Attitudes, as I will define them here, have three components: a cognitive component, an affective component, and a motivational component. The cognitive component consists of an awareness or recognition of the significant features of the situation we are considering. For example, the cognitive component of an attitude of compassion includes an acute awareness of an individual's suffering and of that individual's desire for happiness. The affective component of an attitude consists of the emotional response that accompanies the recognition contained in the cognitive component. In the case of compassion, we feel the individual's pain and her desire for its cessation. The motivational component of an attitude consists of a desire to see the situation we are considering resolved in a particular manner. In the case of compassion, we desire to see the individual relieved of her suffering and established in a state of happiness. The motivational component will often result in behavior designed to bring about the preferred solution, but not always. For example, I may have compassion for an individual who is suffering, but lack the resources to help her myself. Or I may believe that under the circumstances it would be best for that individual to take the initiative to solve her own problems, or to be helped by someone else. It is important to recognize that the desires that constitute the motivational component are intrinsic to an attitude, whereas behavior (or even a disposition to behave in a particular manner) is not. Behavioral factors are always at least somewhat contingent on external circumstances. This said, however, it is also important to notice that in the absence of countervailing considerations, the motivational component of a sincerely held attitude will result in an intention to act, which in turn will lead to action in the absence of external impediments.

On the virtue-ethical approach developed here, I will identify three different types of attitudes, which I will call integrated, conflicted, and fragmented attitudes. In an integrated attitude, the cognitive, affective, and motivational components are inseparable from one another. They are fully harmonious and constitute three aspects of one unified psychological state. Morally ideal attitudes are always integrated attitudes. In the ideal case, we have a full and accurate recognition of the morally salient features of a situation, and our feelings and motives are fully appropriate to the features of the situation that we have recognized. Thus there is no room for the kind of "malady of the spirit" that Stocker has identified. Our reasons and motives for acting are unified.

It is important to understand the difference between an agent who holds an integrated moral attitude and an agent who merely calculates his duty by a moral principle and wills himself to comply with the results. Consider a father who holds an integrated attitude of profound love for his children. A father of this sort will recognize the value and uniqueness of his children and the importance of their flourishing. He will also have deep, persistent feelings of love and affection for his children, and he will be consistently motivated to spend time with them, to protect them, to participate in their lives, and to raise them as well as he can. This unified state of heart and mind will show in his facial expressions, in his tone of voice, in what he says to his children, in how he phrases his thoughts, in his playfulness, in his eagerness to be with them, in the attention and guidance he gives, and so on. His integrated attitude will be evident on a daily basis as he interacts with his children, and it will have an enormous impact on their lives. There is clearly a world of difference between a father of this sort and the father who merely complies with the categorical imperative or the principle of utility in discharging his parental duties. It should not take much reflection at this point to recognize the primary importance of integrated moral attitudes. In a very real sense, they create much of the fabric and quality of our lives. It is therefore important that we cultivate in ourselves morally worthy integrated attitudes in response to wrongdoing.

My central concern will be to examine forgiveness and resentment as integrated attitudes, but it will also be helpful to briefly consider conflicted and fragmented attitudes. Conflicted attitudes, as I will define them here, are attitudes in which there is a lack of harmony either between different components of the attitude or within one or more of the components. For example, a conflict arises between different components of an attitude in an alcoholic who recognizes on a cognitive level that alcohol is very damaging to him, but is still motivated to consume it. A conflict arises within a single component of an attitude if the alcoholic both loves and hates alcohol on the affective level, or both desires to stop drinking and desires to continue drinking on the motivational level.

In a fragmented attitude, one or more of the components of the attitude is suppressed, or missing for some other reason. For example, an individual with post-traumatic stress disorder may have a strong emotional and motivational response to a situation without knowing why. Here, the cognitive component is suppressed. Or an individual who escapes her feelings by retreating into intellect may have a strong cognitive understanding of a situation while the affective component of her attitude is suppressed. Fragmented attitudes are much more common than we might like to think. We often have an intellectual understanding of a situation before we have an integrated attitude about it. In a recent discussion of self-respect, Robin Dillon considers the case of a woman who knows intellectually that she has reason to take pride in her achievements but who does not feel this truth on an affective level. Dillon comments, "Intellectual understanding involves having beliefs which one has reason to accept as true, then coming by inference to have other beliefs which one takes to be true in virtue of their logical relations to warranted beliefs, where believing...need not engage the emotions. Experiential understanding involves experiencing something directly and feeling the truth of what is experienced."[1] As we begin to consider the integrated attitude of forgiveness, then, it is important to bear in mind that integrated attitudes require experiential understanding, and that they take time to cultivate.

We are now in a position to consider the relationship between attitudes and character traits. I want to suggest that we can best understand character traits as attitudes that have been sufficiently ingrained or internalized that they constitute a fairly regular response to a given type of recurring situation. Virtues are sufficiently ingrained, integrated attitudes that are morally worthy, and vices are ingrained attitudes that are morally flawed in some significant respect. An attitude is morally worthy if we have a full and accurate recognition of the morally salient features of a situation, if our feelings are appropriate to these salient features, and if our motives correspond to the way in which the situation could most appropriately be resolved. All three of these components are required for an attitude to be fully worthy. Therefore virtues are integrated attitudes. Whether or not a given character trait is a virtue therefore depends on the moral assessment of the attitude that the character trait regularly manifests, and the central task of virtue ethics is to determine which attitudes are actually morally worthy. We can then proceed to cultivate morally worthy attitudes in ourselves. I will argue here that an integrated attitude of unconditional genuine forgiveness is morally worthy, and that it is therefore important that we try to cultivate this attitude in ourselves as a regular response to wrongdoing. I will summarize this claim by saying that forgiveness is a virtue.

It will be helpful to elaborate briefly on three aspects of this analysis at this point.[2] First, as Aristotle pointed out, there are many ways to miss the mark. Due to the complexity of human life and the various psychological pressures that we face, we will often find ourselves holding attitudes that may resemble morally worthy attitudes or virtues in some respects. However, on further examination we will see that they are actually false approximations of worthy attitudes, and clearly defective in one way or another. For example, an individual may seem to be generous if she makes a donation to charity, but her attitude will be defective

---

[1] Robin Dillon, "Self-Respect: Moral, Emotional, Political," p. 239.
[2] I thank an anonymous reader from Cambridge University Press for drawing my attention to the need to clarify the first two points.

if her only thought in doing so is to win the admiration of her friends. We may or may not call her generous or say that she has performed an act of generosity, but in either case her underlying attitude clearly fails to constitute the kind of morally worthy attitude that we should strive to cultivate in ourselves. Likewise an individual may seem to be courageous if he dares to jump off a ninety-foot cliff into a pool of water for fun, in spite of the fact that others have been killed or paralyzed by making this jump.[3] Again, we may or may not call him courageous or say that his action took courage, but clearly the attitude he exhibited is not the kind of attitude we would want to ingrain in ourselves. Rather, his attitude is defective from a moral point of view in that he fails to recognize that his own life and health are more important than anything that could be gained by making this jump.

On the virtue-ethical approach I am proposing here, our goal is to identify morally worthy attitudes to cultivate in ourselves. Given this goal, we will want to set aside the types of attitudes that are clearly defective in one respect or another, and focus our attention instead on reasonable candidates for morally worthy attitudes. To facilitate this task, I will refer to formulations of attitudes that are reasonable candidates for morally worthy attitudes as "genuine" or "true." For example, I will say that while the attitude adopted by the person who jumps off the cliff may be courageous in a sense, it is not genuine courage. Genuine courage requires a clear recognition of the values that are at stake in a given situation, and of their relative importance. Likewise in Chapter 3, I will set aside false approximations of a worthy attitude of forgiveness, and articulate a conception of genuine forgiveness that is a reasonable candidate for a morally worthy attitude to adopt in response to wrongdoing. We can then attempt to determine whether an attitude of genuine forgiveness or an attitude of resentment is the more morally appropriate response to wrongdoing in particular types of situations. The same procedure will be followed in Chapter 4 in our discussion of self-forgiveness.

Second, on the virtue-ethical approach developed here, we should understand that the extent to which we have ingrained a morally worthy attitude in ourselves is a matter of degree. Therefore the possession of a virtue is a matter of degree, and we would have to employ a threshold criterion to determine when a particular person possesses a particular

---

[3] I have actually seen several people do this at Hamilton Pool near Austin, Texas.

virtue. Given the human condition, we can expect that most people will experience some complexity and variation in their thoughts and feelings. For example, even a very generous person may have moments in which she experiences a selfish thought or impulse. Likewise, brief thoughts or feelings of resentment may well resurface from time to time in a person who has virtuously forgiven her offender. An adequate formulation of a threshold criterion for the possession of a virtue must take this factor into account. However, given that our purpose here is not to determine when a particular person can be said to possess a particular virtue, but rather to determine which character traits we should attempt to cultivate in ourselves, we need not articulate this kind of threshold criterion any further. Instead, we can focus on determining the morally appropriate attitude to adopt in response to wrongdoing.

Finally, there has been much discussion recently of the "fundamental attribution error" and its implications for virtue ethics. Gilbert Harman defines the fundamental attribution error as "the error of ignoring situational factors and overconfidently assuming that distinctive behavior or patterns of behavior are due to an agent's distinctive character traits."[4] He argues that any version of virtue ethics that depends on attributing character traits to individuals is called into question by this error. A full discussion of Harman's position is out of place at this point, but it is important to recognize that the virtue-ethical approach employed in this book does not fall prey to this error. The focus here is not on attributing character traits to individuals. I agree that this practice is often harmful and epistemically suspect. Rather, the focus here is on examining the integrated attitudes we might adopt in response to wrongdoing in order to determine which is the most worthy of cultivating in ourselves. Not only does this task avoid the fundamental attribution error; it is also an essential task for moral agents to undertake. An individual who does not examine her own attitudes from a moral point of view is seriously remiss, as is the individual who never attempts to cultivate morally worthy attitudes in herself. To say that we should not attempt to develop morally worthy attitudes in ourselves because there are no such things as character traits would be to abandon the attempt to develop ourselves as moral agents who can recognize the morally salient features of recurring situations and respond appropriately.

---

[4] Gilbert Harman, "Moral Philosophy Meets Social Psychology: Virtue Ethics and the Fundamental Attribution Error," p. 316.

THE ATTITUDES OF FORGIVENESS
AND RESENTMENT DEFINED

Bearing in mind the general characterization of attitudes and character traits just outlined, let us now turn to the specific attitudes of resentment and forgiveness. My goal here is not to identify the "essence" of forgiveness or resentment. Both Nebblet and Scarre have pointed out the difficulties of this task.[5] Nor is my goal to provide a lexical analysis that captures all (or most) of the legitimate senses of these terms, as Scarre attempts with his "family resemblance" characterization of forgiveness.[6] My aim in this book is to provide a systematic answer to the question of how we ought to respond to wrongdoing, starting from basic attitudes. In keeping with this aim, I will offer what might be called a "precising" analysis of the attitudes of forgiveness and resentment. The analysis offered here should coincide with our ordinary understandings of forgiveness and resentment. But rather than trying to capture every possible meaning of these terms, I will define them in a manner that will help us to answer the substantive questions before us and to address the central issues that separate retributivists and advocates of the paradigm of forgiveness.

As we attempt to determine the morally appropriate attitude to adopt in response to wrongdoing, we will clearly want to consider the integrated forms of the attitudes of forgiveness and resentment. Although the three components of an integrated attitude are inseparable aspects of a unified psychological state, we can gain an understanding of these attitudes by examining each of the components in turn. I will start by examining the attitude of resentment, because forgiveness is generally understood as a foreswearing of this attitude.

1. Resentment

An attitude of resentment (again, insofar as it is of interest to us here) is intimately connected to morality. Rawls remarks, "In general, guilt, resentment, and indignation invoke the concept of right..."[7] More specifically, resentment is a response to wrongs committed against us, or

---

[5] William R. Neblett, "Forgiveness and Ideals," p. 269, and Geoffrey Scarre, *After Evil*, p. 25–27.
[6] Geoffrey Scarre, *After Evil*, Chapter 2.
[7] John Rawls, *A Theory of Justice*, p. 484.

against those close enough to us that we are personally affected by their suffering. We feel guilt when we do wrong ourselves, we feel indignation when we hear about wrongdoing in general, and we feel resentment, in particular, when we are wronged. Murphy says, "In my view, resentment (in its range from righteous anger to righteous hatred) functions primarily in defense, not of all values and norms, but rather of certain values of self. Resentment is a response not to general wrongs but to wrongs against oneself…"[8] In addition, as Griswold points out, an attitude of resentment is directed toward the offender. He says "We do not resent the action; we resent you for doing it, you as its author."[9] The cognitive component of resentment, then, includes the recognition that an individual has wrongfully harmed us (or someone close to us), or has, at the very least, extended a morally inappropriate attitude toward us (or someone close to us). It includes the recognition that the offender is a moral agent who could have and should have done otherwise. It includes the recognition that in harming us and/or regarding us in this manner, the offender has failed to accord us sufficient concern and respect. And it includes the awareness that as a moral agent, the offender is now responsible for acknowledging the wrong, addressing it to the best of his ability, and refraining from further behavior of this sort. (If the offender is dead or has otherwise lost his moral agency, the cognitive component will obviously not include this last element.)

The affective component of an attitude of resentment consists of a feeling of moral anger, with which we are all familiar. As Murphy indicates, there is a range or continuum here from mild righteous anger to righteous hatred. Depending on the circumstances, the injured person may feel a variety of other negative emotions toward the offender. For example, the victim may feel contempt for the drunk driver who injured her, personal hatred toward a spouse who cheated on her, or outrage toward the newcomer who wrongfully usurped a benefit she has sought for a long time.

The motivational component of an attitude of resentment, in its most general form, consists of a desire for the moral order to be restored. Murphy remarks that resentment "stands as a testimony to our allegiance to the moral order itself." He says, "Moral commitment is not

---

[8] Jeffrie G. Murphy, *Forgiveness and Mercy*, p. 16.
[9] Charles Griswold, *Forgiveness*, p. 25. Here Griswold plausibly opposes Jean Hampton, who argues that the object of resentment is the wrong action rather than the offender. See Hampton, *Forgiveness and Mercy*, p. 60.

merely a matter of intellectual allegiance; it requires emotional allegiance as well, for a moral person is not simply a person who holds the abstract belief that certain things are wrong. The moral person is also motivated to do something about the wrong…"[10] Judith Boss further points out that resentment need not entail motivation to retaliate for the wrong: "Resentment is not the same as vindictiveness or a desire to 'get even' or to retaliate, as many people assume."[11] In support of this claim, she quotes psychologist Maria Fortune as saying that victims of domestic abuse "rarely feel vengeful; they simply want the abuse to stop."[12] Nevertheless, resentment is often accompanied by a desire for punishment – often enough that Griswold describes this attitude as "a reactive as well as retributive passion that instinctively seeks to exact a due measure of punishment."[13] Again, there is a range or continuum of motivations that may be part of an attitude of resentment. Depending on the circumstances, the person who resents an offender may desire to have him stop perpetrating the wrong, repent, acknowledge the wrong, apologize, make substantive amends, undergo punishment, or suffer some kind of harm in turn.

Given that the cognitive component of an attitude of resentment includes a salient awareness of the offender as a moral agent who is obligated to acknowledge and address the wrong, the motivational component of this attitude, in Strawson's terms, takes on the character of a "demand" rather than a simple desire. Further, Strawson points out that the attitudes of resentment and indignation are accompanied by at least a partial withdrawal of goodwill toward the offender. He says, "Indignation, disapprobation, like resentment, tend to inhibit or at least to limit our goodwill towards the object of these attitudes, tend to promote an at least partial and temporary withdrawal of goodwill; they do so in proportion as they are strong; and their strength is in general proportional to what is felt to be the magnitude of the injury and the degree to which the agent's will is identified with, or indifferent to, it." He adds that these are not contingent connections, but rather "precisely the correlates of the moral demand in the case where the demand is felt to be disregarded."[14] In an attitude of resentment, then, the recognition of the offender as a moral agent who is

[10] Jeffrie G. Murphy, *Getting Even*, pp. 19–20.
[11] Judith A. Boss, "Throwing Pearls to Swine: Women, Forgiveness, and the Unrepentant Abuser," p. 236.
[12] Maria M. Fortune, "Justice-Making in the Aftermath of Woman-Battering," p. 242.
[13] Charles Griswold, *Forgiveness*, p. 39.
[14] P.F. Strawson, "Freedom and Resentment," p. 21–22.

obligated to respect moral requirements incorporates a *demand* that he acknowledge his wrong in some appropriate manner. Further, this demand is accompanied by at least a partial withdrawal of goodwill toward the offender until he does so (or until the moral order has been reasserted or reestablished in some way). Finally, the extent to which goodwill is withdrawn is proportional to the gravity of the offense and the moral depravity of the offender's current attitude toward it.

2. Forgiveness

Forgiveness is generally understood as a change of heart in which an initial attitude of resentment is overcome and replaced with a positive attitude toward the offender. Jessica Wolfendale writes, "Forgiveness is most commonly defined as a change of heart where the victim renounces negative feelings toward the wrongdoer and accepts them back into the moral community – accepts them as a person."[15] Interestingly, there are persons who are able to maintain continuous compassion for the offender in the face of serious victimization. For example, the Tibetan monk, Lopon-la, was taken as a political prisoner by the Chinese, imprisoned for eighteen years, forced to denounce his religion, and brutally tortured many times during his imprisonment. When Lopon-la was finally released and reunited with the Dalai Lama, the Dalai Lama saw that he was still the same "gentle monk." He asked Lopon-la if he was ever afraid during his imprisonment. Lopon-la responded "Yes, there was one thing I was afraid of. I was afraid I may lose compassion for the Chinese."[16] As will become apparent, Lopon-la on my view exhibited the morally ideal response to wrongdoing. He never lost his compassion and never held an attitude of resentment toward his offenders. However, the overwhelming majority of us will experience an initial attitude of resentment if we are wronged in a nontrivial manner. Thus forgiveness, when it is justified, may be considered a corrective attitude that replaces an initial attitude of resentment that we no longer find worthy. Likewise for many of us, courage often replaces an initial attitude of fear that we find unworthy, generosity often replaces an initial attitude of self-centered attachment that we find unworthy, and so on for many if not all of the virtues.

[15] Jessica Wolfendale, "The Hardened Heart: The Moral Dangers of Not Forgiving," p. 348.
[16] His Holiness the Fourteenth Dalai Lama and Victor Chang, *The Wisdom of Forgiveness*, pp. 47–48.

It should be noted at this point that we cannot fairly require ourselves to have a morally ideal set of attitudes from the beginning, as this would be impossible for the vast majority of us. Thus it is not generally wrong or immoral to hold an initial attitude of resentment, fear, self-centeredness, and so on. What is important is that we evaluate these attitudes as we go along, and make an effort to inculcate in ourselves the attitudes that we find to be morally worthy through this kind of assessment.

Pamela Hieronymi has recently emphasized that the change of heart involved in forgiveness must involve a shift in judgment. With regard to the overcoming of resentment involved in forgiveness, she says that "all too often philosophers see forgiveness primarily as a matter of manipulating oneself out of this unpleasant and potentially destructive emotion. Yet if both resentment and forgiveness admit of justification ... then forgiving will entail more than figuring out how to rid oneself of certain unfortunate effects.... Genuine forgiveness must involve some revision in judgment or change in view. An account of genuine forgiveness must therefore *articulate* the revision in judgment or change in view."[17]

We will soon address the moral reasons for finding an initial attitude of resentment unworthy and for replacing it with an attitude of forgiveness. For now, let us consider the change in view or judgment that takes place when we forgive–or in other words, the difference between the cognitive components of an attitude of resentment and an attitude of forgiveness. The cognitive component of an attitude of forgiveness includes the central beliefs that constitute the cognitive component of an attitude of resentment. When we forgive, we understand that the offender's act was wrong, that the offender is a moral agent who could have and should have done otherwise, and that as a moral agent, the offender is responsible for addressing the wrong to the best of his ability. However, the person who forgives holds an additional set of beliefs that are even more salient.[18] When we forgive, our most salient beliefs are those that we hold about the offender as a person. The cognitive component of an attitude of forgiveness includes an acute or salient awareness of the offender as a sentient being who is capable of experiencing happiness and misery, and who, like us, wants to experience happiness. It includes an acute awareness that like us, the offender is subject to various needs, pressures, and confusions in life and is vulnerable to error. And it includes a salient recognition that

---

[17] Pamela Hieronymi, "Articulating an Uncompromising Forgiveness," pp. 529–530. See also C. Allen Speight, "Butler and Hegel on Forgiveness and Agency," p. 308.

[18] I owe this formulation to an anonymous reader for Cambridge University Press.

the offender is a valuable human being with a moral status equal to our own. We see clearly that the offender is an autonomous moral agent with the same basic capacity for moral choice, growth, and awareness that we have. In an integrated attitude of forgiveness, we will have an experiential understanding of these salient features of the offender as a person and an appreciation of their overriding importance.

The affective component of an attitude of forgiveness consists of feelings of compassion and kindness toward the offender (as opposed to the moral anger that constitutes the affective component of an attitude of resentment) and respect for his personhood. As with an attitude of resentment, a continuum of feelings is possible here, ranging from some respect and compassion to deep love, respect, and caring. And depending on the circumstances, we may experience a variety of other positive emotions toward the offender. For example, we may have feelings of parental love when we forgive our child for a transgression, of romantic love when we forgive our spouse, or of renewed joy, interest, and affection when we forgive a friend.

Finally, the motivational component of an attitude of forgiveness consists of a desire that things go well for the offender, and that he flourish as a person. I will refer to this component as real goodwill toward the offender. The specific form that this desire takes may range from the general desire that we would have for any individual to have a good life and grow as a person, to the deep personal commitment we make to the growth and flourishing of our loved ones. It might be suggested that a simple absence of ill will should suffice for forgiveness. Clearly the overcoming of ill will is an important step to take in cultivating an attitude of forgiveness. However, given that our goal here is to find a morally worthy response to wrongdoing, it will be more helpful to define forgiveness in terms of the presence of real goodwill toward the offender. A salient awareness of the intrinsic worth of the offender, of his capacity to experience pleasure and pain, of his desire for happiness, and so on will most appropriately lead to a desire for his flourishing as a person. Apathy or indifference toward persons and their flourishing is not a morally worthy attitude and does not qualify as a virtue.

A brief comment is in order about the type of respect accorded to the offender in an attitude of forgiveness. Stephen Darwall's distinction between evaluative respect and recognition respect is of central importance here.[19] He identifies evaluative respect as the respect or admiration

---

[19] Stephen L. Darwall, "Two Kinds of Respect."

we have for individuals in virtue of their positive qualities and achievements. Obviously we will not want to evaluate the offender's wrong act or the attitudes that led to it in a positive manner, although we may well admire other things about the offender. It is not evaluative respect that is involved in an attitude of forgiveness, but rather recognition respect. Recognition respect is respect for an individual's basic status as a person. For a Kantian, recognition respect is respect for persons as ends in themselves, or as autonomous moral agents who possess equal intrinsic worth. For a Christian, recognition respect may be respect for each individual as a child of God. For a Buddhist, recognition respect may be respect for the equal Buddha Nature of each being. However it is cashed out, it is important to understand that the recognition respect incorporated in an attitude of forgiveness is respect for our basic nature and status as persons. Unlike evaluative respect, it does not depend on our actions, attitudes, or character traits.

CONTROVERSIAL ASPECTS OF THE NATURE OF FORGIVENESS

So far, I have offered a general conceptual analysis of the attitudes of resentment and forgiveness. Although there seems to be relatively little controversy about the nature of resentment, several aspects of the nature of forgiveness have been the subject of debate in recent literature. By clarifying the nature of forgiveness as it is to be understood here, we can avoid unnecessary confusion as our discussion progresses.

1. Forgiveness as a Response to Wrongdoing

First, because the subject of this book is response to wrongdoing, the issue of forgiveness, insofar as it interests us here, will arise only when a moral agent is judged to have committed an offense. All things considered, his act must have been negligent, reckless, or willfully wrong. Where there is no wrongdoing, there is nothing for the injured person to forgive, although there may be much for her to accept. There is nothing to forgive (but much to accept), for example, when our one-year-old child damages the television set while our back is turned for an instant, or when a driver with no history of coronary disease has a heart attack while driving and injures us severely. Forgiveness is an issue only when a moral agent commits an offense, without justification and in the absence of an exculpating excuse.

2. Who Can Forgive?

Clearly the immediate victim of an offense is properly situated to forgive the offender, but there has been much debate as to whether one person can forgive on behalf of another. Some have questioned, for example, whether the father of a child who was paralyzed by a drunk driver could forgive the drunk driver on behalf of the child.[20] Others have questioned whether political leaders can forgive on behalf of their constituents.[21]

In this book I view forgiveness as an internal change of heart, as opposed to a performative, or speech act, in which forgiveness is bestowed on an offender. (I will say more about the reasons for adopting this approach later.) On this internal understanding of forgiveness, it is clear that each individual must decide for herself whether or not to forgive. As autonomous moral agents, we are ultimately responsible for determining our own attitudes. No one can legitimately choose for us whether we will hold an attitude of resentment or an attitude of forgiveness.

In discussing the question of who can forgive, Trudy Govier points out that there are often multiple victims of a single act of wrongdoing.[22] She identifies three categories of victims. A primary victim is a direct or immediate victim of a wrong. A secondary victim is a family member or close friend of a primary victim who is personally affected by the wrong. A tertiary victim is a member of a community who is deeply affected by harm to a leader or highly visible member of that community. Govier says, "Secondary and tertiary victims are also victims. Insofar as they experience loss, grief, pain, and suffering, they may also feel moral anger and resentment of the wrongdoer."[23]

Taking the discussion further, we can identify two kinds of resentment that may be experienced by secondary and tertiary victims. The first is resentment for harm done to them. For example, the father of the paralyzed child may resent the drunk driver for the overwhelming medical expenses that he now has to bear, or for the enormous amount of time and energy he must now devote to helping his child cope with the paralysis. Or a Tibetan citizen may resent the Chinese for depriving him of the opportunity to attend teachings that would have been

---

[20] David Novitz, "Forgiveness and Self-Respect," p. 302.
[21] See, for example, Trudy Govier, *Forgiveness and Resentment*, Chapter 5, and Carol Quinn, "On the Virtue of Not Forgiving."
[22] Trudy Govier, *Forgiveness and Resentment*, p. 93–94.
[23] *Ibid.*, p. 93.

presented by the Dalai Lama in Tibet were it not for the Chinese invasion. The second kind of resentment that secondary and tertiary victims may experience is resentment for harm done to the primary victim.
Because we care very deeply about some people and identify closely with
them, we will feel significant grief and loss, and then resentment, when
they are harmed. The father of the paralyzed child will be devastated
by the child's anguish and by the loss of opportunities in the child's life.
And Tibetan citizens who are genuinely devoted to the Dalai Lama will
be deeply saddened by the fact that the Dalai Lama was forced to flee
from his own country and live his life in exile. Both may then experience
resentment or outrage pursuant to these feelings.

It is important to recognize, however, that whatever kind of victim
we are, and whatever kind of resentment we experience, we alone can
choose whether to retain that resentment or attempt to replace it with
an attitude of forgiveness. No one can legitimately make this decision
for us, or forgive "on our behalf." It is also important to recognize that
there is no contradiction if one victim chooses to forgive the perpetrator
of a particular act of wrongdoing, and another does not. For example,
the paralyzed child may forgive the drunk driver, while the father does
not, or the father may forgive, while the child does not. In the latter
case, the father does not forgive the drunk driver on behalf of the child.
Rather, the father has chosen, for himself, to regard the drunk driver
with respect, compassion, and real goodwill. It is possible that a person who knows the victim very well can guess, with some degree of
reliability, that the victim would forgive the perpetrator when it is no
longer possible to consult the victim on this matter. For example, suppose that the drunk driver actually kills the child instead of just para-
lyzing her, and suppose also that the child was a very forgiving person.[24]
The father could then tell the perpetrator that he strongly believes that
the child would have forgiven him. However, the father in this case is
simply referring to the kind of attitude he believes that the *child* would
have adopted, rather than making a decision to forgive "on the child's
behalf."

Minas and Scarre (among others) have raised the question of what
happens to an offender who repents and wishes to be forgiven when
the victim is no longer able to forgive. Scarre offers a case in which
an offender decides to repent and seek forgiveness just as the victim is
dying, and arrives at the victim's deathbed a short time after her death.

[24] This example was suggested to me by Kate Padgett-Walsh.

Minas allows for a family member or close friend to step in and forgive the offender on behalf of the victim in this type of case. Scarre holds that the offender must recognize that he has lost his chance for forgiveness, and live the rest of his life without ever being forgiven.[25]

Again, if we understand forgiveness as an internal change of heart, it will be clear that we cannot forgive on one another's behalf. If we have done wrong, we must accept the victim's decision about whether or not she will forgive, and we must accept the fact that the victim may never be willing or able to forgive us. At the same time, however, we are responsible for working on our own attitudes. Rather than allowing our attitudes toward ourselves to be determined by the victim's decisions, we must determine for ourselves the appropriate attitude to adopt toward our own wrongdoing. In Chapter 4 I will argue that an attitude of self-forgiveness is always appropriate and desirable from a moral point of view for a repentant offender who has done his best to address the wrong, whether or not his victim has chosen to forgive him.

3. The Motive for Forgiveness

There has been much discussion about what counts as a legitimate motive for forgiveness. In *Forgiveness and Mercy,* Jeffrie Murphy points out that although forgiveness involves overcoming negative emotions toward the offender, there are methods of overcoming negative emotions that would not count as forgiveness. We have not forgiven the offender if we simply take a pill or undergo hypnosis to eliminate our resentment in order to better get on with our lives.[26] Nor have we forgiven the offender if we simply forget about the incident, but would resent him again if we were to be reminded of the incident at some point in the future. Authors have subsequently questioned whether we have a legitimate instance of forgiveness if the victim forgives in order to make herself feel better, if she forgives in order to feel morally superior to the offender, or even, as Novitz suggests, if she forgives to relieve her own feelings of guilt and shame at taking pleasure in the offender's discomfort.[27] Some authors contend that because forgiveness is other-directed, legitimate instances of forgiveness cannot be motivated in these ways. For instance, Novitz remarks that "if forgiveness is a virtue, it should not be motivated by a

[25] Geoffrey Scarre, *After Evil*, p. 69–70, and Anne Minas, "God and Forgiveness," p. 149.
[26] Jeffrie Murphy, *Forgiveness and Mercy*, p. 22–23.
[27] David Novitz, "Forgiveness and Self-Respect," p. 308.

desire to free oneself from guilt or shame. Forgiveness, at least as traditionally construed, is not self-interested but other-regarding....."[28]

In considering this question, it is important to distinguish between the intrinsic nature of a particular attitude and the impetus for cultivating that attitude. The attitude of forgiveness itself, as it has been defined here, is clearly other-regarding. We can see this by reviewing each of its components. The most salient elements of the cognitive component include a recognition of the *offender's* personhood, an awareness of the *offender* as a sentient being who wants to be happy, and an understanding of the *offender* as a human being subject to various needs, pressures, and confusions, and vulnerable to error. The affective component consists of respect and compassion *for the offender*. And the motivational component consists of real goodwill *toward the offender*.

The impetus for cultivating an attitude of forgiveness is often much more complex, as is the case with other virtuous attitudes. Very few of us are born with a set of virtuous attitudes fully intact. And very few of us go through life cultivating virtuous attitudes in a completely methodical manner, in which we systematically assess the various attitudes we could adopt in the situations we encounter and then choose to adopt the most worthy. As human beings, our moral development is typically somewhat erratic and psychologically complicated. Most of us probably begin to cultivate virtuous attitudes to obtain our parents' approval, or at least to avoid their disapproval. As we gain independence and encounter various situations in our lives, we typically encounter conflicting emotions, adopt various attitudes, find ourselves dissatisfied with some of them, and revise them over time. As autonomous moral agents, our goal is to cultivate attitudes that we find to be morally worthy, but the process of achieving this goal is often one of trial and error, as we make our way imperfectly through life's challenges.

A victim of serious wrongdoing may find herself in so much pain that she enters therapy, seeks religious counsel, or finds some other resource to help her deal with the situation she is facing. As she explores the situation in depth, she may come to see the offender as a fellow human being who warrants respect, compassion, and real goodwill. The fact that she was seeking relief from her pain when she began the process that resulted in her adopting an attitude of genuine forgiveness does not change the intrinsic nature of the attitude of genuine forgiveness that she finally adopts.

---

[28] *Ibid.* See also Molly Andrews, "Forgiveness in Context," p. 83, and Joanna North, "Wrongdoing and Forgiveness."

It may seem that the situation is different if the victim is motivated to feel superior to her offender, but I think the same analysis applies. A victim of serious wrongdoing may feel deeply shamed by the offense and experience a desire to alleviate this shame. She may try to feel better about herself by taking the moral high ground and attempting to forgive. In doing so, she may start to feel morally superior to her offender. However, if she actually adopts an attitude of forgiveness as it has been defined here, she will have to view the offender as a person with a moral status equal to her own. Holding the offender in contempt, or seeing him as having less worth as a person because of his offense, is antithetical to an attitude of forgiveness and incompatible with each of its components. In order to forgive, she will have to transcend her initial impetus to feel superior. But the fact that she reaches an attitude of forgiveness through a process involving a temporary feeling of superiority that is later rejected does not change the intrinsic nature or the moral worth of the attitude of forgiveness she finally adopts. Of course, if the final attitude she adopts is an attitude of moral superiority, then this attitude is clearly defective from a moral point of view.

Returning to Murphy's point about forgiveness, it is certainly true that we cannot forgive by taking a pill or conditioning ourselves not to think about the wrong through hypnosis, or by simply forgetting about the wrong. As Heironymi points out, genuine forgiveness does involve a shift in judgment. More holistically, we can say that it involves a change in all three components of our initial attitude toward the offender. Although the impetus for examining and realigning our attitudes may vary from case to case, what is required for genuine forgiveness is that at some point in the process we examine the attitudes of resentment and forgiveness and determine for ourselves which is more appropriate from a moral point of view. In the end, if we choose to adopt an attitude of forgiveness, it is because we see that the offender warrants respect, compassion, and real goodwill.

4. Forgiving and Forgetting

We often hear the phrase "forgive and forget." Although most authors agree on this point, it is worth emphasizing that forgiveness does not entail amnesia. When we forgive, we normally remember what has happened in the past, and it may be important for us to do so. The wife who is battered by her husband one night should not forget the incident entirely if she forgives her husband, as she must remember to take steps to protect herself in case he does it again. When we forgive, we do not forget the incident; instead, we no longer remember it vindictively. We hold an attitude of real goodwill toward the offender and we regard the incident of wrongdoing in an objective manner with an eye to what we can learn from it. There is an element of truth to this familiar phrase, however. An attitude of resentment tends to keep the incident before our minds in a way that an attitude of forgiveness does not. When we forgive, we make peace with the past and no longer feel a need to concern ourselves with it, beyond drawing on it in ways that are beneficial in planning for the future.

5. Forgiveness and Reconciliation

Some authors have seen reconciliation as a basic component of genuine forgiveness, or at least of a paradigmatic case of forgiveness. For instance, Carol Quinn says that "Genuine forgiveness is tremendously difficult, requiring 1) *a letting go* of anger, resentment, and other sentiments; 2) *a freeing up*, by recovering lost control and lost or compromised dignity; and 3) *a reconciliation*. This third step is most difficult, and requires compassion, understanding, and most importantly, a restoration of basic trust."[29] Claudia Card offers five features of a clear or paradigmatic case of forgiveness, with the fifth feature being an "offer to renew relationship or accept the other as a (possible) friend."[30] And Robert C. Roberts says that "the teleology of forgiveness is reconciliation – restoration or maintenance of a relationship of acceptance, benevolent attitude, and harmonious interaction."[31]

Reconciliation is often the result of forgiveness, as we can easily see by looking at our own personal relationships. Human beings quarrel, forgive, and continue with their personal relationships on a regular basis. Nevertheless, there are many cases in which persons forgive without restoring specific personal relationships, and rightly so. If Jack and Mary argue constantly, they may forgive each other for wrongs they have done to one another, and still decide it would be best to terminate their relationship. A battered wife may forgive her husband and still decide to divorce him, recognizing the need to protect herself and

---

[29] Carol Quinn, "On the Virtue of Not Forgiving," p. 222.
[30] Claudia Card, "The Atrocity Paradigm Revisited," p. 211. I refer to the wording she gives here rather than the wording in her book *The Atrocity Paradigm* because it is more recent.
[31] Robert C. Roberts, "Forgiveness," p. 299.

promote her own welfare. She does not need to stay with her husband in order to forgive him, nor does she need to develop a blind, irrational trust that he will never be violent again. In some cases of wrongdoing, we may decide to terminate a personal relationship even when we have never experienced any resentment. My grandfather had a partner in his surgical practice whose drinking interfered with his work. He liked this man very much and never felt resentment toward him, but sadly had to terminate the partnership because of the unacceptable risk to the patients. Many factors govern the wisdom of maintaining particular personal relationships, and it is simply a mistake to believe that forgiveness must always result in the restoration of these relationships.

Scarre also argues that it is a mistake to view forgiveness as the restoration of "some valued status quo ante," as sometimes there is no such valued status quo ante to restore. The offender and victim may be strangers, or they may have had an awful relationship such as slave and slave owner. Further, the offender may be dead, in a coma, or impossible to locate.[32] It is also worth noting that forgiveness between strangers may create a friendship that did not exist prior to the wrong. For example, when Bill Pelke forgave Paula Cooper, a stranger who murdered his grandmother in order to obtain money to play video games, he started communicating with her, and they became good friends.[33]

It seems, then, that there is no necessary connection between forgiveness and the restoration of particular personal relationships. Personal relationships between the victim and the offender may be restored, terminated, or created when forgiveness takes place, or they may never exist at all. However, forgiveness as it has been defined here does entail respect, compassion, and real goodwill toward the offender. These attitudes may constitute a form of reconciliation very broadly construed, as Roberts's remark suggests. Although it does not necessarily restore particular personal relationships, forgiveness does provide a foundation for all of us to wish each other well and live in mutual respect, peace, and harmony in spite of wrongs that have been committed in the past.

6. Forgiveness, Punishment, and Restitution

Given that forgiveness requires respect and compassion for the offender and a desire that he flourish as a person, it may seem that the person who

---

[32] Geoffrey Scarre, *After Evil*, p. 23.

[33] For a personal account of this process, see Bill Pelke, *Journey of Hope*.

forgives must refrain from imposing any negative consequences on the offender as a result of his offense. Asking for restitution and/or pressing criminal charges may seem incompatible with real goodwill for the offender. In fact, Claudia Card lists as the fourth feature of a paradigmatic case of forgiveness "remission of punishment, if the forgiver has any control there."[34]

Respect, compassion, and real goodwill for the offender do require that we refrain from imposing negative consequences on him *if there are no countervailing considerations*. However, it is important to remember that if these attitudes are morally appropriate responses to the offender as a person, then they are morally appropriate responses to all persons. If we hold these attitudes, we will be reluctant to impose burdens on anyone. However, we may do so in some cases if this is the only way to prevent greater or equal suffering for others. Thus forgiveness is fully compatible with punishment or restitution that is imposed in order to prevent equal or greater harm to others, in a manner that reflects the basic attitudes of respect, compassion, and real goodwill for the offender. On the other hand, I will argue that an attitude of forgiveness is incompatible with many retributive justifications of punishment. I will discuss the implications of an attitude of unconditional genuine forgiveness for the practice of punishment in some detail in Chapter 7.

7. Forgiveness, Attitudes, and Speech Acts

There has been some dispute as to whether forgiveness can best be defined as an internal change of attitudes or as a speech act or performative in which the injured person bestows forgiveness on the offender by saying "I forgive you" (or something similar). Several authors have pointed out that it is quite possible to say "I forgive you" to an offender whom we really haven't forgiven at all, and toward whom we still harbor a great deal of resentment. Thus there is more to forgiveness than a speech act. Novitz explains this point as follows: "Sometimes, it is true, I may appear to forgive just by saying 'I forgive you' – where this performative utterance is thought to constitute and exhaust the act of forgiving. But it does not do so. All that it can do is renounce the claims that I have on you. What it cannot ensure is that I will somehow relinquish the hard feelings that your action occasioned. Since ... one mark of having forgiven a person ... is that one no longer harbors feelings of anger or

---

[34] Claudia Card, "The Atrocity Paradigm Revisited," p. 211.

bitterness, and since the utterance 'I forgive you' cannot ensure this, it is much more like an act of pardoning than it is like forgiving."[35]

However, the performative sense of forgiveness has some importance as well. Dzur and Wertheimer argue as follows: "It may be thought that to say 'I forgive you' without experiencing the relevant emotions is empty. But that is false. The request for and granting of forgiveness has behavioral consequences. If V says 'I forgive you,' V cannot continue to express a desire to see O suffer, or to demand additional apologies. If O says, 'Please forgive me,' O cannot later say, 'I didn't do anything wrong.'"[36]

A complete lexical analysis of forgiveness will include both senses of the term. But again, our purpose here is not to offer a lexical definition of forgiveness, but rather to address the substantive moral question of how we ought to respond to wrongdoing. In this context, viewing forgiveness as a performative puts the cart before the horse. We must first determine whether an *attitude* of forgiveness is an appropriate response to wrongdoing in a given type of situation, or whether a retributive attitude is called for. If a retributive attitude is called for, it will generally not be morally appropriate to say to the offender, "I forgive you." (Exceptions are possible. For example, we should probably say "I forgive you" if a credible terrorist demands that we say this and threatens to unleash a nuclear holocaust if we do not.) If an attitude of forgiveness is appropriate in a given situation, then we can go on to consider whether it is appropriate to perform the corresponding speech act as well. The analysis here is more complex. If we have forgiven the offender and it would be beneficial to tell him so, then the speech act will be appropriate. If we have forgiven the offender, but it would be detrimental at this point to tell him that we have done so, then the speech act should probably be withheld. For example, suppose that a child has committed a relatively serious offense and his mother has sent him to his room to think about the wrong. As soon as the door closes behind the child, the mother realizes that she has forgiven him. She should probably not burst into the room at this point and say "I forgive you," as it would be detrimental to the child to disrupt his contemplation of the wrong.

If we believe that an attitude of forgiveness is morally appropriate in a given situation, but we have not yet managed to overcome our resentment, we will have to decide whether it is better to be honest with the offender or to offer him the peace of mind that he might gain from

[35] David Novitz, "Forgiveness and Self-Respect," p. 301–302.
[36] Albert Dzur and Alan Wertheimer, "Forgiveness and Public Deliberation," p. 12.

hearing us say "I forgive you." There are situations in which honesty will be the best policy. There are also situations in which it may be best to offer the offender peace of mind. For example, if Jane's father begs her forgiveness on his deathbed for a prior offense, and Jane believes forgiveness is appropriate but has not yet overcome her resentment, it may be best for her to tell her father that she forgives him.

Given that we must know whether an attitude of forgiveness or an attitude of resentment is morally appropriate in order to determine whether a speech act of forgiveness is appropriate, there is good reason to define forgiveness as an attitude here. This approach will facilitate our overall examination of response to wrongdoing.

8. Groups and Forgiveness

It seems clear that groups can be wronged, where the size of the group may range from two persons to several generations of the entire global community. For example, if one member of a couple is significantly harmed, the other is likely to be harmed as well. Acts of discrimination often affect all those who share the characteristic on the basis of which the discrimination occurs. Acts of war generally harm entire countries. And the unchecked emission of greenhouse gases is now almost certain to harm entire future generations across the globe for some time to come.[37] It also seems clear that groups can do wrong. A group of persons can get together purposefully to commit some kind of wrongdoing, and any number of people can inflict harm collectively, through behavior that is negligent or willfully wrong.

Perhaps the most confusing question about forgiveness, and the last question I will consider in this section, is whether groups can forgive and/ or be forgiven. Let us first consider the question of whether a group can be forgiven. Forgiving individuals is relatively straightforward in that we know that the offender is responsible for his own wrongdoing and that he is the person to be forgiven. Forgiving groups can be more complicated. We often do not know which persons in the group are responsible for the act of wrongdoing, whether everyone in the group endorsed the decision to commit it (or even knew about this decision), or whether some members of the group actually tried to prevent it. When we forgive groups, it seems reasonable to hold that we forgive those individuals

---

[37] Kate Padgett-Walsh rightly recommended that I clarify the point that the size of groups can vary widely, and some of the ways in which groups can be harmed.

in the group who are responsible for the wrong. Govier objects to this position as follows: "A victim might wish to forgive in the aftermath of institutional wrongdoing without knowing just which individuals within that institution had wronged her. For example, an African American woman not permitted to enter medical school in the 1950's might have long resented that treatment. Were she later to seek to overcome her feelings of resentment and anger, she might not know just which individuals made the decision that so affected her. If she is to forgive, she must somehow forgive the collectivity – a group or institution."[38]

While it is true that we often do not know specifically which individuals have harmed us in this type of situation, I think we can still understand forgiveness of groups in terms of forgiving individuals who make up the group. Suppose that I feel some general resentment toward academia for residual sexist attitudes in this institution. In this case I may know specific individuals within academia who hold sexist attitudes, and here forgiveness is unproblematic. I may also recognize that there are many individuals unknown to me who have contributed to the problem in some way.[39] Without knowing specifically who these individuals are, I can imagine such persons and recognize that they have a moral status equal to my own. I can recognize the importance of their growth and flourishing. I can appreciate that, like the rest of us, they are subject to various needs, pressures, and confusions, and I can imagine which of these pressures may have led to their problematic attitudes. Further, I can recognize that these individuals desire their own happiness and are vulnerable to error, just like the rest of us. I do not need to know who specifically these individuals are in order to forgive them. By working in this way I can overcome my resentment and regard all members of academia with respect, compassion, and real goodwill. I can then turn my attention to positive pursuits, which may include thinking of ways to improve the academic experience for everyone.

The procedure described here allows us to recognize that some members of a group may not have contributed to the wrong in question, and that some may actually have worked very hard to prevent the wrong from occurring. In order to forgive a group by the procedure just described, we need only believe that some members of the group contributed to the wrong. This point is important whether the wrongful behavior is a

---

[38] Trudy Govier, *Forgiveness and Revenge*, p. 84.
[39] Carla Fehr has pointed out to me that many persons are complicit in this form of wrongdoing by failing to speak out against it.

matter of unstructured actions and attitudes that emerge in a group, or a matter of policy that is adopted through the group's official decision-making procedures. It seems problematic either to resent or forgive all of academia for sexist attitudes when many members of academia are trying very hard to eradicate these attitudes. And it seems problematic either to resent or forgive the United States as a whole for the invasion of Iraq or the rejection of the Kyoto Protocol when many U.S. citizens were strongly opposed to these decisions. Although they resulted from our official decision-making procedures, they are certainly not the actions that many of us wanted to take.

If this line of reasoning is correct, then forgiving groups poses no special problems. However, the question of whether groups can forgive is more difficult. Both Desmond Tutu's book *No Future without Forgiveness*, and his work with the Truth and Reconciliation Commission (TRC) in South Africa have demonstrated the enormous potential that forgiveness has in politics. Trudy Govier is clearly inspired by Tutu's work, and attempts to defend the possibility of group forgiveness on philosophical grounds. She identifies three forms of skepticism about group forgiveness – human nature skepticism, fundamental skepticism, and moral skepticism – and attempts to refute each of them in turn.

Human nature skepticism is "the view that forgiveness is for saints and moral heroes and is not achievable by the ordinary people who will constitute the majority of group members."[40] In response, Govier argues persuasively that this form of skepticism is based on a subtly prescriptive and damaging view of human nature. If we believe that human nature is such that most of us cannot forgive, we will tend not to try to forgive, and we will be encouraged to hold onto resentment. It is equally possible to view human nature as forgiving and to develop a culture that supports and encourages forgiveness, as has been done in South Africa.

Fundamental skepticism holds that "since groups do not have minds, they cannot have feelings and attitudes; since forgiveness involves changing our feelings and attitudes, groups cannot forgive."[41] In response to fundamental skepticism, Govier points out, again correctly, that there is a sense in which groups can be understood to have attitudes, both distributively and collectively. A group has an attitude distributively if most people in the group hold this attitude. A group has an attitude collectively if the attitude is endorsed by the group, in the sense that it is

---

[40] Trudy Govier, *Forgiveness and Revenge*, p. 95.
[41] *Ibid.*, p. 79.

articulated in some way by duly appointed leaders of the group and not repudiated afterward by a substantial number of citizens. And in either of these senses, a group's attitudes can change over time.

Moral skepticism is the view that even if it is logically and psychologically possible for groups to forgive, "it would not be morally appropriate for them to do so. Only individuals can be victims of wrongdoing, and only victims are entitled to forgive."[42] Govier recognizes that Tutu and the TRC have been criticized on these grounds. She quotes one young South African woman as objecting as follows: "What really makes me angry about the TRC and Tutu is that they are putting pressure on us to forgive. For most black South Africans the TRC is about us having to forgive... I don't know if I will ever be ready to forgive. I carry this ball of anger inside me and I don't even know where to begin dealing with it... The oppression was bad, but what is much worse, what makes me even more angry, is that they are trying to dictate my forgiveness."[43] Govier responds to this problem by reminding us that there are not only primary victims of wrongdoing, but also secondary and tertiary victims. In cases of serious political oppression, a large portion of the population will be at least tertiary victims, if not primary or secondary victims as well. She argues that "even if we grant the assumption that victims have a special prerogative to forgive, there remains moral space for groups to forgive, because – distributively and collectively – groups can be victims." Given that many of the primary victims are dead in cases of serious political wrongdoing, she adds that "to restrict all forgiveness to primary victims is, in effect, to recommend non-forgiveness and enduring hatred and resentment, for the many large-scale political offenses characterized by killing."[44]

Here I think Govier's argument moves too fast. It is true that in many cases of serious political wrongdoing, virtually all the members of the injured group will be tertiary victims. However, this fact alone does not open up "moral space for groups to forgive." Any individual member of the group can forgive the primary, secondary, or tertiary harm that was inflicted on her. But the question at issue is whether a duly appointed leader of a group can forgive, on behalf of other members of the group, those who have wrongfully harmed them. The force of the objection raised by the young South African woman quoted earlier is that *she*

[42] *Ibid.*, p. 92.
[43] *Ibid.*, p. 94.
[44] *Ibid.*

should be free to decide for herself whether she will forgive the various kinds of harm that were inflicted *on her.*

I want to suggest that this problem about group forgiveness stems from the fact that resentment, as we saw earlier, is a response not to general wrongs but to wrongs done to us personally. When we ourselves are wrongfully harmed, it is certainly our prerogative to determine whether or not we will forgive, and to take the time we need to heal from the wrong. Others cannot forgive on our behalf, or force or pressure us to forgive, without violating our autonomy in this regard. Nevertheless, it is clear that the work of Desmond Tutu and the TRC has great value. I believe the solution to this paradox is to recognize that while an attitude of forgiveness pertains to wrongs done to us personally, it is based on the more general attitudes of respect, compassion, and real goodwill. I will argue in Chapters 3 and 7 that respect, compassion, and real goodwill are morally appropriate attitudes to extend to all persons despite any wrongdoing they may have committed. They are morally appropriate attitudes for individuals to adopt toward those who have wronged them personally, and they are also morally appropriate attitudes for groups to adopt toward any individuals who are guilty of wrongdoing. It is true that as autonomous moral agents, each of us is responsible for determining our own beliefs and attitudes. However, it is also true that groups are responsible for adopting morally appropriate beliefs and attitudes, even if some individual citizens disagree with them. For example, it is appropriate for the state to endorse the moral belief that persons have a right not to be tortured, even if there are some citizens who disagree with this belief. Therefore, if it can be argued that respect, compassion, and real goodwill are morally appropriate attitudes to extend toward all persons regardless of any wrongdoing they may have committed, it will follow that groups (including states) ought to adopt these attitudes toward all wrongdoers. And this argument holds in spite of the fact that groups are not morally entitled to forgive, on behalf of individual citizens, the wrongs that those individuals have suffered personally.

If this line of reasoning is correct, then we can respect individual victims and their prerogative to decide for themselves whether or not to forgive whatever wrongs they have suffered and at the same time decide publicly (or as a group) to extend respect, compassion, and real goodwill to those who have committed these offenses. In doing so, we clearly do not recommend "non-forgiveness and enduring hatred and resentment for the many large-scale political offenses characterized by killing," as Govier fears. Further, we can give a resounding endorsement to the model provided for us by the pioneering efforts of Tutu and the TRC, although we may want to revise this model in hindsight to provide more recognition of the individual victim's prerogative to make her own decision about forgiveness. Although I cannot make the case here, I believe that this group did a remarkable job of proceeding with respect, compassion, and real goodwill for offenders and victims alike, and achieved results that were highly beneficial for all. Likewise, we can endorse the political attitude expressed by President Lincoln in his famous phrase, "with malice toward none, with charity for all...," concerning the way to proceed in the aftermath of the Civil War.[45] And we can endorse the goodwill extended by the Allies to Germany and Japan after World War II. I will return to the issue of public response to wrongdoing later in the book when we consider the implications of the paradigm of forgiveness for legal and social policies. Let us now turn to the moral analysis of the basic attitudes of forgiveness and resentment.

[45] For an enlightening discussion of this and other instances of what might be considered political forgiveness, see Patrick Glynn, "Towards a Politics of Forgiveness."

3

The Moral Analysis of the Attitudes of Forgiveness and Resentment

In this chapter I provide a moral analysis of the attitudes of resentment and forgiveness. I begin with a brief defense of the choice to undertake this analysis from the perspective of virtue, rather than from the perspectives of duty or utility. Then I outline a process of addressing the wrong that many individuals will need to complete before they decide either on an attitude of forgiveness or on an attitude of resentment in response to the wrong perpetrated against them. This process will be important regardless of whether we endorse the paradigm of forgiveness or a retributive defense of resentment. I then proceed to analyze the moral appropriateness of the attitudes of resentment and forgiveness for the individual who has completed the process of addressing the wrong, or for the individual who does not need to do so. The compatibility of each of these attitudes with self-respect, respect for morality, and respect for the offender as an autonomous moral agent is examined in turn. I conclude with a summary of the moral orientation toward persons embodied in each of these basic attitudes.

THREE APPROACHES TO THE MORAL ANALYSIS OF FORGIVENESS

Geoffrey Scarre suggests that there are three potentially promising perspectives from which to approach the moral assessment of forgiveness – the perspectives of duty, virtue, and utility.[1] Whereas Scarre rejects the duty-based and virtue-based approaches and develops a utilitarian

---

[1] Geoffrey Scarre, *After Evil*, p. 37.

analysis of forgiveness, I develop a virtue-based analysis of forgiveness and set aside the approaches based on duty and utility. I do not attempt to defend the decision to do so in depth, as such a defense would require a long and laborious excursion into ethical theory. Instead, I leave it to the reader to judge at the end of the book whether the virtue-oriented approach developed here is successful. However, it will be worthwhile to indicate briefly at the outset some of the central concerns about the duty-based and utilitarian analyses of forgiveness, and to respond to two of the central objections to the virtue-oriented approach raised recently by Scarre, Garrard, and McNaughton.

There are a number of reasons to question the feasibility of a duty-based analysis of forgiveness. First, as many authors have pointed out, we do not have complete control of our thoughts and feelings. Therefore, when forgiveness is construed as an internal change of heart, we will not necessarily be able to forgive on command. If *ought* implies *can*, then it seems that strictly speaking we could at most have a duty to try to forgive. In some cases it seems reasonably plausible to claim that we have a duty of this sort. For example, if an offender wrongs us in a relatively trivial manner, and then apologizes many times and goes way out of his way to make amends, it seems that we really ought to try to forgive him. On the other hand, in cases of serious wrongs, it seems unfair to say that in addition to having to absorb a major loss, the victim acquires a "duty" to try to forgive the offender. If this latter intuition is correct, then a duty-based analysis of forgiveness would apply only to cases of lesser wrongdoing.

Scarre identifies a further problem with the duty-based approach to forgiveness that arises even in cases of less serious wrongs. He says that "it is often said that granting forgiveness is closely akin to giving a gift. On this view, when the person offended forgives the offender, she grants a boon rather than performs a duty or satisfies a right."[2] Basically it seems that the offender has no right to our forgiveness. Rather, in view of his offense, it seems that it would be nice or generous of us to forgive him. In this case we would not have a duty to forgive.

We could attempt to avoid this difficulty by regarding forgiveness as an imperfect duty rather than as a perfect duty. If we have an imperfect duty to help others, then no particular individual has a right to our help, and anyone we choose to help receives a gift. Likewise, if we have an imperfect duty to forgive, then the offender has no right to our forgiveness and receives a gift if we forgive him. While this strategy

---

[2] *Ibid.*, p. 39.

seems plausible initially, I think it is problematic. Kant's two paradigmatic examples of imperfect duties in the *Groundwork* are helping others and developing our talents. It is impossible to fulfill these imperatives completely, and therefore we must make choices in implementing them. However, the situation is fundamentally different with forgiveness. For most of us it is possible to forgive every time we develop a significant resentment. Further, it seems counterintuitive to say that we can appropriately choose whom to forgive and whom to resent on the basis of personal preference, whereas it seems very plausible to say that we can make choices about helping others or developing our talents on this basis. I feel no guilt about making charitable donations to environmental and Buddhist organizations as a matter of personal preference, or about developing my abilities in philosophy as opposed to my somewhat stronger mathematical abilities, simply because I like philosophy better than mathematics. But if, for example, a woman chooses to forgive men much more frequently than women simply because she is attracted to men, then she may seem less than fully admirable.

Although they do not bear on the question of whether we actually have a duty to forgive, two further cautionary points should be made about viewing forgiveness as a duty. First, regarding forgiveness as a duty is likely to lead to a kind of premature forgiveness that will be described in the next section. I will argue that a victim of wrongdoing may need to work through a process of addressing the wrong if she is to respect herself and reach a state of genuine forgiveness. If so, she must be able to explore her thoughts and feelings about the wrong openly, and in her own time as she completes this work. It is both morally problematic and counterproductive to pressure victims through the process of addressing the wrong, and this process can easily be derailed if the victim is driven by the thought that she has a duty to forgive.

Second, regarding forgiveness as a duty may be misleading in that it suggests that forgiving involves some kind of sacrifice, or something that we have to do for others even if we don't want to. I want to suggest, to the contrary, that far from being a sacrifice, reaching a state of genuine forgiveness is a gift for the person who forgives as well as for the offender. It is both pleasant and beneficial for the injured person to reach this state. As we come to understand the nature and benefits of genuine forgiveness more fully, we will be no more inclined to view forgiveness as a duty than we will be inclined to say that we have a duty to take a vacation.

The utilitarian approach to forgiveness also seems problematic. Scarre summarizes it abstractly as follows: "Utilitarians believe that forgiveness derives its value from its propensity to make the world a better place. Whether forgiveness is called for in a given case depends on whether granting it is likely to produce more good than refusing it."[3] One problem with the utilitarian analysis is that it seems to result in the kind of "malady of the spirit" that Stocker has identified, in which our reasons for taking a particular action fail to coincide with our motives for doing so. Scarre recognizes that on the utilitarian analysis, forgiveness may lack spontaneity and be too calculating, particularly in the context of intimate personal relationships. He responds that if utilitarian calculations damage the quality of our personal relationships, then a consistent utilitarian will reject calculations in this domain in favor of the cultivation of dispositions that enhance personal relationships – including a disposition to forgive.

While this response seems plausible and maintains the consistency of the utilitarian position, it fails to solve the problem at hand. Suppose that a husband forgives his wife for some offense that she has committed against him. Ideally, it seems that he will be motivated to forgive her because he has compassion and respect for her and genuinely wishes her well. If he has cultivated the traits recommended in Scarre's analysis, he may well be so motivated. However, on Scarre's analysis, his *reason* for forgiving her would be that the best consequences will be produced overall if husbands cultivate a general disposition to forgive their wives. Thus his motive for forgiving and his reason for forgiving will diverge, and his overall state of heart and mind will not be harmonious. This result might be avoided if we adopt some version of self-effacing consequentialism, but self-deception (or mass deception) seems no more attractive than a divergence between our motives and reasons.

Scarre recognizes another potential objection to the utilitarian analysis of forgiveness. The objection is that on the utilitarian account, "forgiveness appears to concern not just the offender but everyone else as well."[4] He responds again that utility may well be maximized if we set aside utilitarian calculations concerning the rest of the world in our intimate personal relationships, and cultivate dispositions, such as the disposition to forgive, that will enhance our happiness overall in this domain.

While this response goes some distance toward meeting the objection, it does not go all the way. Suppose I am wronged by an unpopular

---

[3] *Ibid.*, p. 46.
[4] *Ibid.*, p. 47.

colleague, Max. Max is old enough to retire comfortably and with full retirement benefits, but he is still able to perform well at his job. Suppose also that if I maintain an attitude of resentment toward Max, then everyone else in the department will feel free to do the same, with the result that Max will feel alienated enough that he prefers to retire. On the other hand, if I forgive Max, others will feel uncomfortable expressing their negative feelings about him, and he will continue to work. Finally, suppose that utility would be maximized if Max were to retire, that all of these facts are apparent to me, and that I am fully capable of making this judgment while maintaining a general disposition to forgive in my intimate personal relationships. On the utilitarian analysis it seems that the external factors in this case determine that I should maintain an attitude of resentment toward Max, and this result seems problematic. In Strawson's terms, by proceeding in this manner I adopt the objective attitude toward Max. Rather than relating to him directly as a person and respecting him as an autonomous moral agent, I regard him as someone to be managed or manipulated in such a way as to produce the best consequences overall. In Kantian terms, I use him as a mere means to this end.

These general objections to the utilitarian analysis, and others, are by now thoroughly familiar, and I will say no more about them here. Suffice it to say that the utilitarian analysis of forgiveness seems to raise the same kinds of problems that are encountered by this theory in other areas. It is also interesting to note that while Scarre presents a very careful and thorough utilitarian analysis of response to wrongdoing, his conclusions differ significantly from my own. He argues that forgiveness is justified in some cases but not in others, whereas I argue that unconditional genuine forgiveness is always appropriate and desirable from a moral point of view. He also suggests that punishment can be justified, in part, "as a means for releasing justifiable anger or resentment...,"[5] whereas I hold that punishment cannot be justified in this way. Therefore, in comparing the utilitarian analysis of forgiveness with the virtue-based approach developed here, the reader can assess the plausibility not only of the two different theoretical approaches, but also of the different practical conclusions that emerge from them.

Before we begin the virtue-based analysis of forgiveness, it will be helpful to consider an objection to this approach raised by Scarre and, in a slightly different form, by Garrard and McNaughton. Scarre cites

---

[5] *Ibid.*, p. 120.

an objection to Aristotelian virtue ethics raised by Robert Nozick. The objection is that on this theory, moral deliberation is basically egocentric, and fails to take sufficient account of others. In Nozick's words, "another person's moral claim then constitutes a tenuous side-effect of your own pursuit of your own good."[6] Scarre then remarks, "One reason why virtue-ethicists fall into this trap is that they need to provide a criterion for distinguishing virtues and vices that is consistent with their claim that the evaluation of character is prior to that of acts. Evaluating character independently of acts inevitably focuses attention on the value of virtue to its possessor rather than on the beneficial effects that virtuous agents produce."[7]

While this criticism may (or may not) apply to Aristotle's position, it is critical for our purposes here to understand that virtue ethics is *not* inevitably centered on the value of virtue to its possessor. Nor need it fail to take sufficient account of others. The virtue-ethical approach developed here does not fall into this trap. Here, virtues are defined in terms of morally appropriate attitudes. Whether or not an attitude is morally appropriate is determined by whether it incorporates a correct cognitive recognition of the morally salient features of the situation in question, and by whether the affective and motivational components respond appropriately as well.[8] The value of a virtue to its possessor plays no role in this assessment. Clearly the possession of morally appropriate attitudes will often lead us to a concern with consequences, both for others and for ourselves. For example, we cannot have respect and compassion for others without concerning ourselves with the ways in which their lives are made better or worse. Nor can we have self-respect without paying some attention to our own needs. However, on the virtue-ethical approach suggested here, attitudes are not assessed in terms of their instrumental value to us, nor are they assessed in terms of their instrumental value in maximizing utility. Rather, they are assessed in terms of the intrinsic appropriateness of the responses they embody to the morally salient features of the type of situation in question. The attitudes we

---

[6] Robert Nozick, *Philosophical Explanations*, p. 41.
[7] Geoffrey Scarre, *After Evil*, p. 43.
[8] More broadly construed, the moral appropriateness of an attitude is determined by whether it is compatible with the recognition of all forms of intrinsic value, and a correct assessment of which values are more fundamental in situations in which they come into conflict. Because responding to wrongdoing concerns moral agents, both as wrongdoers and as injured persons who must determine how to respond to wrongdoing, we need not consider respect for other kinds of intrinsic value here.

are examining here – forgiveness and resentment – will be assessed by ascertaining whether they are morally appropriate responses to persons who are guilty of wrongdoing. More specifically, they will be assessed in terms of whether they incorporate sufficient respect for the victims of wrongdoing, the requirements of morality, and the status of the offender as a moral agent and sentient being. The assessment of attitudes, and by extension, character traits, is prior to the assessment of acts in this sense. If our attitudes are morally appropriate in the sense just described, then the actions that stem from them will be morally appropriate as well.

Garrard and McNaughton present a slightly different version of this objection. They say that "we wish to put to one side a certain kind of reason for forgiveness, one advocated by many writers on this topic (especially Holmgren 1993). The thought here is that a major reason for forgiveness is that it is good for the forgiver – it lifts the burden of hatred and resentment from her shoulders and allows her to move on in her life. But this is an attitude-focused reason for forgiving and we are seeking an object-focused one. Attitude-focused reasons for actions are reasons for getting oneself into a particular psychological state, in this case having a forgiving attitude. To adopt a forgiving attitude in order to make oneself feel better is to act on an attitude-focused reason. Object-focused reasons reveal the way in which the relationship that actually holds between the victim and the offender makes a forgiving response appropriate."[9]

This passage seriously misconstrues the type of moral analysis I presented in the article cited and the moral analysis I wish to develop in more depth here. The moral appropriateness of an attitude clearly does not turn on whether adopting that attitude makes us feel better. I believe that adopting an attitude of unconditional genuine forgiveness does make us feel better, but this is not why it is a morally appropriate attitude. Rather, the appropriateness of this attitude depends on whether it is compatible with the forms of respect listed earlier. In the terminology suggested by Garrard and McNaughton, attitudes, as I construe them, are object-focused. An attitude of unconditional genuine forgiveness is morally appropriate because it responds appropriately to *the offender as a person*. By adopting this attitude (and by performing the actions that stem from it), we relate ourselves properly to the offender as an autonomous moral agent and as a sentient being. If my arguments are correct, then, the objections raised by Scarre, Garrard, and McNaughton

---

[9] Eve Garrard and David McNaughton, "In Defense of Unconditional Forgiveness," pp. 51–52.

will not apply to the virtue-ethical analysis of forgiveness proposed here. Although much more could be said about the strengths and weaknesses of these three approaches, let us now turn to the virtue-based analysis of response to wrongdoing.

THE PROCESS OF ADDRESSING THE WRONG

As I have said, my purpose here is to outline a broadly coherent position on how we ought to respond to wrongdoing. We are now in a position to begin this outline for cases in which we, as individuals, must respond to wrongs perpetrated against us. (I will consider the morally appropriate response to wrongs that we have perpetrated against others in Chapter 4, and social policies that can best be adopted in response to wrongdoing in Chapters 7 and 8.) In many cases when we have been wrongfully harmed by another, we will have to undertake a process of addressing the wrong, and this process is the first step we ought to take in responding to the offense. We may not need to undertake this process if the wrong is relatively trivial, if we are advanced spiritual masters like the Dalai Lama or Lopon-la, or if we have become very adept at responding to wrongdoing. However, for many of us who experience nontrivial wrongs, part or all of this process will be important, and it should precede the cultivation of the final moral attitude we choose to adopt toward the offender.[10]

This process is significant in its own right as the first step in responding to wrongdoing for many victims. In addition, failure to recognize the nature and importance of this process may lead to unnecessary confusion in the moral analysis of the final attitude that can best be adopted in response to wrongdoing. More specifically, it may lead us to confuse an attitude of forgiveness that constitutes a reasonable candidate for a morally worthy response to wrongdoing – an attitude of *genuine* forgiveness – with other attitudes that may resemble genuine forgiveness in some ways, but that are clearly defective in one way or another. (Robert Enright refers to these defective types of forgiveness as "pseudo-forgiveness."[11]) In addition to outlining the process of addressing the wrong, therefore, I will clarify the concept of genuine forgiveness in this section.

---

[10] The more extensively we cultivate virtuous attitudes in ourselves, and the more carefully we think about response to wrongdoing, the more quickly this process will go. As we progress, we may be able to reach a state of genuine forgiveness very quickly.

[11] See Robert D. Enright and Richard P. Fitzgibbons, *Helping Clients to Forgive*.

Self-respect is the primary virtue that governs the process of addressing the wrong. Given that self-respect is a fundamental component of both the paradigm of forgiveness and of retributivist defenses of the attitude of resentment, it is likely that advocates of either of these positions could endorse the process I will describe in this section. Further, it is important to remember that retributivists will advocate forgiveness in some cases – most typically, in cases in which the offender truly repents and does his best to make amends for the wrong. Therefore the concept of genuine forgiveness is also likely to be important for advocates of attitudinal retributivism.

One caveat is in order before we proceed. The following outline of the process of addressing the wrong is not meant to imply that the injured person should take these distinct steps, or take them in this order. Healing from victimization is a complex and multifaceted task, and may be quite idiosyncratic. Further, this is one of the points at which a full development of the paradigm of forgiveness will draw heavily on the empirical sciences. Psychological research will provide us with important information about how the process of addressing the wrong can best be structured. For examples of valuable studies of this sort, let me refer the reader at this point to Robert Enright and Richard Fitzgibbon's excellent work *Helping Clients to Forgive* and to Fred Luskin's groundbreaking study *Forgive for Good*. While psychologists will tell us how we can most effectively structure the work of addressing various sorts of wrongs, my goal here is simply to identify the elements of the process an individual may need to complete if she is to respect herself and truly forgive her offender.

The first task for the victim in the process of addressing the wrong is to recover her self-esteem. As Murphy points out, every act of wrongdoing carries with it the implicit message that the victim does not warrant a full measure of respect. In Murphy's words, the message is "I count and you do not, and I may use you as a mere thing."[12] For example, if John rapes Jane, he is implicitly claiming that her needs and feelings don't count, or at the very least, that they don't count as much as his. And depending on how the crime is committed, the claim may be much more disparaging than this. Thus the victim must clarify for herself that she is just as valuable as every other person, that she has the same moral status as everyone else, and that her needs and feelings matter very much.

[12] Jeffrie G. Murphy, "Forgiveness in Counseling," p. 44. See also Jean Hampton, *Forgiveness and Mercy*, p. 83.

If the victim attempts to forgive the offender before she understands this point, her forgiveness is not fully appropriate. Suppose that Jane attempts to forgive John, vaguely agreeing with his implicit claim that his needs are more important than hers, or worse, vaguely agreeing that she deserved to be raped. Here, Jane obviously fails to respect herself sufficiently, and her attempt at forgiveness is morally problematic in this regard. If she is to respond appropriately to the incident of wrongdoing, the victim must first be clear in her own mind about her own worth. Further, the type of forgiveness described here is problematic in that it amounts to condoning the wrong rather than actually forgiving the offender for having committed it. Therefore, in order to reach an attitude of genuine forgiveness, the victim must understand the nature of the wrong, and to do so she must understand her own status as a person.

A second task for the victim follows immediately from the foregoing discussion. She must come to recognize that the act perpetrated against her was wrong, and she must also understand why it was wrong. That is, she must understand that she has certain rights and that anyone who violates those rights wrongfully harms her. If the injured person fails to understand that the offender's act was wrong, then her response to the incident will again be morally inappropriate in that it fails to incorporate sufficient self-respect. Further, any attempt to forgive in this case will be problematic in that it will amount to condoning the offense rather than forgiving the offender for having committed it.

Third, it is important for the victim of wrongdoing to acknowledge her true feelings about the incident. She is likely to have a variety of reasonable emotional responses to the incident of wrongdoing – grief over her loss, anger toward the offender, feelings of betrayal, and other emotions, depending on the circumstances. In healing from her victimization, it is important that the injured person allow herself to experience reasonable feelings of this sort. These feelings will connect her to the reality of what has happened and help her to appreciate more fully both the nature of the wrong and her own status as a person. (Exaggerated or excessive feelings, such as homicidal rage toward the offender, should clearly be regulated rather than indulged uncritically.)

For a variety of reasons, the victim may want to shut down her feelings and attempt to forgive her offender immediately. For example, she may feel she has a duty to forgive, or that forgiving is the Christian thing to do. She may feel that it is wrong to be angry at family members, at friends, or at anyone at all. Or on some level, if her grief or anger is significant, forgiving the offender may seem easier than experiencing these intense emotions. However, the victim fails to respect herself sufficiently if she attempts to forgive in this manner. Not only does she treat herself in a psychologically destructive manner by shutting down her emotions, she also deceives herself about the true nature of her feelings. In order to respect herself as an autonomous moral agent, she must explore her own thoughts and feelings fully, and determine for herself how she wants to respond to the wrong. This type of forgiveness is inappropriate, then, to the extent that it is incompatible with the victim's self-respect. Further, we should recognize that if we are to forgive in a worthy manner, we will not simply refuse to recognize our negative feelings toward the offender. Instead, we will experience an actual change of heart, in which these negative feelings are overcome and replaced on a spontaneous level with real goodwill toward the offender. Returning to our discussion of attitudes in Chapter 2, we can express this point by saying that genuine forgiveness, or the kind of attitude that we should strive to cultivate in ourselves, is an integrated moral attitude. The victim who shuts down her feelings in an attempt to forgive will at best achieve only a fragmented attitude in which the affective component is suppressed.

Fourth, the victim of wrongdoing faces the task of assessing her situation with respect to the offender. The offender may have attitudes and behavior patterns that are likely to harm her again in the future, and it is important for her to determine the steps she needs to take to protect herself from further victimization. It is also important for her to take her own need for rewarding personal relationships seriously. If she has a personal relationship with the offender, she needs to consider, in light of the offense, whether there is a significant problem in the relationship that needs to be addressed or whether the relationship should be redefined or terminated.

If the victim attempts to forgive without considering her own needs for protection and rewarding personal relationships, she again fails to respect herself sufficiently. Further, her forgiveness will be problematic if she deceives herself about the offender's attitudes and behavior patterns. A morally worthy attitude of forgiveness will not be based on self-deception or on a blindly unrealistic hope that the offender will be different in the future. Rather, it will be based on the victim's recognition of the offender as he actually is – as a sentient being and moral agent with a status equal to her own.

Fifth, depending on the circumstances it may be important for the victim to express her beliefs and feelings to the wrongdoer. She may need to tell him that his action was wrong, that it is not acceptable for her to be treated in this manner, that she feels hurt about the incident, and so on. If the victim does feel a need to express her beliefs or feelings, then it is important that she do so, unless this course of action would be dangerous or detrimental to herself or others. At the very least she should not withhold her feelings, thinking they are not important or not as important as the wrongdoer's. If the victim withholds something she needs to say in this manner, she fails to respect herself. Further, the incident will not be over for her in this case, and she will not achieve the true internal resolution of the incident that an integrated attitude of forgiveness requires. The victim who fails to achieve a true internal resolution of the issue will achieve at best a conflicted attitude in which she has mixed feelings about the offender and the offense.

The final task for the victim of wrongdoing is to determine whether she wants to seek restitution from the offender or to press criminal charges. In order to respect herself, the victim must recognize that she has been wrongfully harmed and is owed restitution for any substantive losses she has incurred as a result of the offense. Respect for her own integrity also requires that she look objectively and with compassion at the wrongdoer's situation. If the offense was a criminal act, she must consider the needs of society as well. She must then make a reasoned judgment about how she wants to proceed. If the victim bypasses this task in an attempt to forgive her offender, she again fails to respect herself. Further, in this case the victim will not achieve the full internal resolution of the issue that an integrated attitude of forgiveness requires. Again, her attitude at best will be conflicted.

In many cases, the steps outlined here will be central to the victim's self-respect and to her healing from the act of abuse perpetrated against her. For many victims, then, these steps are the first steps to be taken in responding to wrongdoing. It is important to emphasize that a variety of attitudes may arise during the process of addressing the wrong. The victim is very likely to adopt a temporary attitude of resentment and to experience other negative emotions as she works her way through this process. Again, we should not condemn these feelings in ourselves or others while we are doing the work of addressing the wrong. When the wrongdoing is serious, these feelings are normal human reactions to a difficult situation. More importantly, they are part of a process that may enable the victim to adopt an attitude toward her offender that is truly worthy from a moral point of view. As I argued in Chapter 2, it is important to distinguish the attitudes and motives that arise temporarily in the process of addressing the wrong from the moral worth of the attitude that the victim finally chooses to adopt toward the offender.

Once the victim has taken the steps just described, she has done what she needs to do for herself. She has also avoided a number of errors that may lead to premature forgiveness, or to an attitude that may resemble a worthy attitude of forgiveness in some respects, but one that is clearly defective in one way or another. At this point, the injured person is in a position to drop the focus on herself and to consider the moral attitude she wishes to cultivate toward the offender. We should recall here that some victims will be able to reach this point without completing the process just described. If the wrong was not serious, if these victims are advanced spiritual masters, or if they are very adept at responding to wrongdoing, they will be able to avoid the kinds of errors described above and focus much more quickly and directly on the moral attitude they wish to adopt toward the offender.

If the injured person wishes to forgive the offender at this point, her forgiveness will be genuine. As we can now define the term, a victim's forgiveness is genuine only if she regards herself with sufficient self-respect, and if she does not condone the wrong, engage in self-deception, or evade any of the issues she needs to address with the offender as a result of his offense. The victim who reaches a state of genuine forgiveness does not deceive herself about her own status as a person or about the nature of the wrong. She does not deceive herself about her feelings concerning the offense, or about the wrongdoer's attitudes and behavior patterns. Instead, she forgives him with a clear understanding of these matters, knowing that she has addressed with him the issues that need to be addressed, and that she has taken the steps she needs to take to honor her own needs. In this case, when she forgives the offender she will adopt an integrated attitude of genuine forgiveness.

In the remainder of this chapter, I will assess the moral appropriateness of an attitude of resentment and an attitude of genuine forgiveness for an injured person who has completed the process of addressing the wrong, or for a victim who does not need to undertake this process. Before we leave the process of addressing the wrong, however, I want to emphasize its importance. Jeffrie Murphy has stressed, and rightly so, that great moral harm can accompany premature forgiveness. He points out that battered wives who are encouraged to be forgiving may stay with their husbands and incur further abuse, which may well be fatal for them. He also reminds us that "slavery, oppression, and victimization are made worse, not better, when people are rendered content in their victimization."[13] Although it has not received much attention, the process of addressing the wrong is of fundamental importance for many injured persons. Victims who need this process must take it seriously, and should be encouraged to complete it prior to adopting a final attitude of forgiveness.

DIVERGENCE OF THE PARADIGM OF FORGIVENESS AND ATTITUDINAL RETRIBUTIVISM

Whereas advocates of both attitudinal retributivism and the paradigm of forgiveness can endorse the process of addressing the wrong just described, they will part company on the question of whether the victim who has completed this process (or who does not need to do so) should adopt an attitude of resentment or forgiveness. Some authors hold that forgiveness is appropriate only if certain conditions are met, and that an attitude of resentment is otherwise called for. The most common position among them is that forgiveness is appropriate only if the offender repents. Murphy, in his early work, holds that forgiveness is appropriate only if the wrongdoer repents, if he meant well, if he has suffered enough already, if he has undergone humiliation, or if he has been a loyal friend in the past.[14] Richards holds that forgiveness may be appropriate if the wrong was not recent or serious, if the wrongdoer repents, if he had an excuse, if he was a loyal friend, or if one engages in the same behavior oneself.[15] Hieronymi suggests that forgiveness is appropriate only if the offender repents, or perhaps if the victim receives "strong community support," such that the community affirms the wrongness of the offense, the worth of the victim, and the offender's status as a moral agent.[16] And Griswold holds that "the agent requires reasons in order to commit to giving up resentment," which are present if the wrongdoer repents and goes through various steps of accepting responsibility for the wrong, reforming his character, and offering the victim an extensive apology in a respectful and caring manner.[17] Each of these criteria (except Richards's last) centers on the actions, attitudes, or positions of the wrongdoer (or in Hieronymi's case, perhaps also of the members of the community).

---

[13] Jeffrie G. Murphy, "Forgiveness in Counseling," p. 46.
[14] Jeffrie G. Murphy, *Forgiveness and Mercy*, p. 24–29.
[15] Norvin Richards, "Forgiveness."
[16] Pamela Hieronymi, "Articulating an Uncompromising Forgiveness," p. 553.
[17] Charles Griswold, *Forgiveness*, p. 49. See pp. 49–52 for an explanation of these steps.

The paradigm of forgiveness, as I develop it here, holds rather that the moral appropriateness of forgiveness turns only on the internal preparation of the person who forgives. If the victim has completed the process of addressing the wrong, or if this process is unnecessary, then it is always morally appropriate and desirable for her to forgive, regardless of whether the offender repents and regardless of what he has done or suffered. Therefore, in the context of the position I am developing here, forgiveness can be viewed as both unconditional and unilateral.

However, a caveat is in order about the use of the term "unilateral." Much has been made in recent literature of the distinction between unilateral and bilateral forgiveness. It is important to remember that on the virtue-ethical approach developed here, attitudes are primary. First we develop and cultivate morally worthy attitudes in ourselves and then we work from these attitudes to determine morally appropriate actions and social policies. I will argue in the remainder of this chapter that adopting an attitude of unconditional genuine forgiveness toward the offender is always morally appropriate for the victim who has completed the process of addressing the wrong (or who does not need to do so), whereas maintaining an attitude of resentment toward the offender until he has met certain conditions is not. Thus the victim can and should cultivate an attitude of genuine forgiveness unilaterally, without waiting for any particular response on the part of the offender.

However, the victim's unilateral cultivation of an attitude of unconditional genuine forgiveness does not preclude what is commonly referred to as "bilateral" forgiveness. Once the victim has adopted an attitude of unconditional genuine forgiveness toward the offender, her interactions with him can take a variety of forms. The offender may repent and apologize to the victim, and the victim may then tell the offender that she forgives him (bilateral forgiveness). The victim may initiate an open and compassionate discussion of the wrong with the offender in hopes that the offender will repent and that some kind of social relationship between them can be restored (invitational forgiveness).[18] Or the victim and offender may never engage in an open discussion of the wrong (because the offender is dead or otherwise incapacitated, or because he does not believe that he did anything wrong, or because he is not sorry for having committed the wrong, or for some other reason), while the victim forgives the offender nonetheless. This latter situation is often

---

[18] For an excellent discussion of invitational forgiveness, see Trudy Govier and Colin Hirano, "A Conception of Invitational Forgiveness."

referred to as "unilateral" forgiveness in the literature because the victim forgives the offender without engaging in any kind of interactive process with him. In the analysis I am developing here, however, forgiveness should be understood as unilateral in a broader and more internal sense. On my analysis, the victim *unilaterally* cultivates *her own* attitude of genuine forgiveness *independent* of the offender's actions and attitudes, and then is able to interact with the offender in the variety of ways described, depending on the circumstances. Thus the key distinction for our purposes here is the distinction between unconditional and conditional forgiveness, and the central question is whether the victim who has completed the process of addressing the wrong should forgive the offender unconditionally, or whether she should maintain an attitude of resentment toward the offender until he meets certain conditions.

In the remainder of this chapter I will begin the defense of the paradigm of forgiveness by offering a defense of the basic attitude of unconditional genuine forgiveness. In keeping with the virtue-ethical approach I have described, I will attempt to show that an attitude of unconditional genuine forgiveness is fully compatible with self-respect, respect for morality, and respect for the offender as a moral agent and as a sentient being. It is therefore a virtue, or a morally worthy attitude that we should strive to cultivate in ourselves as a regular response to wrongdoing. Further, I will argue that an attitude of resentment toward an unrepentant offender is to some extent incompatible with these three forms of respect, and is therefore not fully appropriate for the victim who has completed the process of addressing the wrong or for the victim who is able to adopt an attitude of genuine forgiveness directly. For simplicity of argument, I will address the case of an unrepentant offender, assuming that he has not been exempted from resentment by any of the special conditions cited earlier by various authors as possible reasons for forgiveness. If I can show that unconditional genuine forgiveness is warranted in this case, then we need not concern ourselves with any of these other conditions. The argument will show *a fortiori* that unconditional genuine forgiveness is uniformly appropriate and desirable from a moral point of view. Let us begin by examining the compatibility of the attitudes of resentment and unconditional genuine forgiveness with self-respect.

FORGIVENESS, RESENTMENT, AND SELF-RESPECT

Those who believe that an attitude of resentment is morally appropriate toward an unrepentant offender offer a number of reasons for believing that forgiveness may be incompatible with self-respect in this type of situation. Murphy, Haber, and Hieronymi (among others) argue that forgiveness may be incompatible with self-respect because by forgiving we acquiesce in, or at least fail to protest, the claim implicit in the act of wrongdoing that disparages our worth. Murphy says, "Wrongdoing is in part a communicative act, an act that gives out a degrading or insulting message to the victim – the message 'I count and you do not, and I may use you as a mere thing.' Resentment of the wrongdoer is one way that a victim may evince, emotionally, that he or she does *not endorse* the degrading message..."[19] Haber argues that in responding to an unrepentant offender "bad feelings are ... not only natural ... but called for as an expression of aversion to mistreatment."[20] And Hieronymi says that "resentment protests a past action that persists as a present threat. The levelheaded among us might now ask, how can a past action pose a present threat? I suggest that a past wrong against you ... makes a claim. It says, in effect, that you can be treated in this way, and that such treatment is acceptable."[21] Each of these authors recognizes that the offender's apology and repentance might serve to denounce the claim and thereby obviate the need for the victim to adopt an attitude of resentment. However, if the offender does not repent, an attitude of resentment may be called for to perform this important function.

I have argued, to the contrary, that an attitude of genuine forgiveness toward an unrepentant offender is fully compatible with the victim's self-respect, whereas an attitude of resentment is not. By adopting an attitude of resentment to protest the claim implicit in the act of wrongdoing, the victim assigns far too much power and importance to the offender's problematic attitudes, and fails to assign sufficient importance to *her own* assessment of her worth. The victim who has completed the process of addressing the wrong (or the victim for whom this process is unnecessary) will *know* that she has a moral worth and status equal to that of any other person, and that she deserves to be treated with respect. She will know that the act perpetrated against her was wrong, and she will understand why it was wrong. If she truly respects herself, she will be secure in these judgments and will not feel threatened by the wrongdoer's confused attitudes. Rather than reacting to his implicit false claim, she will recognize his confusion for what it is and go on to determine her own position independent of his wrongful behavior. Of

[19] Jeffrie G. Murphy, "Forgiveness in Counseling," p. 44.
[20] Joram Graf Haber, *Forgiveness*, p. 88.
[21] Pamela Hieronymi, "Articulating an Uncompromising Forgiveness," p. 546.

course, she will want to take note of the offender's problematic attitudes and behavior patterns in order to take reasonable steps to protect herself and to honor her own need for rewarding personal relationships. But the person who has completed the process of addressing the wrong will already have performed these tasks. There is no reason at this point to regard the wrongdoer's implicit claim as a threat. Having taken the steps she needs to take to secure her own interests, and having assessed the situation for herself, the victim is free to extend to the offender an attitude of respect, compassion, and real goodwill.

A number of objections have been raised to this line of reasoning. Murphy concedes that some victims may have sufficient self-esteem to see that their status and dignity is not lessened by the wrong, but he is concerned that other victims may not. For victims in the latter category, he argues that maintaining an attitude of resentment may be a mark of self-respect.[22] I believe Murphy is correct in thinking that an attitude of resentment may be a mark of self-respect in a victim who fails to recognize her own worth and status as a person. In this case, an attitude of resentment may actually be desirable in that it is preferable to the victim's having no self-respect at all, or not recognizing that she was wrongfully harmed. However, a victim who fails to recognize her own worth and status as a person has clearly not completed the process of addressing the wrong, and clearly needs to do so. If she is to respect herself sufficiently, the victim who fails to recognize her own worth must continue with the process of addressing the wrong until she does come to appreciate her true status as a person. She must recognize for herself that the claim implicit in the act of wrongdoing is false. Once she does so, she will no longer need to maintain an attitude of resentment toward the offender.

Murphy further objects to my claim that adopting an attitude of resentment assigns far too much power and importance to the wrongdoer's confused attitudes and in doing so takes power away from the victim. He argues as follows: "But surely this is not always the case. If the offender greatly wants to be forgiven by me and I am not much interested in forgiving him – at least until he repents – then it seems to me that the balance of power is in my favor and not in favor of the offender."[23]

---

[22] Jeffrie G. Murphy, "Forgiveness in Counseling," p. 45.
[23] *Ibid.*, p. 47. Murphy actually refers in the text to a statement of the argument by Robert D. Enright, but it is the same argument.

Again there is a sense in which Murphy is correct. If the victim chooses to engage in a power struggle with the offender, she may well gain the upper hand by refusing to forgive. The question is whether she truly respects and empowers herself by proceeding in this manner. I submit that she does not. By engaging in a power struggle of this sort, the victim focuses her attention on the fact that the wrongdoer failed to respect her and did something wrong. She also orients herself toward using resentment and rejection to manipulate the offender into acknowledging her worth, or toward dominating him in some other way. She does not respect herself or enrich her life by doing so. Rather, she will enhance both her self-respect and the quality of her life if she assesses the incident of wrongdoing for herself and puts the offender's confusion in proper perspective. She can then forgive the offender and devote her time and energy to her own positive pursuits.

Further objection to the line of reasoning I have presented can be derived from Hieronymi's remarks. As I indicated, she views resentment as a protest against the claim implicit in the act of wrongdoing. She recognizes that she needs to argue that "being threatened by another's disregard does not betray a failing or weakness." Her response is as follows: "At first cut, I will suggest that, contrary to the advice we give school children, we ought to care about what other people think. To not care about what you think is to not care about you. To disregard your evaluation is to disregard you ... I may, in the end, think your evaluation mistaken and wrong. If I think it is importantly wrong ... I will protest it."[24] Hieronymi also suggests that we should care about and protest the claim implicit in the wrong because it threatens the "public understanding" of our moral status and carries a "broader, social meaning," given that "one's identity is at least partially constituted by how one is perceived by others."[25]

Hieronymi is clearly correct in thinking that we should care about the offender and respect him as a moral agent. An attitude of forgiveness, as defined here, incorporates both a fundamental respect for the offender as a moral agent and a sincere desire that he grow and flourish as a person. In adopting an attitude of genuine forgiveness toward the offender, we do not let go of the wrong because we discount the offender as a person. Instead, we simply recognize that the claim implicit in the act of wrongdoing is false. In order to respect the offender as a moral

---

[24] Pamela Hieronymi, "Articulating an Uncompromising Forgiveness," p. 549.
[25] *Ibid.*, p. 550.

agent, we need not protest every important claim he makes that we find incorrect. If we did have to do this in order to take persons seriously as moral agents, we would have to spend our entire lives protesting the thousands of importantly incorrect claims that moral agents make all over the world every day. Again, if we truly respect ourselves, we will not live our lives in reaction to the beliefs, actions, and attitudes of others. Rather, we will make our own pro-active decisions about how we will spend our time and energy.[26]

There may be some cases in which it is important to protest a public misunderstanding about our moral status, but even in cases of this sort, an attitude of resentment is not called for. The Dalai Lama, Desmond Tutu, Nelson Mandela, Mahatma Gandhi, Martin Luther King, and others have all worked very effectively to correct public misunderstandings about the moral status of various groups of persons while maintaining an attitude of respect, compassion, and real goodwill toward those whose attitudes were in need of correction. There may also be cases in which there is a need to protest a private misunderstanding of our worth. For example, if Jane's husband cheats on her, she need not mount a campaign to inform the public that she has a worth and status that her husband has failed to recognize. However, she may need to convey *to her husband* that she has a status equal to his and that he must respect her needs. But in this case, what is called for is not an attitude of resentment, but rather an attitude of dignity, in which the individual maintains, with firmness and quiet self-confidence, her own belief in her own worth. And an attitude of dignity is fully compatible with an attitude of unconditional genuine forgiveness. (Further, we should recall that if Jane has completed the process of addressing the wrong, she will have already said what she needs to say to her husband.)

The concern that our identities are at least in part socially constituted is often raised in connection with the compatibility of forgiveness and self-respect. Govier seems to share the view that social identities

---

[26] Nietzsche makes this argument in explaining why the "noble" or "higher" man will eschew revenge and considerations of "justice." It is important to recognize that although the position I am developing here coincides with Nietzsche's view in this respect, it differs from his position in at least two important ways. First, I believe that the argument I make here applies to all moral agents who have completed the process of addressing the wrong (or who do not need to do so), rather than only to an elite group of men. Further, on my position in adopting an attitude of unconditional genuine forgiveness, we do not see the offender as being inferior to ourselves. Rather, we view him as a person with a moral status equal to our own. See Friedrich Nietzsche, *On the Genealogy of Morals*, pp. 72–73.

are important here. She says: "After the wrongdoing, things must some-how be put right, and a central dimension of that putting right is the *vindication* of the victim, the showing that the victim did not deserve to be treated in this way, that the person has human dignity and was worthy of respect."[27] She goes on to argue that as a victim, one need not adopt an attitude of resentment to vindicate oneself. Instead, one can "seek to build oneself up and assert or reassert one's own self-respect." In connection with this point, Govier offers us the example of Samuel Pisar, a Holocaust survivor who went on to receive a doctorate and sig-nificant notoriety in the field of international law. Regarding Pisar, she says: "His entire adult life was an ongoing attempt to vindicate himself, to prove that he was a worthy human being, fit to be alive, and capable of making important contributions to the world."[28]

Govier succeeds in showing that the victim need not adopt an attitude of resentment in order to vindicate herself. However, it is important to recognize that Pisar's strategy for vindication, as brave as it was under the circumstances, may also fail to evince sufficient self-respect. If we truly recognize and respect our own worth, we will feel no need to spend our lives proving to others that we have it. This crucial part of our iden-tity is *not* socially constituted. Each of us has an intrinsic worth and moral status equal to that of every other person, regardless of what other people think and regardless of how they behave. Once we recognize this point, we can guide our lives by our own interests and passions, rather than by the perceived need to prove our worth to others. We will have no further need to vindicate ourselves, either by adopting an attitude of resentment or by amassing a public record of achievement. (Of course, if we respect ourselves we will devote our energy to worthwhile causes, and we may go on to accomplish great things. But we will do so because we believe that what we are doing is worthwhile, rather than to prove to others that we have worth.) It is important to recognize that our lives may be described as socially constituted in many important respects. For example, we may be a father, mother, husband, wife, physician, athlete, custodian, consumer, citizen of a particular country, dog owner, friend, volunteer, and so on. Our lives are extensively interdependent and incor-porate a multitude of complex relationships, each of which creates for us various opportunities and responsibilities. However, none of these factors affects our basic moral status or our intrinsic worth as persons.

---

[27] Trudy Govier, *Forgiveness and Revenge*, p. 20.
[28] *Ibid.*, p. 21.

Rather, if any social arrangement fails to respect our basic moral status as persons, we have reason to believe that the arrangement is morally problematic.

A final question may be raised about the argument that by continuing to resent the offender, the victim assigns too much importance to the offender's attitudes and fails to honor her own assessment of her worth. It might be objected that if the reasoning outlined here is correct, then we may assign too much importance to another person's beliefs when we adopt positive reactive attitudes as well – for example, attitudes of gratitude, admiration, or love.[29] If a victim's attitude of resentment is morally problematic in that she simply reacts to the offender's wrong rather than thinking pro-actively about her own life and her own assessment of her worth, then perhaps some of her positive attitudes are also too reactive.

It seems clear that a lack of self-respect can sometimes lead to excessive gratitude or excessive admiration, in a manner that could well be described as overly reactive. And, arguably, love betrays a deficiency of self-respect when it is overly dependent, involves idealization, or becomes obsessive. In each of these cases, the person who holds the attitude in question reacts too strongly to another individual, and in doing so, fails to pursue her own life in a fully autonomous manner.

However, I do not believe that these positive attitudes generally involve the kind of reactivity and deficit of self-respect that occur in an attitude of resentment adopted by the victim who has completed the process of addressing the wrong. To see this point, it will be helpful to distinguish between an attitude that is *reactive* and an attitude that is *responsive*. We might say that healthy attitudes of gratitude, admiration, and love *respond* to the actions or attitudes of another. However, they need not be reactive in any negative sense of the word. An individual who has cultivated morally worthy attitudes in herself will clearly be responsive to other persons (and to many other things as well – to animals, to the beauty of the world around her, to moral values, and so on). She will be sensitive and responsive to the needs of others, she will admire their positive qualities, she will appreciate the things they do for her, she will love those who are close to her, and so on. None of these attitudes involve any lack of self-respect on the agent's part, and all are fully compatible with a pro-active orientation toward her own life. She can hold these attitudes while she has confidence in her own assessments of the world, and while

---

[29] This point was suggested to me by an anonymous reader for Cambridge University Press.

she focuses her attention on her own positive pursuits. The situation is different however, if she adopts a continuing attitude of resentment toward someone who has wronged her after she has completed the process of addressing the wrong. By maintaining an attitude of resentment, the victim in this case reacts to the offender's confusion rather than responding to what is truly of value in her life.

Both Novitz and Murphy raise a different concern about the compatibility of forgiveness and self-respect. The worry is that in forgiving the offender we may lose track of our own interests and thereby fail to respect ourselves. Novitz emphasizes the importance of empathy in reaching a state of genuine forgiveness. He then remarks that "empathy is believed to undermine one's sense of self – and not without reason, for whenever we empathize we run the risk of losing ourselves in the other; of failing, that is, to attend sufficiently to our own needs and desires..."[30] Murphy makes a similar point in offering a story about Ralph, who was repeatedly sexually abused by his father when he was young. As an adult attempting to cope with the abuse, Ralph changed his last name and broke off relations with his father. After years of separation, Ralph's father, without expressing any remorse for his past actions, requests reentry into Ralph's life because he believes he would look more respectable to his new wife and her children if he were in contact with his son. Ralph's minister tells Ralph that it is his duty to forgive his father and "welcome him back into family life – at least on limited terms," but Ralph is concerned that if he does so, he will suffer more psychological damage.[31]

While this concern is important, it does not show that unconditional genuine forgiveness is incompatible with self-respect. The victim who has completed the process of addressing the wrong has already regained her self-esteem and considered her own needs for protection, rewarding personal relationships, and restitution. In forgiving the offender, she does not disregard these needs. Rather, she honors her own needs *at the same time* that she empathizes with and forgives the offender. In Ralph's case, it seems reasonable to believe that he may in fact suffer further kinds of abuse if he reunites with his father. The important point to recognize is that Ralph can choose not to reconcile with his father, or he can choose to set any boundaries on the relationship that he deems appropriate, at the same time as he extends to his father an attitude of

---

[30] David Novitz, "Forgiveness and Self-Respect," p. 310.
[31] Jeffrie G. Murphy, "Forgiveness in Counseling," p. 48.

unconditional genuine forgiveness. To forgive another person is not to do whatever that person wants you to do. It is not to abandon all thought of your own needs, to "lose yourself" in the other person, or to ignore the reality of the other person's current attitudes and behavior patterns. Rather, to forgive someone is to extend to that person an attitude of respect, compassion, and real goodwill, regardless of his past or current actions and attitudes.

Finally, Scarre suggests that both holding and expressing an attitude of resentment may be important in some cases, and that failure to do so may constitute a deficiency of self-respect. He says, "Someone makes an insulting remark: you are not affronted. He forcibly removes your goods: you let them go … He hits you in the face: you turn the other cheek to him. Such a level of indifference … would raise serious question whether you cared for anyone or anything, including yourself…. you *ought* to get angry over bad things which are done to you and yours."[32]

In response to this argument, it is important to recognize that an attitude of unconditional genuine forgiveness does not require passivity in the face of wrongdoing. It is possible for us to maintain an attitude of respect, compassion, and real goodwill toward a wrongdoer at the same time as we attempt to prevent him from wrongfully harming us or others. We can also request restitution for the harm after it has been inflicted while maintaining these attitudes. There is a kind of peace and letting go that accompanies unconditional genuine forgiveness, but it should not be confused with passivity or lack of respect for or caring about ourselves or others. In completing the process of addressing the wrong, the victim does what can be done to honor her own needs. Adopting an attitude of resentment toward the offender after this process is complete does not evince some kind of extra or deeper respect or caring about herself. Instead, it merely evinces continuing (and I would suggest fruitless) moral anger toward the offender.

If my arguments in this section have been correct, an attitude of unconditional genuine forgiveness is fully compatible with the victim's self-respect. Regardless of whether the offender repents, and regardless of what he has done or suffered, the victim evinces true self-respect by adopting an attitude of genuine forgiveness after she completes the process of addressing the wrong (or when she does not need to undertake

---

[32] Geoffrey Scarre, *After Evil*, p. 101. See also Charles Griswold's worry that by forswearing resentment on an ongoing basis, "we are dressing up servility as a virtue." *Forgiveness*, p. 66.

this process). Further, by adopting an attitude of resentment after she completes this process (or when she does not need to undertake it), the victim fails to respect herself sufficiently in that she reactively assigns too much importance to the wrongdoer's confused attitudes and fails to accord enough importance to her own assessment of her worth as a person. As I have noted, Hieronymi challenges those who endorse an attitude of unconditional genuine forgiveness to articulate the change in judgment that occurs when we forgive. We are now in a position to articulate this change as it pertains to self-respect. When we hold an attitude of resentment, as Hieronymi suggests, we view the disparaging claim implicit in the offense as a threat. We believe that we need to fight back and protest it, at least until our worth is acknowledged by the offender, or perhaps by widespread support in the community. However, by working through the process of addressing the wrong, we put ourselves in a position to revise this judgment. As we work through this process, we establish for ourselves that we have a worth equal to that of any other person. We also take the steps we need to take to protect ourselves from further abuse and to honor our own needs. We then recognize that instead of fighting back against the offender and trying to get him to acknowledge our worth, we can simply trust our own assessment of our worth. At this point, there is no reason to resent the offender or to regard his implicit claim about us as a threat. Instead, we can put his confusion in perspective, extend toward him an attitude of respect, compassion, and real goodwill, and turn our attention to our own positive pursuits. Let us now consider the question of whether the attitudes of forgiveness and resentment are compatible with respect for morality.

FORGIVENESS, RESENTMENT, AND RESPECT FOR MORALITY

Attitudinal retributivists also argue that forgiving an unrepentant offender may be incompatible with respect for morality. Several authors have argued that an unrepentant offender implicitly endorses his own wrong, and that by forgiving the offender under these circumstances, the victim endorses or condones the wrong as well. She therefore fails to show sufficient respect for the requirements of morality. For example, Hieronymi says of an unrepentant offender, "I remain unable to forgive him because, given his lack of remorse and 'public' reluctance to acknowledge the wrong, it looks to me as though abandoning my anger and so 'forgiving' him would amount either to *condoning the wrong*, giving up on him, or discounting myself"[33] [my emphasis]. This argument seems to start from a premise that J.L. Mackie makes explicit in his defense of retributivism. He says: "It is involved in the very concept of wrongness that a wrong action calls for a hostile response."[34] Peter French also states that "if we have a concept of moral wrong at all, it includes the notion that whatever is morally wrong must be met with an antagonistic response from the members of the moral community."[35]

There is certainly an element of truth in these claims. All members of the moral community should definitely oppose wrong actions. Further, no member of the moral community should ever condone a wrong action, or be indifferent as to whether or not it is committed. But there is a significant gap between these claims and the claim that we must resent unrepentant offenders.[36] In fact, this inference fails because we cannot infer from the fact that a "hostile" response toward a wrong act is called for that a hostile response toward the person who committed the wrong act is called for. In Augustine's terms, we cannot infer from the fact that we should "hate the sin" that we should also "hate the sinner."

The notion that the victim condones the wrong by forgiving the unrepentant offender is seriously mistaken, at least when the victim has completed the process of addressing the wrong or has no need to do so. The victim who has completed the process of addressing the wrong fully understands that the act perpetrated against her was wrong, and she understands why it was wrong. She has explored her negative feelings about the offense, and has made a reasoned decision as to whether she will seek restitution for the harm that was wrongfully inflicted on her. There is no sense in which the victim condones the wrong by forgiving the offender at this point, regardless of whether the offender repents and regardless of what he has done or suffered. When the victim extends an attitude of real goodwill toward the offender, she recognizes the wrongness of *the offense* at the same time that she extends an attitude of respect, compassion, and real goodwill toward *the offender*.

A number of authors have argued that it is problematic to regard the unrepentant offender as separate from his offense, or in other words to

[33] Pamela Hieronymi, "Articulating an Uncompromising Forgiveness," p. 541.
[34] J.L. Mackie, "Morality and the Retributive Emotions," p. 214. Mackie later acknowledges that he finds retributivism to be paradoxical.
[35] Peter A. French, *The Virtues of Vengeance*, p. 97.
[36] There is an even larger gap between these claims and the conclusion that Mackie and French wish to draw from them: that retributive punishment is justified. We will examine retributive justifications of punishment in Chapter 7.

separate the sinner from the sin. They argue that in order to respect the offender as a moral agent, we must recognize and then resent his identification with the wrong act that he has chosen to commit and has not yet chosen to renounce. I believe this argument is profoundly mistaken. We will consider it in some detail in the next section, as it is based on the requirement that we respect the offender as a moral agent.

There is one further argument that has been proposed to show that genuine forgiveness may be incompatible with respect for morality. Some have suggested that by forgiving an unrepentant offender, we fail to respect morality sufficiently by failing to *express* our disapproval of wrong acts. Consider the following passage, in which Govier addresses the question of how we should respond to unrepentant offenders who have committed very serious wrongs: "We may rightly regard a perpetrator as *conditionally unforgivable* if that perpetrator has not acknowledged, and does not morally regret, the wrongdoing. In such a case we may say that the perpetrator has not separated himself or herself from the evil acts committed, and thus inherits the unforgivability of the acts. Failure to forgive perpetrators in these circumstances *expresses* our conviction that those acts, and any person still identified with them, are profoundly evil." [my emphasis] She regards such perpetrators as in principle forgivable, but holds that forgiving them should be "conditional on their remorse and moral transformation."[37]

Although this argument seems more plausible than the simple argument that we condone the wrong by forgiving an unrepentant offender, I believe it fails as well. It is interesting that Govier applies this line of reasoning only to very serious wrongs. When a less serious wrong is committed, it seems that we need not always express our conviction that the act was wrong. Further, it sometimes seems morally inappropriate to do so. If my brother is in desperate financial straits and takes some cash from my wallet without my consent, I need not confront him and tell him that his act was morally wrong. By confronting him, I may cause a breach in our relationship that prevents me from helping him in the future. I may be able to enhance his moral and personal growth much more effectively by saying nothing about the offense and talking to him amicably about how he could solve his financial problems in a way he can be proud of. There are of course cases of less serious wrongdoing in which it will be appropriate for us to express our conviction that the act was wrong. And as Govier suggests, in cases in which an unrepentant

---

[37] Trudy Govier, *Forgiveness and Revenge*, p. 117.

offender has committed a very serious wrong, it seems important to express this conviction. The problem with her argument, however, is that we can express our opposition to seriously wrong acts (and to less serious wrongs when it is appropriate to do so) without hating or resenting the wrongdoer. We can explain to the wrongdoer that his act was wrong and why it was wrong at the same time that we regard him with respect, compassion, and real goodwill.

It is possible that an offender may *mistakenly* interpret an expression of forgiveness as a sign that the forgiver accepts or condones the wrong act. It is also possible that the offender may feel, again mistakenly, that he has no reason to examine and reform his behavior if the victim has already forgiven him. Griswold suggests that "'forgiveness' that requires *nothing* of the offender ... does communicate to her, as well as to everyone else, that she is not being held accountable."[38] And Murphy remarks, "What if confronting resentment gives some wrongdoers incentives to repent and reform? If so, then a hasty forgiveness might contribute to their further moral corruption by depriving them of this important incentive."[39] Undeniably there are possibilities of this sort. However, they do not indicate that an attitude of unconditional genuine forgiveness is incompatible with respect for morality, or that we ought to adopt an attitude of resentment toward unrepentant offenders.

To grasp this point, we must distinguish clearly between the moral appropriateness of *holding* a given attitude and the moral appropriateness of *expressing* that attitude in a particular set of circumstances. As we have seen, on the virtue-ethical approach adopted here, the moral appropriateness of *holding* an attitude of unconditional genuine forgiveness depends on whether this attitude embodies self-respect, respect for morality, and respect for the offender as a moral agent and sentient being. If the arguments in this chapter are correct, then an attitude of unconditional genuine forgiveness does incorporate these forms of respect. It is therefore always appropriate and desirable from a moral point of view for the victim who has completed the process of addressing the wrong (or who does not need to undertake this process) to *hold* an attitude of unconditional genuine forgiveness.

The victim who holds an attitude of unconditional genuine forgiveness holds an integrated attitude of respect, compassion and real goodwill toward the offender. As I have argued, the motivational component

[38] Charles Griswold, *Forgiveness*, p. 64.
[39] Jeffrie G. Murphy, "Forgiveness in Counseling," p. 46.

of this attitude includes a desire that the offender grow and flourish as a person. Thus the person who holds this attitude will have a genuine concern for the offender's moral development. Acting from this motivation, she will refrain from expressing her forgiveness in cases in which the offender is likely to misinterpret this expression as accepting or condoning his wrongful behavior. Further, she may even pretend to be angry with the offender if this is the only way that he might pay sufficient attention to his own moral development, as Murphy suggests. It is important to recognize, however, that in these cases the way in which the victim *expresses* herself to the offender derives from the attitude she *holds* toward him – an attitude of unconditional genuine forgiveness. Here, her moral stance toward the offender is significantly different than it would be if she simply holds an attitude of resentment toward him. The person who holds an attitude of genuine forgiveness acts from an overall state of heart and mind characterized by real compassion for the offender and a sincere, holistic concern for his growth and flourishing as a person. The victim who holds an attitude of resentment acts from an overall state of heart and mind characterized by moral anger, partial withdrawal of goodwill, and a demand that the moral order be restored.

Christopher Bennett has recently offered a more complex analysis of retributive reactive attitudes as expressions of our moral disapproval of the offender. He offers us the story of Bryson, who comes to work late every day and who cheats on his long-term partner, Kate. When he arrives at work one morning, late again, his co-workers refuse to talk to him and give him the cold shoulder. Bryson is then left to figure out whether they are angry about his lateness, his affair, or both. He must therefore examine his behavior carefully and make some needed reforms. This case illustrates the cycle or dialectic of retribution. Bennett remarks that "withdrawal is our most natural *expression of moral disapproval*."[40] It is "the outward face of a particular emotional state … namely, blame," and it "expresses the alienation of the offender from the moral community."[41] In this respect, retributive reactive attitudes can be seen as "properly backward-looking, justified by a past wrong and not simply by the likelihood of getting the offender to behave differently."[42] Therefore we can regard these attitudes as deserved, or as intrinsically appropriate from a moral point of view. Nevertheless, Bennett argues

[40] Christopher Bennett, "The Varieties of Retributive Experience," p. 149.
[41] *Ibid.*, p. 150.
[42] *Ibid.*, p. 152.

that retributive reactive attitudes are also constructive or purposeful in that they aim to get the offender to repent, make amends, and ultimately to overcome his alienation from the moral community.

Although Bennett's analysis seems insightful as a *description* of the nature of retributive reactive attitudes, it does not suffice to justify them.[43] His analysis has two components: one based on the appropriateness of retributive reactive attitudes and one based on their constructive aims. If the arguments presented in this chapter are correct, then contrary to Bennett's assertion, retributive attitudes are not intrinsically appropriate from a moral point of view. Let us turn, then, to the constructive component of the analysis, based on the supposed good that may come from expressing our moral disapproval of the offender. The first thing to notice about this part of the analysis is that, like the positions we have just considered, it fails to distinguish between *holding* an attitude and *expressing* that attitude. The fact that we might achieve some good by turning a cold shoulder to an offender does not justify *holding* an attitude of blame or resentment toward him, because if it is really necessary to turn a cold shoulder in order to bring about his moral transformation, we can do so at the same time that we hold an attitude of unconditional genuine forgiveness.

However, it is also important to question whether we should routinely express ourselves to offenders by withdrawing our goodwill, however "natural" this mode of expression may seem. Let us return to the story of Bryson and consider how we would prefer to respond to him if we hold an attitude of unconditional genuine forgiveness. If we hold an attitude of unconditional forgiveness toward Bryson, we will definitely hope that he will recognize that his behavior is wrong, make amends, and correct his attitudes and behavior patterns in the future, just as Bennett suggests. But otherwise our response is likely to be different. Bennett acknowledges that the withdrawal of goodwill as an expression of moral disapproval can be "tremendously distressing" and involve significant pain. If we regard Bryson with the compassion and real goodwill that are embodied in an attitude of genuine forgiveness, we will be motivated to spare him this kind of pain if possible. Because we have sincere concern for him, we will want to address him as gently and respectfully as we can. Further, if we respect him as a moral agent, we will be motivated to address him directly as such, and to avoid interacting with him in a manner that is manipulative. In this case it seems that our response to

---

[43] Bennett recognizes this point himself in this article.

Bryson would be to take him aside and explain to him, in a direct, compassionate, and respectful manner, that we need him to come to work on time so that he does not impose an unfair burden on others, and that we are concerned that Kate may be deeply hurt by his affair at some point in the future. To respect his autonomy, we might also explain to him that if he does not regularly come to work on time, unfortunately, we will have to let him go and hire someone else who will be more punctual. And we can add that we hope he is able to make the needed correction and stay on. He can then make his own choice about this matter. In contrast, having the entire office turn a cold shoulder to Bryson seems manipulative, disrespectful, and devoid of genuine concern for him. Not only do we lack justification for *holding* retributive reactive attitudes, then, we also have reason to question whether the routine expression of these kinds of attitudes constitutes a morally desirable form of communication. At the very least, it seems that an expression of resentment or anger constitutes a mode of communication that should be used only as a last resort (and not as a regular response to offenders), and then only when we *hold* an attitude of unconditional genuine forgiveness and are motivated by real goodwill for the offender.

Drawing again on a possible interpretation of Govier's and Griswold's arguments, we may extend the objection we are considering beyond the way in which the victim expresses herself to the offender to the way in which she expresses herself to the moral community as a whole. Perhaps in order to respect morality we must communicate to all members of the community that we abhor seriously wrong acts, and therefore we must maintain an attitude of resentment toward unrepentant perpetrators of serious moral wrongs. I believe this argument fails as well. It is clearly important for all members of the moral community to express opposition to moral wrongdoing, and especially to very serious moral violations. However, we need not hate or resent offenders to communicate our opposition to wrong acts. As we have seen, leaders such as His Holiness the Dalai Lama and Desmond Tutu provide counterexamples to this assertion, given that they have publicly communicated strong opposition to wrong actions without any resentment. Neither of these leaders is a stranger to the worst kinds of moral horrors. Yet both have done a great deal to communicate opposition to such acts while maintaining an attitude of unconditional genuine forgiveness toward those who have committed them. The fact that both of these leaders have received the Nobel Peace Prize demonstrates the effectiveness of their approach to communicating respect for morality to the global moral community.

As members of the moral community, there is much that we can do to express our opposition to wrong acts and to help prevent them from occurring. I will discuss the steps we can take to prevent wrongdoing in more detail in Chapter 7. Briefly, we can express our commitment to human rights and basic moral principles in a wide variety of ways, ranging from ratifying political documents that express these commitments to discussing our moral convictions with other individuals. We can engage in local, national, and global dialogues about moral standards and about the damage that moral violations inflict on victims. We can mount various initiatives to study conditions that tend to result in wrongdoing and to determine means of eradicating these conditions. And we can launch initiatives to find effective methods for inculcating attitudes of respect and compassion for all persons, and to make these techniques available to everyone. In addition to all this, hatred and resentment of wrongdoers seems to add nothing to our commitment to upholding moral standards. At best, resenting wrongdoers is a clumsy and inarticulate way of expressing our opposition to moral wrongdoing. A clear, calm, respectful statement of why the act is wrong, coupled with diligent pursuit of constructive methods of enhancing moral behavior, seems much more effective. Further, as I will argue in the next section, an attitude of resentment is ultimately incompatible with respect for the offender as a person. Thus, by adopting an attitude of resentment toward the offender, we ultimately fail to respect morality by adopting a morally inappropriate attitude ourselves.

Finally, it might be objected that although we can express our opposition to wrongdoing without engaging in negative responses toward the offender, we cannot do so *proportionately*. In order to express our appreciation for morally worthy acts proportionately, we must go beyond a calm verbal expression of our attitude. For example, when we consider the enormous sacrifice and generosity that was required of our parents to raise us from infancy to adulthood, we will realize that it is not enough simply to say "thank you." Rather, to express our gratitude proportionately, we must go some distance toward responding in kind. Likewise, we may fail to express our opposition to wrongdoing proportionately if we fail to inflict some negative response on the offender.[44]

This objection is interesting, but I believe it fails as well. It is undeniably important that we express ourselves fully and proportionately with regard to actions and attitudes that have real moral significance – either

---

[44] This objection was also suggested to me by an anonymous reader for Cambridge University Press.

positive or negative. But I think the analogy between positive and negative responses to significant moral actions ends here. We are fully capable of expressing verbally how seriously we take horribly wrong acts, and we can articulate verbally which acts are more seriously wrong than others, and why. Further, we can express the strength of our opposition to wrong acts proportionately by the extent of the diligence with which we pursue the constructive suggestions outlined earlier. I will also argue in Chapter 7 that as a matter of social policy, we should require the perpetrators of such acts to make restitution to those they have wrongfully harmed. All of this can be done while we hold an attitude of respect, compassion, and real goodwill toward the offender.

But to inflict hatred, resentment, or other negative responses on the offender simply in order to express our opposition to wrong acts proportionately is more problematic. Perhaps these forms of expression are more dramatic, but they are also seriously burdensome to the offender. And in the absence of some countervailing consideration such as preventing greater or equal harm to others, they seem to be incompatible with respect, compassion, and real goodwill for the offender. Therefore additional justification is required for expressing our proportional opposition to wrongdoing in this manner. On the other hand, expressing gratitude or love by offering substantive benefits to those we appreciate is clearly morally permissible. It is also fully compatible with respect, compassion, and real goodwill for these persons.

In sum, it seems that we have no reason to believe that an attitude of unconditional genuine forgiveness is incompatible with respect for morality, provided that we can show that it is morally appropriate to separate the sin from the sinner. An argument to this effect will be presented in the next section and developed further in Chapter 5. If these arguments are successful, then regardless of whether the offender repents and regardless of what he has done or suffered, the victim fully respects morality by adopting an attitude of genuine forgiveness. Again, Hieronymi has challenged those who endorse an attitude of unconditional genuine forgiveness to articulate the change in judgment that occurs when we replace an attitude of resentment with an attitude of forgiveness. We are now in a position to articulate this change as it pertains to respect for morality. When we hold an attitude of resentment, we feel threatened by the wrong. It contravenes our moral standards, which we rightly hold to be very important, and we believe we must respond with anger or resentment unless the offender repents. As we examine the wrong and think carefully about the offender, we come to see that while the act was

wrong, the offender is a *person* who is distinct from the act he has committed. We recognize that we can oppose the wrong act at the same time
that we respond to the offender *as a person* with respect, compassion,
and real goodwill. Let us now turn to the crucial question of whether the
attitudes of resentment and forgiveness are compatible with respect for
the offender as a moral agent.

FORGIVENESS, RESENTMENT, AND RESPECT FOR THE OFFENDER

I believe that the central difference between attitudinal retributivists
and those who endorse an attitude of unconditional genuine forgiveness lies in their different conceptions of what is required to respect the
offender as a moral agent. Those who believe that an attitude of resentment toward unrepentant offenders is morally appropriate hold that
this attitude embodies respect for the offender as a moral agent who is
responsible for his own actions and attitudes. As we have seen, Strawson
contrasts reactive attitudes with what he calls the "objective attitude."
To adopt the objective attitude toward the offender is to see him as "an
object of social policy," or as someone "to be managed or handled or
cured or trained; perhaps simply to be avoided."[45] When we adopt this
attitude, we objectify the offender by regarding him in the same way
we would regard an animal or an object – as something to be managed
or manipulated in such a way as to bring about the results we want.
In doing so, we fail to respect the offender as an autonomous moral
agent. In contrast, Strawson speaks of the reactive attitudes of resentment, indignation, and disapprobation as follows: "The holding of them
does not, as the objective attitude does, invoke as part of itself viewing
their object other than as a member of the moral community. The partial
withdrawal of goodwill which *these* attitudes entail, the modification
they entail of the general demand that another should, if possible, be
spared suffering, is, rather, the consequence of *continuing* to view him
as a member of the moral community; only as one who has offended
against its demands."[46] In the same vein, Haber asserts that by adopting an attitude of resentment, "we indicate that we have an attitude of
regard for wrongdoers, in the sense that we do not look at them as mere
things whose movements happen to cause injury."[47]

[45] P.F. Strawson, "Freedom and Resentment," p. 9.
[46] *Ibid.*
[47] Joram Haber, *Forgiveness*, p. 82.

The connection that these authors (and others) have seen between an attitude of resentment toward an unrepentant offender and respect for that offender as an autonomous moral agent seems clear enough. As autonomous moral agents, we are responsible for conforming our actions and attitudes to the requirements of morality. In the absence of excusing conditions, we also determine what our actions and attitudes will be. Therefore, to respect the offender as a moral agent, we must regard him as the author of his offense and of the wrongful attitudes that led to it. And if he does not repent – if he is indifferent to the fact that he has wrongfully harmed someone, or worse, if he is pleased that he did so – then we must regard him as the author of this attitude as well. By resenting the offender, we therefore respect him as a moral agent who chooses his own actions and attitudes and who is accountable for the extent to which they deviate from the requirements of morality. As we saw in the last section, it is for this reason that many authors believe that it is morally problematic to "separate the sin from the sinner." We respect the offender's moral agency by recognizing that *he* is responsible for creating this separation, and by holding him accountable for renouncing his offense.

An attitude of resentment thus regards the unrepentant offender as the author of his own wrongful actions and attitudes, or, in Murphy's words, as "psychologically identified with the sin."[48] The moral anger and partial withdrawal of goodwill that are embodied in an attitude of resentment evince our judgment or evaluation of the offender as such. The offender is seen as someone we must protest against or oppose, as someone who is bad, or, as Roberts says, as someone who is "alien, unworthy, and due to be punished."[49]

Many authors, some quite sympathetic to forgiveness, others less so, seem to endorse a position of this sort. They hold that the attitude we adopt toward the offender ought to reflect our overall evaluation or judgment of the offender as a moral agent. For example, Tara Smith (who is less sympathetic to forgiveness than some) holds that when we consider forgiving the offender, "The primary question is not: 'Should I continue this relationship?' but 'How should I evaluate this person?'" She adds that forgiveness "is the judgment that a person's immoral action should not be treated as proof of a grave moral defect or an irredeemably bad character."[50] Jean Hampton (who is quite sympathetic to forgiveness)

---

[48] Jeffrie G. Murphy, "Forgiveness in Counseling," p. 46.
[49] Robert C. Roberts, "Forgiveness," p. 292.
[50] Tara Smith, "Tolerance & Forgiveness: Virtues or Vices," p. 37.

says that "to forgive someone for an action or trait is a way of removing it as evidence of the state of her soul, so that one is able to judge her favorably without it."[51] Joanna North (also generally sympathetic to forgiveness) suggests that we ought not forgive an unrepentant offender who is guilty of a very serious wrong, because such a wrong "weighs far more in the balance than all other aspects of the wrongdoer's past and personality put together." In such cases, she says, "the reframing process, far from allowing us to separate the wrongdoer from his actions, serves to reinforce the *identification* of the wrongdoer with his action. The more we understand, the more we come to regard the wrongdoer as culpable, as wholly and utterly bad."[52] Charles Griswold (who again is less sympathetic to forgiveness than some) argues that if the victim is to have reason to give up her resentment toward the offender, the offender must meet certain conditions that "warrant a change of belief about 'the bad person's' character." Griswold clearly states that this change does not involve "dividing off the deed from the doer," which "invites the thought … that the sinner is always to be *excused* or pardoned." Rather, it involves an assessment of the offender as a "whole person."[53] And most recently, Lucy Allais says: "My suggestion is that when you forgive the perpetrator your attitude towards her as a person is no longer the negative one that her wrongdoing supports; in other words, the act is disregarded in your ways of regarding and esteeming her…"[54] She specifically sees the shift from resentment to forgiveness (at least in part) as a change in one's affective attitude of *evaluative* respect for the offender.

Although the line of reasoning outlined here is widely accepted, it is also seriously flawed. The first premise of this line of reasoning is plausible. In order to respect the offender as a moral agent, we must regard him as an individual who chooses his own actions and attitudes (in the absence of excusing conditions) and who is responsible for those choices. However, it does not follow that an attitude of resentment toward unrepentant offenders is morally appropriate. Strawson points out that an attitude of resentment avoids objectifying the offender by regarding him as something to be managed or manipulated in such a way as to bring about the results we want. However, an attitude of resentment may embody another, more subtle form of objectification that is equally problematic from a moral point of view. While it is reasonable to claim

[51] Jean Hampton, *Forgiveness and Mercy*, p. 86.
[52] Joanna North, "The Ideal of Forgiveness," p. 27.
[53] Charles Griswold, *Forgiveness*, p. 64.
[54] Lucy Allais, "Wiping the Slate Clean: The Heart of Forgiveness," p. 79.

that the offender is responsible for his actions and attitudes, we also objectify the offender in a way that is morally problematic if we conflate him with his actions and attitudes. In adopting an attitude of resentment, we may commit this moral error. We slide from the reasonable belief that the unrepentant offender is responsible for the offense and his current lack of remorse for it to the vague claim that he is "identified with" them. We then judge the conglomerate to be "bad," "unworthy," "wholly and utterly bad," and so on. Finally, we respond with anything from moral anger to retributive hatred, and with a corresponding degree of withdrawal of goodwill.

I want to suggest that it is not only possible to distinguish between a person and his actions and attitudes – it is both conceptually and morally imperative that we do so. A person is not in any sense the same thing as the attitudes he adopts or the actions he performs. If we hold that an individual is in some sense identical to the attitudes he currently holds, then the concepts of moral growth, moral agency, and moral responsibility are rendered incoherent. For moral growth to take place, there must be an agent of that growth who first holds a given attitude, then evaluates it, and finally replaces it with another attitude that is more morally appropriate. And it is critically important for the retributivist to recognize that if she holds that an individual is in some sense identical to his current attitudes, she makes the notions of moral agency and moral responsibility incoherent. For the retributivist to hold that resentment is the morally appropriate response to an unrepentant offender, she must hold that the offender is a moral agent who is responsible for his offense and his lack of remorse regarding it. However, if the offender is in some sense identical to his current attitudes, then he cannot choose to hold these attitudes, nor can he choose to change them. Instead, he simply is these attitudes. In order for moral agency and moral responsibility to exist, there must be an agent, distinct from his actions and attitudes, who chooses which actions to perform and which attitudes to adopt.[55]

We will examine the compatibility of the attitudes of forgiveness and resentment with plausible conceptions of personal identity and moral responsibility more fully in Chapter 5. In this section I will examine the compatibility of these attitudes with respect for the offender as both a sentient being and a moral agent. Let us begin with respect for the

---

[55] This paragraph and much of the material in this section is taken from my "Forgiveness and Self-Forgiveness in Psychotherapy." Jessica Wolfendale applies this point about objectification very nicely to the most serious offenders in her interesting article, "The Hardened Heart: The Moral Dangers of not Forgiving."

offender as a sentient being. When we conflate the offender with his wrongful actions and attitudes, we fail to regard him as a sentient being or subject of experience. When I write a philosophy paper, I am not in any sense the same thing as the action of writing that paper. Rather, I am the experiencing subject who hopes that the paper will turn out well, who fears that it will not, who agonizes over the problems that arise, who gets excited when a point becomes clear, and so on. Nor am I in any sense the same thing as the attitude I hold toward the paper. If I hold an attitude of concern about the paper's worth, I am not this attitude. Rather, I am the subject who experiences the pain and anxiety of holding this attitude, and who hopes that it will turn out to be groundless. Likewise, the offender is not in any sense the same thing as his actions and attitudes. Rather, he is a sentient being – a *subject* of experience who deals with various needs, hopes, pressures, and confusions, and who ultimately wants to be happy. To fail to view the offender in this manner is to fail to recognize and respect him as a sentient being. It is also to objectify him by equating him in some sense with his actions and attitudes.

If we objectify the offender by conflating him with his actions and attitudes, feelings of hostility or anger are likely to arise, and reasonably so. As Mackie and French point out, wrongful actions and attitudes call for a hostile response from members of the moral community. If we make the mistake of regarding the offender as in some sense the same thing as his wrongful actions and attitudes, then we will naturally (but mistakenly) feel hostility or anger toward him as a person as well. On the other hand, when we regard the offender as a sentient being – as an experiencing subject who is not in any sense the same thing as his actions and attitudes – compassion will naturally follow. Lawrence Blum defines compassion as shared regard for the other as an equal.[56] As sentient beings ourselves, we are generally familiar with the kinds of needs, pressures, feelings, and so on that the offender experiences. Instead of looking down on the offender, we can understand him as an equal – as someone like us who experiences the same kinds of needs and emotions that we experience. Many authors have described in detail the kind of reframing process we can undertake to understand what the offender was experiencing and to thereby engender compassion for him.[57]

---

[56] Lawrence Blum, "Compassion."
[57] For two excellent discussions of this process, see Joanna North, "The Ideal of Forgiveness," and David Novitz, "Forgiveness and Self-Respect."

As we have noted, Hieronymi points out that it is a serious mistake to view forgiveness merely as a means for manipulating our emotions in such a way as to avoid holding a painful and potentially destructive attitude of resentment. What she fails to recognize, however, is that a reframing process – a process in which we look at things from the offender's point of view and come to understand what he was experiencing – is not merely a way of manipulating our emotions in order to avoid holding unpleasant attitudes. Rather, it is a perspective that is *required* of us if we are to recognize and respect the offender as a sentient being, and to avoid objectifying him by conflating him with his actions and attitudes. It seems, then, that an attitude of genuine forgiveness toward an unrepentant offender is fully compatible with recognition of and respect for the offender as a sentient being, whereas an attitude of resentment is not.

A parallel analysis will show that when we conflate the offender with his wrongful actions and attitudes, we fail to respect him as a moral agent. Again, when I write a philosophy paper I am not the same thing as the action of writing that paper. Instead, I am the *agent* who takes the action of writing it. I am the agent who decides to undertake this particular project, the agent who evaluates various sections of the paper and decides which are acceptable and which need to be redone, and so on. Nor am I the same thing as the attitude I hold toward the paper. Instead, I am the agent who develops this attitude, whether it is despair, concern, excitement, pride, or some other attitude. I am also the agent who at some point will assess this attitude and attempt to replace it if I find it to be problematic. By the same token, the offender is not in any way the same thing as his actions and attitudes. Rather, he is a moral agent who has chosen certain actions and attitudes and who has the capacity both to assess these choices and to make new choices in the future. To fail to regard him as an agent of choice who is distinct from the actions and attitudes he has chosen is simply to fail to respect him as a moral agent.

Again, if we objectify the offender by conflating him with his actions and attitudes, it is very likely that we will sit in judgment of him and respond with hostility or resentment if this judgment turns out to be unfavorable. As before, we can draw on French and Mackie to elucidate this point. As moral agents ourselves, as members of the moral community, we can and must evaluate actions and attitudes from a moral point of view. We must determine which actions and attitudes are morally worthy, which are morally neutral, which are wrongful, and which are "wholly and utterly bad." Again, if we make the mistake of regarding the offender as in some sense the same thing as his actions and attitudes, we will naturally (but mistakenly) sit in judgment of him as a person as well. On the other hand, when we regard the offender as a moral agent – as a being who has the capacity for moral choice, growth, and awareness – recognition, respect, and real goodwill for the offender will naturally follow. We will have respect for the offender as an individual who has these basic moral capacities, and we will desire that he grow and flourish as a person.

It is critically important to recognize here that *moral agency* is not the same thing as *moral performance* with regard to choosing our past or current actions and attitudes. Moral agency is simply the *capacity* for moral choice, growth, deliberation, and awareness. The person who chooses to perform a wrong act retains his moral agency (barring some kind of debilitating injury or illness). If he did not, arguably any kind of retributive response to him would be inappropriate. To respect the offender as a *moral agent* is precisely to recognize and respect him as an individual who possesses these basic moral capacities. Further, respect involves the recognition of value. Respect for moral agency is then the recognition of the inherent worth of an individual possessing these basic moral capacities. Recognition of the inherent value of anything will *necessarily* be accompanied by a positive response, rather than a hostile or negative response, to that thing. It will also be accompanied by a desire to see that which is of value preserved, protected, and enhanced. Likewise, recognition of the inherent value of an individual with basic moral capacities will necessarily be accompanied by a positive response toward that individual and a desire to see him grow and flourish as a person. Those who conflate the offender with his offense miss this point. As a result, they confuse recognition respect for the offender as a moral agent with evaluative respect (or lack thereof) for his moral performance.

In connection with our discussion of objectifying the offender by conflating him with his actions and attitudes, it will again be instructive to consider whether the same kind of moral error arises when we adopt positive reactive attitudes. As before, I believe that it is possible for positive reactive attitudes to involve this kind of objectification. For example, people often admire and express favorable reactions to famous persons in various ways without respecting them as sentient beings. They conflate these well-known persons with their positions or achievements, and then respond to them with significant disregard for their feelings, their privacy, their desires to make their own decisions about how they will live their lives, and so on. Likewise if we respond to a person who is known for having performed morally worthy actions simply by heaping praise or admiration on him, we may well be objectifying him and failing to respect him as a moral agent. If we respect him as a moral agent, we will not conflate him with his positive actions and attitudes. Nor will we simply sit in judgment of him and praise him. Rather, we will recognize that he takes moral values and their instantiation in the world seriously. In this case, most of our energy will be directed toward asking him for his advice on various matters, engaging in worthwhile projects with him, attempting to learn from him, and so on. However, it seems clear that positive reactive attitudes generally do not involve this kind of moral error. It is common to admire others, to feel grateful to them, to love them, and so on, all without objectifying them in the manner described earlier. In general, positive reactive attitudes (including an attitude of unconditional genuine forgiveness) are responsive to persons as sentient beings and moral agents.

The retributivist might object at this point that she can distinguish clearly between the capacity for moral agency and actual moral performance and thereby avoid the error of conflating the offender with his actions and attitudes. And at the same time, she can go on to argue that one way of showing respect for the capacity for moral choice is to respond to the way in which it has been actualized.[58] Thaddeus Metz articulates the notion of recognition respect for persons in this manner in a recent article. Initially he defines his position as follows: "The principle of respect for the dignity of persons, as I understand it, instructs agents to treat other agents as having the highest intrinsic value in the world. An agent, or person, is a being that has the ability to act on the basis of ends it has adopted upon principled deliberation.... This superlative intrinsic value warrants respect, which respect forbids sacrificing it for something worth less than it and, more generally, forbids treating it as a mere means to an end. Respect also requires treating persons as equals ... as well as helping them on occasion to develop their capacity to choose goals or attain the goals they have chosen."[59] Everything that Metz has said about recognition respect for persons is, so far, fully compatible with the notion of recognition respect for persons incorporated in the paradigm of forgiveness.

---

[58] I thank an anonymous reader for Cambridge University Press for calling my attention to this objection, and for referring me to the work of Thaddeus Metz in the discussion that follows.

[59] Thaddeus Metz, "Judging Because Understanding: A Defence of Retributive Censure," pp. 226–227.

However, as Metz continues, his notion of recognition respect for persons diverges sharply from the paradigm of forgiveness. He says: "Furthermore ... respect requires at least institutions (if not individuals) to track the responsible actualization of the capacity for autonomy ... By 'tracking' such a choice I mean not merely reacting to a person in light of a decision she has made, but also responding in kind, i.e., imposing burdens in reaction to wrong choices and not doing so (and perhaps offering benefits) in reaction to right ones."[60] Here I find Metz's conception of recognition respect much more difficult to understand. In respecting persons, it is clearly important to respect our capacity for autonomous choice, but it is also important to recognize that this capacity does not exist in the abstract. Rather, it always exists in the *person* who possesses it. While we can and should separate the offender from his wrongful actions and attitudes, we cannot rightfully separate him from his capacity for principled deliberation and choice, or in other words, from his moral agency. Nor can we rightly separate him from his status as a sentient being. What we must respect, then, is not the abstract capacity to choose, but rather *persons* – developing, experiencing, vulnerable human beings – who possess this capacity. It is not clear to me how we respect a *person* who has the capacity to choose by inflicting burdens on him when he makes wrong choices (unless we must do so to prevent greater or equal harm to others). Again we must recall that respect is a positive response to something of value. If this latter point is correct, it seems instead that we would respect the offender as a valuable human being with a valuable capacity for choice by attempting to help him to use this capacity well, or in other words, by attempting to promote his moral growth and personal flourishing.

It may be helpful here to distinguish between acknowledging the existence of a valuable capacity in persons and actually respecting that capacity. Acknowledging the existence of a valuable capacity in persons is a necessary step in respecting that capacity and the persons in whom it is instantiated, but it is not sufficient. By "tracking" the actual choices that persons make and inflicting burdens and benefits on them accordingly, we clearly acknowledge the existence of the human capacity to engage in principled deliberations and make choices. However, we do not yet respect this capacity or the persons who possess it. To respect persons as beings with the capacity for autonomous choice, we must recognize and appreciate them as beings with this valuable capacity, and we must

<hr />

[60] *Ibid.*, p. 227.

respond to them in a positive manner. In other words, we must allow persons to make their own choices whenever we can without damaging others, we must recognize each person as the author of his own inner moral development, and we must do what we can to promote human growth and flourishing.

It is true that in order to respect an individual's autonomy we must respect his actual choices, again to the extent that we can do so without unjustly burdening others. And Metz goes on to provide four very plausible examples outside of the context of retributivism in which it seems clear that we should allocate burdens to individuals in response to their wrong choices. In reference to one example, Metz argues that persons should be required to make restitution for the losses that they wrongfully inflict on others. In reference to another, he argues that an individual who slacks off should receive lower pay than a co-worker who is very diligent. I agree fully with the practical conclusions that Metz draws here, but not because I think that we respect persons by "tracking" their choices and imposing burdens on them when those choices are wrong. Rather, I will argue in Chapters 6 and 7 that social institutions that respond to our actual choices in roughly this manner are justified because they provide a fundamental benefit for each of us: the opportunity to make the most of our lives through our own choices and efforts.

Garrard and McNaughton have raised a related objection to grounding a defense of unconditional forgiveness in respect for the offender as a moral agent. They say: "Why should we respect the presence of moral agency in those who have put that capacity to so distorted a use? We might rather regard them as being worse than unreasoning brutes ... So respect for persons by itself doesn't seem to provide a reason for conditional forgiveness, let alone unconditional forgiveness." In the same vein, they argue, "We don't withhold admiration and respect from [the virtuous agent] just because she has the capacity for moral change, and hence might become an evildoer. So why should the bare capacity – the mere potential – for moral change in a wrongdoer provide us with a reason to treat him with the respect and good will appropriate to non-offenders – i.e. to forgive him?"[61]

The objection that Garrard and McNaughton raise here again reflects the widespread tendency to conflate the offender with his actions and attitudes, and then to sit in judgment on the conglomerate. As I have

---

[61] Eve Garrard and David McNaughton, "In Defense of Unconditional Genuine Forgiveness," pp. 52–53.

noted, this error leads to the error of interpreting respect for persons as evaluative respect as opposed to recognition respect. Admiration for a virtuous person is a type of evaluative respect. We recognize the virtuous person as having cultivated morally worthy character traits, and respect him for having done so. In a like manner, we would have evaluative respect for an outstanding athlete, or for the artist who paints a beautiful painting. Evaluative respect is properly based on the actions persons have performed and the attitudes they have adopted. Garrard and McNaughton are correct in saying that we do not withhold admiration of a virtuous agent merely because she has the potential for wrongdoing, any more than we would withhold admiration from Lance Armstrong merely because it is possible that he will lose his prowess on the bicycle. But respect for persons is not evaluative respect. It is rather recognition respect for persons as persons – as sentient beings and as moral agents. Regardless of our moral track records and regardless of our achievements in other areas of our lives, we have basic moral capacities.

We might *evaluate* a serial killer as having performed in a manner that is worse than an unreasoning brute. However, we have a kind of recognition respect for serial killers that we do not have for unreasoning brutes. I admire my dogs very much for their loving, enthusiastic, and cooperative attitudes, and I do not admire the attitudes of serial killers. And I would much rather spend time with my dogs than with a couple of serial killers. However, we put vicious dogs down without trials and appeals, without offering a last meal or finding out if they have any last words, and so on, unlike serial killers. The mere capacity for moral agency is something that we consider worthy of recognition respect, and rightly so. Likewise we accord to both dogs and persons a moral status that we do not accord to rocks, sticks, and other physical objects. Being a sentient being also confers on us a moral status that is recognized in recognition respect. We could say that both moral agents and sentient beings have intrinsic value. Alternatively, we could say that it is intrinsically important for beings who are capable of having experiences to have good experiences, and that it is intrinsically important for moral agents to grow and flourish as persons. Either way, the respect, compassion, and real goodwill for the offender embodied in an attitude of unconditional genuine forgiveness is a morally appropriate response to any individual who is both a sentient being and a moral agent, regardless of what that individual has done and regardless of whether he repents.

Finally, it is important to recognize that by abandoning the perspective of judging the offender's moral performance we are not abandoning

the moral point of view. Cheshire Calhoun makes the following suggestion: "What I will suggest is that aspirational forgiveness is achieved by
seeing that, although an agent's wrongdoing fails to make moral sense,
it does make biographical sense. I will also suggest that a commitment
to going beyond a merely minimalist forgiveness is also a commitment to
deprioritizing the moral and to seeing that there may be equally important ways that normal persons of goodwill need to make sense of their
lives."[62] Calhoun is of course correct in saying that when forgiveness
is an issue, the offender has done wrong, and there is no way to make
"moral sense" of the act by construing it as right. She is also correct in
suggesting that we can come to understand why the offender did what
he did from a biographical perspective, and develop compassion for him
by examining his actions in the context of the pressures he has experienced throughout his life. And she is again correct in suggesting that
cultivating an attitude of genuine forgiveness involves an acceptance of
the offender as he is. But there is actually nothing in the process she has
described that involves an abandonment of the moral point of view or
a deprioritizing of the moral. Rather, when we cultivate an attitude of
unconditional genuine forgiveness, we *adopt the moral point of view* and
recognize that from this point of view, it is not appropriate for us to sit
in judgment on the offender as a person. Instead, we ought to respect the
offender as a sentient being and moral agent. We should regard him with
respect, compassion, and real goodwill, regardless of whether he repents
and regardless of what he has done or suffered. Further, we should do
what we can to promote his personal and moral growth.

Before we close our discussion of respect for the offender as a moral
agent, let us consider two alternative proposals. Garrard and McNaughton
suggest that we base a justification of unconditional genuine forgiveness
on human solidarity, or "the sense of a common predicament which we
all share, and which gives us a reason to be concerned for each other."
They elaborate as follows: "More profoundly at work is the sense that
as a group, as a species, we are morally pretty unimpressive; the human
nature which we have in common includes some very dreadful propensities. Our predicament includes the possession of this morally tainted
nature...."[63] This is a valuable suggestion, and it certainly constitutes
an important strategy for starting to cultivate an attitude of forgiveness
in ourselves. By reflecting on our shared predicament, we can develop

[62] Cheshire Calhoun, "Changing One's Heart," p. 92.
[63] Garrard and McNaughton, "In Defense of Unconditional Forgiveness," p. 54.

compassion for the offender. By reflecting in this manner, we can also resist any tendency we may have to sit in judgment on the offender, and to regard ourselves as his moral superior.

However, the fact that we share "some very dreadful propensities" with the offender is not the fundamental basis for the attitudes of respect, compassion, and real goodwill incorporated in an attitude of forgiveness. Shared dreadful propensities are not and cannot be a basis for respect. Respect is an attitude that recognizes and responds positively to something of value, and dreadful propensities do not have value. Garrard and McNaughton therefore remove respect from their account of forgiveness (mistakenly, I believe) and base their defense of unconditional forgiveness instead on solidarity, which they further define as "the concern for the well-being of those who one feels are in the same condition as oneself."[64] However, our shared dreadful propensities in themselves do not provide the basis for an attitude of compassion or concern either. It is very possible for someone such as the Dalai Lama, Mother Teresa, or Jesus Christ, who ostensibly do not have dreadful propensities, to nevertheless have concern and compassion for those of us who do, and to forgive us for our wrongs. It is the fact that we suffer from these propensities and that we fall into them because we think they will alleviate our suffering that evokes compassion. Compassion is an attitude that recognizes and responds to the suffering experienced by sentient beings, and the desire of all sentient beings to be happy. Finally, shared dreadful propensities do not provide a basis for real goodwill toward persons. If we were to reflect only on our shared dreadful capacities, we might reasonably begin to wish for the end of the human race. Real goodwill is based on a desire that sentient beings avoid misery and experience happiness, and also on the desire that moral agents grow and flourish as persons. It is therefore grounded in a recognition respect for persons as sentient beings and as moral agents who have the capacity for moral growth and personal flourishing.

It is true that our shared dreadful propensities put most of us in need of forgiveness at various (and frequent) times in our lives, and that we therefore cannot consistently will a world without forgiveness, as Garrard and McNaughton suggest. And this certainly constitutes a possible reason for adopting an attitude of unconditional genuine forgiveness. However, I do not think it is the most direct, most fundamental, or most compelling reason for doing so. Earlier in their article, as I have

[64] *Ibid.*, p. 51–52.

already noted, Garrard and McNaughton assert that the most compelling justification for unconditional genuine forgiveness will be object-focused, and I am inclined to agree.[65] On the virtue-ethical approach suggested here, we are concerned with inculcating in ourselves the overall state of heart and mind that is most appropriate from a moral point of view. Once the victim of wrongdoing has completed the process of addressing the wrong (or if she has no need to do so), she is ready to drop the focus on herself and to think about the offender as a person. At this point, adopting an attitude of genuine forgiveness is not about her. It is not about her own dreadful tendencies, her own need for forgiveness, or her own probable or actual rational inconsistency in being unwilling to forgive various kinds of offenders. Rather, it is directly and fundamentally about the offender.

Unconditional genuine forgiveness is the morally appropriate attitude for her to adopt at this point *because* this attitude responds appropriately to *the offender as a person*. It responds with compassion to the offender as a sentient being, with respect to the offender as an individual with the capacity for moral choice, growth, and awareness, and with real goodwill to the offender as a person with both of these characteristics. By inculcating in ourselves attitudes that embody these responses to persons, we will again avoid the kind of "malady of the spirit" that Stocker has identified, in which our reasons and motives diverge from one another. On the approach suggested here, our reasons for action, our affective responses, and our motives will all be in harmony, and our thoughts, words, and actions will follow from this unified overall state of heart and mind.

Hagit Benjabi and David Heyd offer us yet another way of justifying forgiveness, although their argument fails to support unconditional genuine forgiveness as a uniform response to wrongdoing. They have suggested that we can freely shift perspectives on the inseparability of the offender and the offense. They say that "the idea of a perceptual shift of attention is different from John McDowell's perceptual analysis of virtue. In McDowell's analysis there is only *one* correct moral reading of a given situation, and in the virtuous mind this perception *silences* all its alternatives. This means that the situation calls for either a negative reaction or, all things considered, for toleration (or forgiveness) ... Our suggestion, based on the analogy to the rabbit-duck case, holds that in forgiveness and tolerance we can and should be able to freely

---

[65] *Ibid.*, p. 55.

switch from the impersonal perspective to the personal.... There is no general and systematic way of combining the impersonal negative judgment of the offensive act with the personal acceptance of its agent as a friend or fellow-citizen."[66] Their argument therefore implies that there is no systematic defense of an attitude of unconditional genuine forgiveness, or, for that matter, of an attitude of resentment. Either attitude may be justified, depending on the perspective we take in a given set of circumstances.

If my arguments here are correct, Benjabi and Heyd's suggestion must be rejected. Part of the problem with Benjabi and Heyd's analysis is that they see forgiveness as a kind of reconciliation, or restoration of a particular relationship. In determining whether or not we wish to engage in a particular relationship with the offender, we do need to determine whether the offender's attitudes and behavior patterns are conducive to the kind of relationship we are seeking. Notice that in doing so we do not objectify the offender by conflating him with his actions and attitudes, nor do we sit in judgment of him as a person. We can assess the possibility of a particular relationship with him at the same time that we recognize his intrinsic worth as a person and regard him with respect, compassion, and real goodwill. However, in Chapter 2 I have rejected the interpretation of forgiveness as reconciliation or restoration of a particular relationship.

If forgiveness is understood as I have defined it here – as an attitude of respect, compassion, and real goodwill toward the offender – then there *is* a systematic way of combining the impersonal negative judgment of the offense with personal forgiveness of the offender. Rather than shifting perspectives freely on the inseparability of the offender and the offense as we shift perspectives freely in the rabbit-duck picture, we *must* regard the offense as wrong and *at the same time* we *must* respect the offender as a sentient being and moral agent. As McDowell has argued, there is only one correct reading of the situation, and it silences the alternatives. To the extent that we conflate the offender with his wrong actions and attitudes and sit in judgment of the conglomerate, we objectify the offender and fail to accord him the respect he is due as a person.

A similar line of reasoning will show that we should also reject Lucy Allais' account of forgiveness. Allais suggests that we understand

---

[66] Hagit Benjabi and David Heyd, "The Charitable Perspective: Forgiveness and Toleration as Supererogatory," pp. 573–574. Here they refer to John McDowell, "Virtue and Reason," p. 335.

forgiveness as in part a shift in our evaluative stance toward the offender. Although she characterizes this shift as a shift in affective attitude, it is still open to rational assessment. In order to explain how we are being rational in taking up a different evaluative stance toward the offender, she points out, correctly, that our judgments of persons' characters are always underdetermined by the evidence. She goes on to say that "while the reasons for which you believe are epistemic, there may be reasons for forming attitudes such as trust, which are not epistemic, so long as they are not *contradicted* by what is epistemically justified. The point of trust, resentment, and gratitude is not to align your mental states with the way the world is, and the intentional content of feelings is partly a matter of focus.... Focus of attention is epistemically optional, and this means that to say that an attitude is appropriate is more like saying that you are entitled to feel it than you ought (epistemically or morally) to feel it."[67]

But if my reasoning here has been correct, the focus of our attention as we overcome resentment and forgive the offender is ultimately *not* something that is morally or epistemically variable or optional. Nor is it something that is to be determined by extrinsic or pragmatic considerations. Rather, the focus of our attention is *intrinsic* to the recognition of the offender as a sentient being and as a moral agent. Although it takes time and effort to forgive, and no one should pressure us into doing so, ultimately the morally appropriate attitude to adopt toward any offender is one of unconditional genuine forgiveness. If we fail to separate the offender from his wrongful actions and attitudes and fail to extend to him an attitude of respect, compassion, and real goodwill, we are missing something that is important from both an epistemic and a moral point of view. Specifically, we are failing to recognize and to respond appropriately to the morally salient characteristics of the offender as a person.[68] Although we may have some latitude in choosing what to focus on as Allais suggests, we are at fault on both epistemic and moral grounds if we choose not to focus on the most morally salient feature of the offender as we determine how we will respond to him – his intrinsic worth as a person.

---

[67] Lucy Allais, "Wiping the Slate Clean: The Heart of Forgiveness," p. 81.

[68] Therefore we must also reject Allais' claim that "the Kantian respect appealed to by Holmgren – the idea that we ought to recognize the perpetrator's humanity and recognize her intrinsic value – is by no means incompatible with judging that she has done culpable wrong *and holding this against her.*" [my emphasis]. Ultimately, an attitude of resentment is incompatible with true recognition respect for the offender as a person. See "Wiping the Slate Clean: The Heart of Forgiveness," p. 41.

We are now in a position to return to Hieronymi's challenge to articulate the change in judgment that occurs when we replace an attitude of
resentment with an attitude of forgiveness, as it pertains to respect for
the offender as a moral agent. When we resent the offender, we see him
as in some sense inseparable from his wrongful actions and attitudes.
We then respond to the conglomerate with moral anger and hostility.
When we forgive the offender, we revise this judgment. We recognize
that while his actions and attitudes were wrong and should be opposed,
the offender as a person is a sentient being and moral agent, and as such
warrants respect, compassion, and real goodwill.

If the arguments in this section have been correct, it is not only possible to separate the sin from the sinner, it is morally important that we do
so. To regard the offender as in any way the same thing as his wrongful
actions and attitudes is to objectify him and to fail to respect him as a
sentient being and moral agent. To the extent that an attitude of resentment involves this kind of objectification of the offender, it is ultimately
inappropriate from a moral point of view. In adopting this attitude, we
slide from a correct recognition of the offender as a moral agent who
chooses his own actions and attitudes to a morally problematic identification of the offender with those actions and attitudes. As a result of
conflating the offender with his actions and attitudes, we respond to the
offender inappropriately. While it is fully appropriate to sit in judgment
of actions and attitudes, it is seriously problematic to adopt this moral
orientation toward persons.

When we reify persons by conflating them with their actions and attitudes, we distance ourselves from them and start to view them as proper
objects of anger, hatred, and opposition. As we do so, we tend to reify
ourselves as well, by conflating ourselves with virtuous attitudes. We
react to the offender with horror and outrage, and in doing so we see
ourselves as virtuous persons who must oppose those who are bad, or
"wholly and utterly bad." At this point, rather than being virtuous, we
have become self-righteous. We then set up a polarized drama, a contest
between good and evil, in which we are the good guys and they are the
bad guys. Offenders become pawns in this drama, and we respond to
them in ways that are disrespectful and manipulative. We exhibit hostility toward them, judge them, rebuff them, reject them, inflict harm on
them, and, in extreme cases, we kill them. What is missing in all of this
is genuine concern and respect for the offender as a person.

An attitude of unconditional genuine forgiveness embodies a significantly different moral orientation toward persons – one that is fully

compatible with respect for the offender as a sentient being and moral agent. In adopting an attitude of unconditional genuine forgiveness, we recognize the offender as a person who is distinct from his actions and attitudes, and we respond to him as such. While we condemn his offense and his wrongful attitudes, we respond to him with respect, compassion, and real goodwill. We are acutely aware that the offender is a sentient being who experiences various needs, feelings, pressures, and confusions in life, just as we do, and that he desires to be happy. We respond to him accordingly, with compassion and a genuine desire for his happiness. Likewise, we are acutely aware of the offender as a moral agent – as an individual with the capacity for moral choice, growth, and awareness. Again, we respond to him accordingly, with respect for him as a being of this sort, and with a genuine desire that he grow and flourish as a person. We do not judge him, reject him, react to him with hostility, or act to harm or kill him (unless we must harm or kill him to prevent greater or equal harm to others, and in this case we will do so only with great reluctance). Rather, we are motivated to do what we can to promote his moral development and to make his life rich and rewarding. Thus the moral orientation toward persons embodied in an attitude of unconditional genuine forgiveness is free of the self-righteousness, judgment, and drama that often emerge in attitudinal retributivism.

We have seen that attitudinal retributivists successfully avoid the kind of objectification of offenders that Strawson articulates in defining what he calls "the objective attitude." While this is an important achievement, attitudinal retributivists commit another, more subtle kind of objectification of the offender that is equally problematic. The attitude of unconditional genuine forgiveness embodied in the paradigm of forgiveness constitutes an advance over attitudinal retributivism in that it avoids both of these forms of objectification.

One final comment about Strawson's objective attitude is in order before we close this discussion. Strawson interestingly suggests that there are situations in which we may want to adopt the objective attitude, not only toward those who are seriously impaired, but toward those who are mature as well.[69] For example, a therapist or a physician may appropriately regard her patient as someone to be cured, rather than as someone to engage with as an equal in a personal relationship, even if the patient is clearly a moral agent and someone who can enter into personal relationships with others. An advocate of the paradigm of forgiveness can

[69] P.F. Strawson, "Freedom and Resentment," p. 9.

accommodate this insight, although perhaps in a different manner than Strawson had in mind. The therapist or physician relates to her patient in a way that is somewhat unique in that she sets aside any focus on herself and instead focuses on the patient's needs in an attempt to promote his welfare. Likewise, when we adopt an attitude of unconditional genuine forgiveness, we do so unilaterally, without conditions attached concerning our own needs or expectations. We reestablish our self-respect and take care of our own needs in the process of addressing the wrong, and we are then free to set aside the focus on ourselves and direct our attention to the offender. Our perspective here is objective in the sense that it transcends the self or ego and focuses on the other.

It is important to recognize that this form of objectivity is not morally problematic, but rather morally admirable. As I have argued, the kind of objectivity embodied in an attitude of unconditional genuine forgiveness does not preclude self-respect or attention to our own needs. It simply allows us to relate to others in such a way that we let go of the preoccupation with ourselves and focus on others' welfare. Of course, in many cases we will want to maintain personal relationships with those whom we forgive, and we will often want to establish limits or conditions on these relationships. But an attitude of unconditional genuine forgiveness itself, as opposed to reconciliation with the offender, will be objective in the sense just described.

In this chapter I have provided some initial justification for pursuing the moral analysis of the attitudes of forgiveness and resentment from the perspective of virtue ethics. I have also outlined a process of addressing the wrong that will be important for many victims of wrongdoing if they are to respect themselves and reach a state of genuine forgiveness. I have then argued that for the victim who has sufficiently completed the process of addressing the wrong, or for the victim who does not need to do so, it will always be appropriate and desirable from a moral point of view to adopt an attitude of unconditional genuine forgiveness. Regardless of whether the offender repents and regardless of what he has done or suffered, an attitude of genuine forgiveness is fully compatible with self-respect, respect for morality, and respect for the offender as a sentient being and moral agent. Further, for the victim who has sufficiently completed the process of addressing the wrong or has no need to do so, an attitude of resentment is ultimately incompatible with these three forms of respect. If the arguments in this chapter are correct, I have provided a defense of the attitude of unconditional genuine forgiveness that is both articulate and uncompromising. The defense of unconditional forgiveness presented here is thoroughly uncompromising in that it is fully compatible with self-respect, respect for morality, and respect for the offender as a moral agent. And it is articulate in that I have explained the changes in judgment that occur when we replace an attitude of resentment with an attitude of unconditional genuine forgiveness. Let us now turn to the moral analysis of the self-referential counterparts of forgiveness and resentment: the attitudes of self-forgiveness and self-condemnation.

4

The Moral Analysis of the Attitudes of Self-Forgiveness and Self-Condemnation

In Chapters 2 and 3 I have defined the attitudes of forgiveness and resentment and provided a moral evaluation of these attitudes. These chapters lay the groundwork for defining and evaluating the attitudes of self-forgiveness and self-condemnation, and our discussion here can therefore be more concise. In this chapter I will provide a brief conceptual analysis of self-forgiveness and self-condemnation. I will then outline the process that the offender must complete in order to adequately address his own wrong. Finally, I will argue that for the offender who has sufficiently completed the process of addressing the wrong, self-forgiveness is always appropriate and desirable from a moral point of view. As with the attitude of unconditional genuine forgiveness, I will defend the attitude of self-forgiveness by arguing that it is compatible with the forms of respect that are required of us in the type of situation at issue: respect for the victims of wrongdoing, respect for morality, and, in this case, respect for ourselves as sentient beings and moral agents. At the same time, I will show that the analogue of resentment, which I will refer to as self-condemnation, is to some extent incompatible with these three forms of respect.

THE ATTITUDES OF SELF-FORGIVENESS AND SELF-CONDEMNATION DEFINED

As I argued in Chapter 3, our initial response to an offender who has wrongfully harmed us tends to be resentment. When we forgive, we replace this initial attitude of resentment with an attitude of respect, compassion, and real goodwill for the offender. In the same manner, when we recognize that we have committed a wrong, we tend to respond at first with feelings of guilt and self-condemnation. In forgiving our-selves, we replace our initial response of self-condemnation with a more positive attitude toward ourselves. Thus, like forgiveness, self-forgiveness can be seen as a corrective attitude.

Let us begin by examining the attitude of self-condemnation. Again, I am not attempting to construct a lexical definition of either self-condemnation or self-forgiveness here. Instead I am attempting to provide an account of these attitudes that will facilitate the substantive analysis of response to wrongdoing undertaken in this book. Insofar as it is of interest to us here, an attitude of self-condemnation is an atti-tude we adopt toward ourselves when we recognize that we are guilty of moral wrongdoing.[1] The cognitive component of this attitude con-sists first and foremost of the salient recognition that we have violated a moral standard and done something wrong or, in other words, that we have performed a harmful act without adequate justification or excuse. It includes the salient recognition that we are moral agents who could have and should have done otherwise. And it includes an acute aware-ness that we have failed to respect the true moral status of the persons, animals, or objects we have harmed. When we have harmed a person or animal, the cognitive component of an attitude of self-condemnation also includes an acute awareness of the suffering we have caused our victim to experience. In order to simplify the discussion that follows, I will consider only the wrongs that we have perpetrated against persons. Self-forgiveness is arguably most problematic in cases of this sort, and the moral analysis presented here should be easily applicable to cases in which we have wrongfully harmed animals or objects.

The affective component of an attitude of self-condemnation consists of feelings of guilt, shame, and self-directed moral anger, with which we are all familiar. Again, there is a continuum of feelings here, ranging from mild or moderate feelings of this sort to feelings of excruciating guilt and outright self-loathing. Robin Dillon describes the range of feelings associated with an attitude of self-condemnation as follows: "Painful feelings of negative self-assessment such as guilt, shame, deep disap-pointment with oneself, self-contempt, self-loathing, as well as remorse,

---

[1] Nancy Snow, and now several others, have pointed out that we often speak of self-forgiveness in nonmoral contexts as well. For example, a football player whose fumble causes his team to lose a game may say that he will never forgive himself for dropping the ball. However, as our focus here is exclusively on self-forgiveness as a response to wrongdoing, I will not consider cases of this sort. See Nancy Snow, "Self-Forgiveness," p. 76.

anguish, despair, [and] self-doubt..."[2] Depending on the circumstances, we may also experience a variety of other emotions in connection with our wrong. For example, if a father seriously abuses his daughter, and his daughter breaks off all contact with him, the father may experience intense regret for the loss of his relationship with his daughter and the opportunity to contribute to her life.

The motivational component of an attitude of self-condemnation consists, as with resentment, of a desire for the moral order to be restored. This desire may take various forms. It may consist of a desire to take the victim's place or to take on her suffering in some other way. It may consist of a desire to undertake some form of penance or to experience the suffering we take ourselves to deserve in view of the wrong we have committed. In its most extreme form, it may even consist of a desire to commit suicide – to terminate our own existence as a person who has perpetrated an act so heinous that we consider it to be unforgivable.

An attitude of self-forgiveness, again insofar as it is of interest to us here, also responds to the fact that we have wrongfully inflicted harm on another without adequate justification or excuse. The cognitive component of this attitude, like the cognitive component of an attitude of self-condemnation, includes the recognition that we have done wrong, and that we are moral agents who could have and should have done otherwise. It includes an awareness of the moral status of the persons we have harmed, and of the suffering they have experienced as a result of our offense. And it includes the awareness that as the perpetrator of the wrong, we are responsible for making amends to those whom we have injured. Unlike an attitude of self-condemnation, however, the cognitive component of an attitude of self-forgiveness also includes a full and salient recognition of ourselves as valuable human beings with the capacity for moral growth, choice, and awareness, who have a moral status equal to that of any other person. (Here again, it is important to understand that this type of regard for ourselves involves recognition self-respect rather than evaluative self-respect.) The affective component of an attitude of self-forgiveness consists of a basic feeling of self-respect and self-acceptance. And the motivational component of an attitude of self-forgiveness consists of the desire to make adequate amends for the wrong and then to focus on the positive pursuits that will make our lives meaningful for ourselves and others. Thus whereas the person who adopts an attitude of self-forgiveness will sincerely regret, on an ongoing

[2] Robin Dillon, "Self-Forgiveness and Self-Respect," p. 63.

basis, the wrong and the suffering that he has inflicted on the victim, he will not hold himself in contempt for having committed it. And rather than desiring to punish himself or perhaps even kill himself, he will want to do what he can for the victim and then live in a peaceful and constructive manner.

Finally, it is important to recognize that we can wrongfully harm ourselves as well as other persons. Kathryn Norlock examines at some length the extremely difficult choices that face some of the victims of serious wrongdoing. She points out that victims of these wrongs may feel that they have made wrong choices themselves under the intense pressures they face. Further, she argues that victims of various types of abuse sometimes make decisions that tend to perpetrate the kind of abuse in question for themselves as well as for others. When these persons make choices that tend to perpetrate their own oppression, they may well need to self-forgive for harming themselves. On the virtue-ethical analysis of self-forgiveness constructed here, there is room for both types of self-forgiveness. As moral agents, we are responsible for determining the attitudes we will adopt toward ourselves in view of the fact that we have harmed others. We are also responsible for determining the attitudes we will adopt toward ourselves in view of the fact that we have harmed ourselves. As Norlock argues, neither type of self-forgiveness is incoherent or insignificant. In the discussion that follows, I will restrict my discussion to cases in which we have harmed others. On the virtue-ethical analysis presented here, the same arguments used to justify self-forgiveness when we have harmed others will justify self-forgiveness when we have harmed ourselves, although some modifications will have to be made to the process of addressing the wrong. I refer readers who are particularly interested in forgiving self-harm to Norlock's excellent analysis, as well as to Claudia Card's insightful discussion of these matters in *The Atrocity Paradigm*.[3]

THE PROCESS OF ADDRESSING THE WRONG

Unlike forgiveness, self-forgiveness must always be preceded by a process of addressing the wrong if the offender is to respect himself and his victim and reach a state in which he can forgive himself in a worthy manner. (Some of the steps may be performed very quickly and easily if

---

[3] See Kathryn Norlock, *Forgiveness from a Feminist Perspective*, pp. 149–154, and Claudia Card, *The Atrocity Paradigm*, chapter 10.

the wrong is trivial, but they must still be performed.) Again, it should be understood that this is not a mechanical process. The way in which an individual addresses a wrong he has committed will be tailored to his own circumstances. Further, as with the process of addressing the wrongs that have been perpetrated against us, a full development of the paradigm of forgiveness will draw heavily at this point on scientific research. Psychologists can provide us with valuable information concerning the most effective ways for individuals in various circumstances to carry out each of these steps, and about how to structure the process as a whole. Here I will simply identify the steps the offender needs to take if he is to reach a state of genuine self-forgiveness and respect his victim, himself, and his moral obligations.

The first task for the offender is to recognize and acknowledge to himself that he has committed a wrong, and to take full responsibility for what he has done. If he does not acknowledge that his act was wrong, he fails to respect both the victim of his wrongdoing and the moral obligations that he violated in committing the offense. By engaging in self-deception regarding his responsibility for the offense, he also fails to respect himself. Further, if he attempts to forgive himself before he acknowledges his responsibility for committing the wrong, his self-forgiveness will be morally problematic in that it will amount to condoning the wrong rather than forgiving himself for having committed it.

The second (and related) task for the offender is to recognize his victim's status as a person. The most severe pain in the process of addressing the wrong will be encountered when the wrongdoer regards his victim as a person, like himself, with her own needs, feelings, and vulnerabilities, and with a moral status equal to his own. Until the offender recognizes his victim's status as a person, he clearly fails to respect her. He also fails to respect his moral obligation to regard others in this manner, and again fails to respect himself by engaging in self-deception. As with acknowledging that the act was wrong, if the offender attempts to forgive himself before he recognizes his victim's status as a person, his self-forgiveness will amount to condoning the wrong, and it will be morally problematic in this regard.

Third, the offender must acknowledge the feelings that arise for him in connection with the offense – compassion for the victim, grief that he has injured her, guilt, revulsion toward the wrong and the attitudes that led to it, and so on. Again, it is important to distinguish between reasonable emotional responses to the wrong and excessively destructive feelings that may arise, such as intense self-loathing, feelings of utter worthlessness, or suicidal feelings. The offender's emotional responses serve to connect him with the reality of what he has done, the value of the victim, and the importance of his moral obligations. Therefore, by denying himself access to these feelings, the offender fails in an important sense to respect his victim and his moral obligations. He also fails to respect himself as a moral agent by denying himself the moral growth he could achieve by experiencing these feelings. Further, by suppressing his feelings in this manner, the offender prevents himself from reaching an integrated attitude of self-forgiveness. Suppressed feelings of guilt and self-contempt will remain in this case, and the offender will not achieve the internal resolution of the issue that an integrated attitude of self-forgiveness requires. At best, he will hold a fragmented attitude of self-forgiveness in this case

Fourth, the offender must address the attitudes and behavior patterns that led him to commit the wrong. If he does not do so, it is likely that he will commit a similar offense in the future. This task can be very difficult, and it is unlikely that anyone can perform it perfectly. What is required of the offender here is that he make a persistent, good faith effort to identify and eliminate the defects of character that led to his wrongdoing. He must be mindful of his own harmful propensities, and take any steps that will be effective in ensuring that he does not harm others in the same manner. If the offender fails to address the attitudes and behavior patterns that led to the wrong, he clearly fails to respect the requirements of morality. He also fails to honor his victim, and to respect others like her whom he may harm in the future. And he clearly fails to respect himself as a moral agent by neglecting his own moral growth. Once again, until the offender addresses the attitudes and behavior patterns that led to the offense, the incident will not be over for him and he will not achieve the true internal resolution of the issue that an integrated attitude of self-forgiveness requires.

Finally, the offender faces the task of making amends for the wrong. He must fully acknowledge the nature of his wrong and express his sincere regret to the victim for having committed it, unless a direct apology would do her more harm than good. It is important to recognize that an adequate apology is specific. The victim is likely to be aware of the various ways in which she was affected by the wrong, and each of the aspects of the wrong should be acknowledged directly. It is not enough to say "I owe you amends for things I've said and done," and to drop the matter there. The very common phrase "I'm sorry *if* I hurt you" is also not adequate. An adequate apology would instead be, "I'm sorry *that* I hurt you in these specific ways." Further, an adequate apology directly states that the act was wrong, in addition to expressing regret that the victim was hurt or offended.[4] In cases in which a direct apology will do the victim more harm than good, the offender must simply correct his behavior and do what he can to improve the victim's life without causing her further suffering.

In addition to apologizing to the victim, the offender must make substantive amends for any losses the victim has suffered, to the extent that he is able to do so. It is important that he ask the victim (again, unless he would cause her further suffering by doing so) what she needs or wants in compensation for her losses. The offender should also have thought about this question in depth, and have ideas of his own to offer as to how he might provide her with adequate restitution. As he considers how he can best make amends for his wrongdoing, he must consider secondary and tertiary victims as well as the primary victim of his offense. In some cases the offender may have inflicted so much harm on his primary victim, and/or on his secondary and tertiary victims, that it is impossible for him to make full restitution, no matter what he does. In cases of this sort, he must simply make a good faith effort to do what can reasonably be expected of him under the circumstances, and to persist in this course of action as long as is necessary to have actually done his best to make full restitution to his victims. In cases in which the wrongdoer has committed a crime, he may also have a criminal penalty to pay in making amends to the community. (I will discuss criminal punishment in some detail in Chapter 7.) Again, it is clear that the offender must take this step if he is to respect his victims, honor his moral obligations, and respect himself as a moral agent. It is also clear that until he takes this step, the incident will not be over for him and he will not achieve the true internal resolution of the issue that an integrated attitude of self-forgiveness requires.

Once the offender has worked through the process outlined here, he has taken the steps he needs to take to address his own wrongdoing. He has done his best to address the offense in a reasonable and responsible manner. He must still complete the course of action he has undertaken as restitution for the harm he has wrongfully inflicted on others, and he must continue to work on the defects of character that led him to commit the offense. However, provided that he has initiated these tasks and made a firm commitment to follow through on them, he is properly

---

[4] For an excellent book-length discussion of apologies, see Nick Smith's *I Was Wrong*.

situated to forgive himself. At this point he has avoided a number of moral errors that often occur when we forgive ourselves. Thus the attitude of self-forgiveness that he adopts will be a reasonable candidate for a morally worthy response to his own wrongdoing. In the terminology introduced in Chapter 2, if he forgives himself at this point, his self-forgiveness will be genuine. He is not condoning his own transgression, or deceiving himself about the nature of the wrong or his feelings about it. Nor is he evading any of his moral obligations, or any of the steps he needs to take to address the wrong appropriately. Rather, as he forgives himself he fully acknowledges the nature of his offense and of the suffering he has inflicted on the victim. He also takes full responsibility for correcting his attitudes and behavior patterns, and for doing his best to make adequate amends for his offense. In the remainder of the chapter, I will assess the moral appropriateness of the attitudes of self-condemnation and genuine self-forgiveness for the offender who has completed the process described here.

DIVERGENCE OF THE PARADIGM OF FORGIVENESS AND ATTITUDINAL RETRIBUTIVISM

As with interpersonal forgiveness, both advocates of the paradigm of forgiveness and attitudinal retributivists can endorse the process of addressing the wrong that has been described. Both types of theorists are concerned with respect for morality, respect for the victims of wrongdoing, and respect for ourselves as moral agents. Attitudinal retributivists and advocates of the paradigm of forgiveness will part company, however, on the question of whether the offender should adopt an attitude of self-condemnation or an attitude of genuine self-forgiveness once this process is sufficiently complete. Advocates of both positions will agree that the offender should adopt an attitude of genuine self-forgiveness if his offense was mild or moderate, if he is able to make adequate amends for the harm he has wrongfully inflicted, and if he has been forgiven by the victim. However, attitudinal retributivists may argue that self-forgiveness is not morally appropriate when the offender is guilty of very serious wrongdoing, is unable to make adequate amends, or has not been forgiven by the victim. In contrast, an advocate of the paradigm of forgiveness will argue that for the offender who has sufficiently completed the process of addressing the wrong, an attitude of genuine self-forgiveness is always appropriate and desirable from a moral point of view, regardless of what the offender has done, regardless of whether he has the capacity to make full restitution for the wrong, and regardless of whether the victim is willing or able to forgive him.

There seems to be no question that genuine self-forgiveness is good for the offender. H.J.N. Horsburgh remarks that "the man who resolutely refuses to forgive himself is often launched on a course of utter self-destruction, and it is this which gives moral significance to the process of self-forgiveness."[5] And Nancy Snow says that "self-forgiveness for moral wrongs is essential for maintaining the capability for moral agency. After a serious moral failure, we must, to regain our bearings as functioning moral agents, be able to recognize and accept our imperfections and forgive ourselves for having them and sometimes acting wrongly."[6] To remain in a state of self-hatred or self-contempt after we have worked through the process of addressing the wrong would be debilitating. It would not only destroy the quality of our own lives, but also significantly undermine our ability to contribute and relate to others. The central question about the moral appropriateness of an attitude of unconditional genuine self-forgiveness is whether this attitude is compatible with respect for the victim, respect for morality, and respect for ourselves as moral agents. Let us examine each of these forms of respect in turn.

SELF-FORGIVENESS, SELF-CONDEMNATION, AND RESPECT FOR THE VICTIM

One of the most pervasive concerns about self-forgiveness is that it may be incompatible with respect for the victim. Some authors have suggested that because the victim is the person who was wrongfully harmed, it is her prerogative to do the forgiving. If the offender pre-empts this right and forgives himself before the victim is willing or able to forgive him, then he fails to respect the victim. Richard Swinburne holds that the victim has special rights in this regard, although the rights are limited. He says that if the victim refuses to forgive the offender, the offender should not forgive himself for a period of time. "But if the apology is pressed and the penance increased, and still the victim refuses to forgive, the guilt disappears."[7] Swinburne also asks whether an offender's guilt remains if he cannot make adequate restitution or apology to his victim,

[5] H.J.N. Horsburgh, "Forgiveness," p. 275.
[6] Nancy Snow, "Self-Forgiveness," p. 76.
[7] Richard Swinburne, *Responsibility and Atonement*, p. 87.

or if his victim is dead. Nancy Snow seems to attribute a special status to the victim as well, by insisting that self-forgiveness constitutes only a second-best alternative to full reconciliation with the victim.[8] This position seems to suggest that the offender should first seek full reconciliation with the victim, and then if she is unwilling or unable to forgive him, he can settle for self-forgiveness as the second-best option. And Charles Griswold writes that when the offender has taken appropriate steps to address the wrong, but the victim is unwilling or unable to forgive him, self-forgiveness "seems once again to constitute an approximation of forgiveness"[9] rather than a paradigmatic case of forgiveness. He adds that if the victim may be able to forgive the offender at some point in the future, then "if self-forgiveness has already lifted the burden of guilt, the address to the injured party looks to be a formality, and a form of disrespect."[10]

There are several points to consider here. Let us begin with the questions about restitution and apology for the wrong. Clearly the offender is morally obligated to make amends to his victim. If he has completed the process of addressing the wrong, he has addressed this issue to the best of his ability. No less is required of him if he is to respect his victim. But what if the offender cannot make full restitution or adequate apology for the wrong, either because the victim is dead or otherwise unavailable, or because a direct apology would do more harm than good, or because the wrong was so serious that it outstrips his ability to atone for it?

If the offender is to truly respect his victim, it must be the case that he would be willing to make full restitution and adequate apology for his wrong if he could. He must honor the victim's status as a person and recognize that she deserves full amends for the harm he has wrongfully inflicted on her. However, the fact that the offender is limited in his ability to atone for the wrong does not imply that he lacks this level of respect. It is his internal attitude rather than his external capabilities that are relevant in this regard. He can deeply respect the victim and at the same time lack the ability to apologize to her adequately and to compensate her completely for her losses.

In order to respect the victim, the offender must also fulfill his moral obligations to her. But we must bear in mind, as Kant pointed out, that "ought implies can." The offender is not obligated to do what he cannot

---

[8] Nancy Snow emphasizes this point a number of times in "Self-Forgiveness."
[9] Charles Griswold, *Forgiveness*, p. 123.
[10] *Ibid.*, p. 124.

do. Once he has done his best to make amends for the wrong, he has ful-filled his moral obligations to the victim.

It is important to recognize that apology and restitution are oriented toward the victim and are undertaken for her sake. They are the means by which the offender alleviates the victim's suffering and makes good her loss, rather than the means by which the offender somehow "lifts the burden of his guilt" or becomes an acceptable person again after the wrong. If we separate the offender from his offense, we will recognize that he does not lose his basic acceptability – his moral status or his intrinsic worth as a person, as a result of his wrongdoing. His moral status as a person – as a sentient being and moral agent – is grounded in his basic capacities: his capacity to experience happiness and misery, his desire for happiness, and his capacity for moral choice, growth, and awareness. It cannot be defeated by his wrong choices, nor can it be increased by an ability to make adequate apology or restitution for the offense. At all times, he possesses a moral status equal to that of every other person. In this case, an offender who is unable to make adequate apology or full restitution for his wrong does not lack sufficient moral status for self-forgiveness, nor does he fail to respect the victim by forgiving himself. In order to respect the victim, he must renounce his wrong and do his best to make amends for it, but he need not renounce himself as a person. In adopting an attitude of genuine self-forgiveness, the offender simply recognizes his intrinsic worth as a person (which he retains regardless of his ability to make amends for the wrong) at the same time that he also fully respects his victim's moral status and intrinsic worth.

Let us now turn to the deeper question of whether the victim has an exclusive right to do the forgiving, and whether the offender fails to respect the victim by forgiving himself when she is unwilling or unable to forgive him. If he is to respect his victim, the offender must recognize the victim's right to decide for herself whether or not she will forgive him. He must respect the fact that the victim needs time to work through her own process of addressing the wrong, especially when the offense was serious, and that she may in fact never wish to forgive him. However, the offender must at the same time recognize his own right and responsibility to determine what his own attitudes will be. As an autonomous moral agent, he is fully responsible for determining his own attitudes. If he simply reacts to the victim's decisions and allows her attitudes to determine his own, he fails in this regard. Thus the responsible offender will not wait to forgive himself until the victim has forgiven him, nor will he refuse to forgive himself on the grounds that it is the victim's prerogative to do the forgiving. Instead, he will respectfully separate himself from the victim's attitudes and work to determine his own. The offender who reaches a state of genuine self-forgiveness determines for himself that in spite of his wrongdoing, he remains a valuable human being who warrants respect, compassion, and real goodwill.

Contrary to Griswold's assertion, the offender can adopt an attitude of genuine self-forgiveness without making further address to the victim a mere formality and a form of disrespect. Suppose that Jason has wronged Erin, and that she is totally unreceptive to any contact with him at this point, although he has reason to believe that she may be able to forgive him at some time in the future. Assuming that Jason has sufficiently completed the process of addressing the wrong and determined that a direct apology would do more harm than good at present, he can adopt, at this point, an attitude of genuine self-forgiveness. Then, as soon as Erin seems receptive to communicating with him, he can respectfully offer her a sincere and thorough apology. He will do so not to "lift the burden of his guilt" and not as a mere formality. Rather, he will do so because he genuinely respects and cares about Erin and believes that she is owed an apology and would benefit from receiving one. It is also important to recognize that if Erin forgives Jason at this point, her forgiveness is not superfluous. If, as I have argued, genuine forgiveness is always appropriate and desirable from a moral point of view, then Erin's forgiveness has a moral significance of its own. Reaching a state of genuine forgiveness will also be beneficial to Erin, and it will make a contribution to whatever kind of relationship (if any) she chooses to have with Jason in the future.

In addition, it is important that the offender forgive himself independently of the victim's decision even if the victim is entirely willing and able to forgive him. Robert Enright has pointed out that the victim's forgiveness can serve as a catalyst for the offender's self-forgiveness. By forgiving him, the victim can help the offender to accept himself and recognize his intrinsic worth as a person in spite of his wrongdoing.[11] In this case, the victim's forgiveness is certainly valuable to the offender. However, the offender must ultimately recognize *for himself* that he is worthy of respect, compassion, and real goodwill in spite of what he has done. If he fails to grasp this truth for himself, and instead relies on the victim to tell him that he is acceptable, his self-forgiveness will not be stable or genuine. It will not be stable because it is grounded in the victim's perceptions and attitudes, which may change depending on what is happening in her life. And it will not be fully worthy from a moral point of view, because in failing to recognize this truth for himself the offender deceives himself about his own status as a person. Further, the offender's self-forgiveness in this case will be problematic in that it is grounded in the victim's moral vision and understanding instead of his own. In short, in order to possess the morally integrated attitude of genuine self-forgiveness, the offender must determine for himself that this attitude is morally appropriate. And he must have the cognitive, affective, and motivational aspects of this attitude firmly in place in his own heart and mind.

Additional problems may arise if the offender fails to forgive himself and instead holds himself hostage to the victim's decision about forgiveness or reconciliation. First, consider a case in which the victim has not yet forgiven the offender, and in which the offender refuses to forgive himself until the victim forgives him. In this case, it is likely that the offender will actively seek the victim's forgiveness so that he can be at peace. As Swinburne suggests, he may press his apology to get the victim to forgive him. In doing so, he may well engage in behavior that is again disrespectful of the victim. If he continues to express his regret strictly for the victim's sake, to promote her welfare and to help her to see that she is truly valuable, then he behaves in a respectful manner. But if he performs acts of penance and presses his apology to get the victim to forgive him, his behavior is self-centered, manipulative, and fundamentally disrespectful of the victim.

An incident in which an offender does not forgive himself independent of his victim's response is described in Simon Wiesenthal's book *The Sunflower*. The incident takes place in a hospital room in Nazi Germany. A Nazi soldier on his death bed recognizes the magnitude of his own wrongdoing and asks for a Jew to be brought into his room. A Jewish inmate in a concentration camp – presumably Wiesenthal – is taken from his work crew and brought to the soldier. The soldier acknowledges his wrongdoing, repents, and then desperately seeks Weisenthal's forgiveness. He says he cannot die in peace until he receives forgiveness from a Jew. Wiesenthal leaves the room without saying a word.

Here the soldier's behavior is doubly disrespectful of Wiesenthal. First, he pressures Wiesenthal to forgive him for selfish reasons – so that he can accept himself and die in peace. In desperately seeking his own ends, he fails to consider Wiesenthal's need to come to terms with the enormous wrongs of the Holocaust in his own way and in his own time. Second, the soldier imposes an unfair burden on Wiesenthal, who is already severely burdened at the time. It is not Wiesenthal's responsibility to assuage the soldier's guilt or to establish for him that he is worthy of respect, compassion, and real goodwill. Rather, it is the soldier's responsibility to recognize these points for himself. If the soldier had managed to forgive himself independently of Wiesenthal's decision about forgiveness, he would not have disrespected Wiesenthal in these ways. Instead, he would have acknowledged the wrong, expressed his deep remorse, and honored Wiesenthal's process of dealing with the wrongs inflicted upon him. And by accepting himself, he could have died in peace.

In some cases, the victim who has not yet forgiven the offender will want the offender to desperately seek her forgiveness. Implicit in the act of wrongdoing is the claim that the victim does not warrant a full measure of respect. If the victim has not yet forgiven the offender, she is likely to be struggling with this claim. She may feel respected or empowered if she can get the offender to apologize profusely, to perform many acts of penance, or to lower or humiliate himself. However, if the offender has worked through the process of addressing the wrong, he will have acknowledged to the victim that his act was wrong and that she deserved to be treated with a full measure of respect. It is now up to her whether or not she accepts the apology. Again, if the offender goes on in the manner just described not for the victim's sake but in order to get the victim to forgive him, his behavior is self-centered and manipulative. Further, by catering to her in this way he enables her to remain stuck in a set of attitudes and behavior patterns that are unproductive for her. She will feel more empowered and be happier in the long run if she stops seeking external validation and recognizes for herself that she is a valuable human being who deserves to be treated well.

Let us now consider a case in which the offender seeks not only forgiveness but also full reconciliation with the victim. In addition to wanting his victim to regard him with respect, compassion, and real goodwill, the offender wants her to resume her former personal relationship with him. It is important to recognize that there is no moral imperative for the offender to seek full reconciliation with the victim. For example, suppose that John is married to Jane, an abusive alcoholic. After a long period of suffering, he lashes out at her in anger and makes some cruel remarks about her alcoholism. Although John's act was wrong, he need not reconcile with Jane. This incident may show him that it would be best for both of them to terminate the marriage. Or, as a result of the incident, Jane may recognize that she is addicted to alcohol, start a reha-bilitation program, and realize in the process of examining herself that she married John for all the wrong reasons and cannot sustain a loving relationship with him. Full reconciliation with the victim is not always the best option for the offender or for the victim.

But suppose that two people have a marriage that is basically good for both of them, and then one wrongfully harms the other. If they wish to reconcile, the quality of their relationship may be damaged if the offender cannot forgive himself independently of the victim's response. In this case, it is again likely that the offender will engage in manipula-tive behavior either to get his wife to forgive him, or if she has already done so, to maintain her acceptance of him. He will approach his wife in need of something from her instead of approaching her to contribute to her life and to share life's experiences with her as an equal. By failing to regard himself with respect, compassion, and real goodwill, he sets himself up to be needy and self-centered in seeking these things from her. On the other hand, if he forgives himself independently of her response, he will come to the relationship as an equal, and with much to offer. Having met his own needs for self-acceptance, he can focus on her and contribute to her life.

Self-forgiveness, then, is not best conceived as a second-rate alternative to full reconciliation with the victim. It is morally important in its own right, regardless of whether the offender and victim choose to attempt reconciliation. If they do choose to reconcile, genuine self-forgiveness provides a firm foundation from which the offender can approach his vic-tim in a respectful manner, secure in himself and able to contribute to the relationship as an equal. It therefore seems that self-forgiveness is not only compatible with respect for the victim; it is also fundamentally important in having respectful interactions with the victim in the future.

It might also be argued that self-forgiveness is intrinsically incom-patible with respect for the victim when the wrong is very serious. To forgive oneself under these circumstances may be to dismiss the victim from one's mind too readily, after seriously damaging her welfare. This argument is not persuasive either. In order to respect the victim under these circumstances, the offender must honestly acknowledge the full extent of his wrong and express his sincere regret for having harmed her so severely. He must also do everything that can reasonably be expected of him to compensate for her losses, and those of any secondary or ter-tiary victims. And he must continue to show great concern for the victim throughout his life, if she is receptive to this kind of contact with him and if she is not seriously abusive to him in return. In no case should he dismiss the victim from his mind, and he must always regret having wrongfully harmed her and having caused her to suffer. However, to respect the victim of his serious wrongdoing, the offender need not hate himself or hold himself in contempt. To fix his attention on the fact that he did wrong, and to dwell on this fact in a state of self-contempt, serves no moral value after he has completed the process of addressing the wrong. Respect for the victim is necessarily a positive attitude that is focused on the victim. It is not a negative attitude centered on the offender and his past moral performance. The offender respects the victim by transcending his focus on himself and showing sustained and profound concern for the victim's needs and feelings, rather than by continuing to dwell on his own shortcomings.

If the arguments in this section are correct, then an attitude of unconditional genuine forgiveness is fully compatible with respect for the victim, regardless of whether the offender has the ability to fully atone for the wrong, regardless of whether the victim has forgiven the offender, and regardless of the gravity of the offense. An attitude of self-condemnation is no more respectful of the victim than an attitude of genuine self-forgiveness. Further, an attitude of self-condemnation is often less than fully respectful of the victim in that it may cause the offender to focus too much on himself, to direct less of his attention to the victim's true needs and feelings, and to manipulate the victim in order to relieve his own guilt or secure his own place in their relationship. In forgiving ourselves we do not think less of the victim. Rather by adopting this attitude toward ourselves, we transcend our egocentric concerns and enable ourselves to focus directly on the victim, in a respectful, caring, and constructive manner.

To return to Heironymi's challenge (which can apply to an analysis of self-forgiveness as well as forgiveness), it seems clear that the defense of self-forgiveness developed in this section is both uncompromising and articulate. It is uncompromising in that it is fully compatible with respect for the victim. And it is articulate in that we can identify the change in judgment that leads us to replace an attitude of self-condemnation with an attitude of genuine self-forgiveness. The change of judgment that takes place in self-forgiveness, as it pertains to respect for the victim, is the recognition that an attitude of self-condemnation is actually not an attitude of respect for the victim. Rather, it is merely an attitude of disrespect for ourselves. An attitude of respect for the victim is focused directly on the victim and her needs, and not on our own moral deficiencies.

SELF-FORGIVENESS, SELF-CONDEMNATION,
AND RESPECT FOR MORALITY

Some authors have questioned whether an attitude of self-forgiveness is compatible with respect for morality. One version of this challenge holds that to forgive oneself may be to condone the wrong. In citing reasons why he hesitates to describe self-forgiveness as a virtue, Horsburgh says that "one recognizes how dangerous it would be if it were felt to be a virtue. For then it would be all too easy to slip into the habit of condoning the injury which one inflicts on others."[12] And Griswold says of self-forgiveness that "it all too easily degenerates into self-interested condonation or excuse-making."[13]

While this line of reasoning poses a significant worry about the offender who forgives himself before completing the process of addressing the wrong, it does not apply to the offender who has completed this process. It is important to remember here that I am endorsing an attitude of *genuine* self-forgiveness, which is a state that we can reach only after sufficiently completing the process of addressing the wrong. If the offender has worked through this process, he has acknowledged to himself that the act was wrong. He also understands why it is wrong, as he has taken care to recognize the victim's true status as a person. He has allowed himself to experience his grief at having caused his victim to suffer, and he has attempted to correct the attitudes and behavior patterns that led him to do so. Finally, he has made a thoughtful, concerted effort to make amends for the wrong. In this case, there is no question of the offender's condoning his own wrong. In reaching a state of genuine self-forgiveness, he extends an attitude of respect, compassion, and real goodwill to himself as a person at the same time that he thoroughly condemns his wrong act. In other words, he separates himself, the "sinner," from the sin. Rather than conflating himself with his past wrong actions and attitudes, he recognizes that he is a sentient being and moral agent who is distinct from those actions and attitudes. Therefore he can forgive himself at the same time that he utterly renounces his offense.

A closely related worry is that if an offender forgives himself, he may commit similar wrongs more easily and readily in the future. However, Enright has pointed out that by recognizing his own worth and status as a person, the one who forgives himself need not "become blind

---

[12] H.J.N. Horsburgh, "Forgiveness," p. 275.
[13] Charles Griswold, *Forgiveness*, p. 122.

to the self's objective failures needing refinement." He adds that "self-forgiveness, not its pseudo form, may be a key for genuine positive change."[14] Someone who reaches a state of genuine self-forgiveness need not neglect the importance of his future moral obligations. In fact, once he has worked through the process of addressing the wrong, he will have done much to cultivate within himself a genuine respect for morality.

It is also unlikely that the offender can cultivate a deeper respect for morality by adopting an attitude of self-condemnation. Feelings of guilt may be useful in motivating the offender to work through the process of addressing the wrong, but beyond this point, it is not clear what purpose will be served by maintaining an attitude of self-contempt. It is possible that negative feelings about himself will motivate the offender to comply with future moral obligations, in that he may wish to avoid the pain of these feelings in the future. But even if the offender were motivated in this manner, it is not clear that complying with a moral rule from such a motive would constitute a deep or meaningful form of respect for morality. Nor would it be an integrated attitude of this sort, given that avoidance of pain is not a motive that is in harmony with a true cognitive recognition of the importance of our moral obligations and those whom these obligations protect.

In contrast, consider an offender who reaches a state of genuine self-forgiveness. The offender who has worked through the process of addressing the wrong has carefully considered his victim's status as a person, as a moral agent and sentient being with needs, hopes, and feelings similar to his own. He has also considered carefully the ways in which his offense damaged the victim and thwarted her hopes for herself. Having developed true respect and compassion for his victim, he will be motivated to avoid hurting others in a similar manner in the future.

In addition to having recognized his victim's status as a person, the offender who forgives himself recognizes his own worth and regards himself with respect, compassion, and real goodwill. As he addresses the defects of character that led to his wrong, he will look honestly at himself and come to understand why he did what he did. Suppose he has stolen something from his victim. If he respects himself, he can begin by acknowledging that he had a legitimate desire for more money to pursue his personal projects, although he attempted to fulfill this legitimate desire in a wrongful manner. With enough self-respect, he can recognize that he has the ability to fulfill his own needs in ways that

[14] Robert D. Enright, "Counseling within the Forgiveness Triad," p. 117.

are compatible with respect for others and respect for his own moral integrity. Or, if it is truly impossible for him to do so, he can recognize that he can make his life meaningful without the material resources he was seeking. He is then likely to feel good about himself and about complying with his future moral obligations. He can also look at some of the basic attitudes that have been driving his negative behavior. Perhaps he felt discounted by his parents in the past, and adopted the mind set that if he didn't matter to anyone else, then no one else would matter to him. When he assesses this attitude with true self-respect, he will recognize that he deserved to be loved, honored, and cared for, even if his parents were not able, for whatever reason, to respond to him in this manner. He can then look at their situation with respect and compassion. By working in this manner, the offender is likely to cultivate within himself genuine respect, compassion, and goodwill, both for others and for himself.

In general, then, it seems that the offender's character defects can be eradicated much more effectively if he regards himself with respect, compassion, and real goodwill instead of with self-contempt. Arguably, the offender evinces greater respect for morality, and for his own moral development by proceeding in this manner than he does by maintaining an attitude of self-condemnation or a fear-based compliance with moral rules. Robin Casarjian, a well-known therapist who writes and teaches about forgiveness, supports this position. She says: "You may think that blaming yourself will motivate you to change or to live up to your true potential.... We have been conditioned to believe that our judgments are necessary, and that they have value, and that if we didn't always judge ourselves, we would never change, we would be unethical, and we would be lazy slobs.... But quite to the contrary, it is our chronic self-judgments that keep us stuck in an often-vicious cycle of act and remorse. What these judgments really do is keep us out of our own heart and separate us from the clarity, love, and natural integrity that is our deepest inclination and highest need to express."[15]

Again, if the arguments presented here are correct, an attitude of genuine self-forgiveness is fully compatible with respect for morality. The offender who forgives himself does not condone his past moral violations or neglect his future moral development. Rather, he condemns his

---

[15] Robin Casarjian, *Forgiveness*, p. 164. Casarjian has taught on forgiveness for the Harvard Community Health Plan, DuPont, the United States Army, and the Massachusetts prison system, among several other organizations.

past moral violations and undertakes a process that is both respectful of the requirements of morality and effective in cultivating morally appropriate attitudes in himself. Further, I argue throughout this chapter that an attitude of genuine self-forgiveness is a morally appropriate attitude for the offender to adopt once he has sufficiently completed the process of addressing the wrong, whereas an attitude of self-condemnation is not. If these arguments are correct, the offender who adopts an attitude of genuine self-forgiveness respects morality in a very direct and fundamental manner – by adopting a morally appropriate attitude and rejecting a morally inappropriate stance toward himself. Thus the account of self-forgiveness developed here is uncompromising in that it is compatible with respect for morality. It is also articulate in this regard. The change in judgment that occurs with regard to respect for morality when we replace an attitude of self-condemnation with an attitude of genuine self-forgiveness comes with the recognition that we have a basic status as sentient beings and moral agents that is distinct from our wrongful actions and attitudes. It results from the recognition that whereas our actions and attitudes were undeniably wrong, we, as persons, warrant respect, compassion, and real goodwill.

SELF-FORGIVENESS, SELF-CONDEMNATION, AND RESPECT FOR OURSELVES

Again, I believe the central difference between those who endorse an attitude of genuine self-forgiveness and those who endorse an attitude of self-condemnation lies in their different conceptions of what is entailed in respecting ourselves as moral agents. Those who endorse an attitude of self-condemnation for offenders who are guilty of very serious wrongs believe that in order to respect ourselves as moral agents, we must regard ourselves as fully responsible for our wrongful actions and attitudes. If we have performed extensive or grievous acts of wrongdoing, we may have no other choice than to regard ourselves with self-contempt. George Harris articulates this position in the following passage: "It is true that I can be justifiably and deeply ashamed about something in my past without being deeply ashamed about who I am at present. But it is not clear to me that if my shame is justifiable enough and deep enough regarding my past that I can make sense of looking at the future with anything other than self-contempt, no matter what I am like now."[16]

---

[16] George W. Harris, *Strength and Dignity of Character*, p. 156.

It is true that if we are to respect ourselves as moral agents, we must regard ourselves as responsible for our past wrongs. However, it does not follow that an attitude of self-contempt or self-condemnation is morally appropriate for the offender who has completed the process of addressing the wrong. Again, a conclusion of this sort would follow only if we objectify ourselves by conflating ourselves with our wrongful actions and attitudes. If we do regard ourselves as in some sense the same thing as our past actions and attitudes, then Harris's position makes sense. In this case, our past record of moral performance takes on a great significance as part of our identity. In fact, to the extent that morality is of overriding importance in our lives, our past record of moral performance may well constitute the most significant component of our personal identity. Just as we appropriately judge the moral worth of various actions and attitudes, if we regard ourselves as at least in part the same thing as our past actions and attitudes, we will also judge the overall records of moral performance that each of us accumulates. If an agent develops a poor moral record, he might improve his moral standing by doing better in the future, in much the same way as a student who has performed poorly in the past might attempt to improve his GPA by receiving A's in his remaining courses. But if the previous moral failures on the record are extensive enough or severe enough, they may overwhelm any future attempts to create an acceptable overall record of moral performance. In this case, an attitude of self-contempt will be morally appropriate in that it is deserved. An offender with such a record ought to adopt an attitude of self-contempt, because this attitude responds appropriately to who he is as a person.

As we saw in Chapter 3, this type of analysis is seriously problematic from a moral point of view. In the case of an attitude of self-contempt, it is morally inappropriate in that it objectifies us by conflating us with our own past actions and attitudes. Although our past wrongful actions and attitudes warrant our condemnation, and in severe cases, our contempt, we as persons do not. Whatever we have done, we remain sentient beings and moral agents. As such, we warrant respect, compassion, and real goodwill. Clearly we must respect ourselves as moral agents, but to respect ourselves as moral agents is *not* to conflate ourselves with our past record of moral performance and to pass judgment on ourselves accordingly. Rather it is simply to respect ourselves as persons who have the *capacity* for moral choice, growth, and awareness. Again, it is important to remember that respect is a positive attitude that responds to that which is of value. To respect ourselves as moral agents is to regard ourselves in a positive manner in light of our valuable moral capacities.

Further, if we are to respect ourselves as moral agents, we must consistently exercise our moral agency in a responsible manner. In order to do so, we must make choices and adopt attitudes that have genuine moral value. To dwell on one's own past record of moral performance, either with a sense of superiority or with a sense of self-contempt, is overly self-absorbed and devoid of any real value. Of course we have every reason to do the best we can in the moral domain. But there seems to be no reason to focus our attention on our past moral track record. It is much more responsible from a moral point of view to focus on ways in which we can enhance our moral growth in the future, make genuine contributions to others, and engage in constructive activities. The offender who adopts an attitude of self-contempt, then, actually disrespects himself as a moral agent by focusing his attention in a way that is devoid of value. In contrast, the offender who reaches a state of genuine self-forgiveness respects his moral agency by using it responsibly. He transcends the focus on himself and his past wrongs, and turns his attention to what is truly of value.

George Harris develops an interesting scenario to support his position. He asks us to consider a hypothetical situation in which Jeffrey Dahmer somehow comes to care sincerely about the persons he brutally murdered. He then suggests that in this case, Dahmer would suffer what he calls a "benign integral breakdown." In a benign integral breakdown, as Harris defines the term, the agent loses his capacity to function effectively. More specifically, he loses his will to live or succumbs to deep clinical depression, insanity, hysteria, debilitating shame, or pervasive self-deception. Further, the breakdown is caused by something *good* about the agent – in this case, his true caring about his victims – and could not be prevented without removing this admirable aspect of his character. If Harris is correct, then Dahmer's inability to forgive himself and live with what he has done would be a good thing, and self-forgiveness would be inappropriate. Further, Dahmer could achieve a stable state of self-forgiveness only if he were to lose his capacity to care about others, and in particular, about his victims.

While it would certainly be very painful for Jeffrey Dahmer to look back on what he had done if he sincerely cared about his victims, it does not seem plausible to hold that something good about Dahmer's character would necessitate a breakdown at this point. One way to approach this point is to imagine ourselves offering advice to Harris's reconstructed Dahmer. It seems clear that we would not advise him to lose his will to live or to succumb to depression, insanity, debilitating shame, or self-deception. Instead we would advise him to undertake the process of addressing the wrong described earlier. We would advise him to acknowledge and take full responsibility for his wrongs, and to carefully contemplate his victims' status as persons. We would advise him to acknowledge his feelings of grief and revulsion toward his past behavior, and to embark on a serious program of moral and personal growth to eradicate the defects of character that led to his wrongdoing. And we would encourage him to do everything he possibly could to make amends to his victims' families throughout the rest of his life. Beyond this, we might suggest to him that he could make a contribution to society by explaining to psychiatrists why he did what he did and how he came to care about his victims. In addition, he might be able to work with other prisoners to good effect, and to form meaningful relationships with those who had also come to regret their past actions. In sum, we would advise him to address his past wrongs to the best of his ability and to turn his attention to the good he can do from this point forward.

To address Harris's concerns, we must consider whether this course of action is compatible with true caring about others and with an appropriate attitude toward oneself. Consider the contrast between the reformed Dahmer who suffers integral breakdown and the reformed Dahmer who instead pursues the more positive path suggested here. Whereas the Dahmer who breaks down certainly exhibits some caring about his victims, this caring is severely attenuated as he focuses extensively on himself and the horror of what he has done. By succumbing to integral breakdown, he prevents himself from being able to make amends to his victims or to contribute anything to anyone else. It seems that the Dahmer who pursues the more positive path exhibits much more unadulterated and mature caring about others, and especially about his victims. He focuses on his victims rather than on himself, does his best to alleviate their suffering, and considers the contributions he can make to them and to others as well. Rather than requiring the removal of the capacity to care about others, it seems that genuine self-forgiveness allows for the full expression of this moral capacity, whereas integral breakdown does not.

It also seems that the Dahmer who pursues the positive path exhibits a more worthy attitude toward himself. Both Dahmers admirably hold themselves responsible for their past wrongs and respect their own moral agency in this way. However, the Dahmer who breaks down abdicates responsibility when it comes to making amends to his victims, whereas the Dahmer who pursues the positive path demonstrates a much more robust sense of personal responsibility for addressing his past offenses. Further, the Dahmer pursuing the positive path respects himself as a moral agent who is capable of moral growth and contribution, whereas the Dahmer who collapses into a debilitating state of self-contempt does not.

It therefore seems that an integral breakdown of the sort Harris imagines is not caused by a true caring about others, but rather by self-absorption. True caring about others leads inevitably to a focus on others and to the positive contributions we can make to their lives. Nor is it caused by a worthy attitude toward ourselves as moral agents. Respect for ourselves as moral agents leads inevitably to using our moral capacities in a responsible, constructive manner. Thus an attitude of genuine self-forgiveness appears to evince both more caring about others and more respect for ourselves as moral agents than any kind of breakdown caused by an attitude of self-contempt.

Robin Dillon has raised another important challenge to the analysis of self-forgiveness presented here. She agrees that we cannot succumb to integral breakdown or lose our ability to function responsibly if we are to respect ourselves as moral agents. However, she argues that an attitude of self-reproach or self-condemnation is sometimes required if we are to respect ourselves properly. Her position derives from a complex analysis of self-respect developed in her earlier work. Most centrally, her position turns on the connection she identifies between recognition self-respect (both agentic and personal) and evaluative self-respect. Briefly, one who has agentic recognition self-respect has "a proper appreciation of oneself as a moral agent," and a recognition that certain actions and attitudes are morally appropriate, whereas others are not.[17] One who has personal recognition self-respect "holds herself (though perhaps not others) to personal standards and expectations the disappointment of which she would regard as shameful or degrading."[18] On the other hand, evaluative self-respect "rests on an evaluation of oneself in terms of the normative self-conception that structures recognition self-respect."[19] According to Dillon, recognition self-respect and evaluative self-respect are necessarily connected. She says that "a recognition self-respecting

---

[17] Robin Dillon, "Self-Forgiveness and Self-Respect," p. 66.
[18] *Ibid.*
[19] *Ibid.*

person commits herself to a conception of the sort of person it would be good for her to be."[20] Further, "one cannot have a normative self-conception without a disposition to assess one's *self and not just one's actions* in light of it, and without being liable, unless one is a saint, to self-reproach."[21] [my emphasis] Therefore, self-reproach, and depending on the circumstances, even punishing self-reproach for the rest of one's life, can be warranted. By adopting this attitude, we manifest proper recognition self-respect, take responsibility for ourselves, and demonstrate commitment to our moral values.

However, Dillon recognizes that there should be limits to self-reproach. As mentioned earlier, she holds that self-reproach is not warranted when it undercuts our ability to function as responsible moral agents. Further, it is inappropriate when it is based on a false or excessively narrow assessment of ourselves, when it is a function of low basal self-esteem, or when it stems from an unhealthy perfectionism or disposition to be overly critical and intolerant. Finally, even when self-reproach is warranted, we can justifiably limit the power it has over us.

While Dillon makes some important points here about the limits to self-reproach, I believe that her basic justification of the attitude of self-reproach is flawed. Let us return to the connection she identifies between recognition self-respect and evaluative self-respect. Dillon is clearly correct in asserting that the person who has recognition self-respect will appreciate herself as a moral agent and recognize that some actions are morally appropriate while others are not. She is also correct in asserting that a person with recognition self-respect will have a normative self-conception and will hold herself (if not others) to certain standards. These things are required of us if we are to respect ourselves as moral agents. There is also an important sense in which she is correct in asserting that when we have a normative self-conception, we must assess ourselves in terms of it. However, it is necessary at this point to distinguish between two very different ways in which we can assess ourselves in terms of our normative self-conception. For convenience, I will refer to them as "improvement-oriented self-assessment" and "judgment-oriented self-assessment." When we engage in improvement-oriented self-assessment, we assess ourselves against our normative self-conception in order to determine if we are actually living up to that conception, or whether we need to make adjustments in our actions and attitudes in the future if

---

[20] *Ibid.*
[21] *Ibid.*, p. 69.

we are to meet the standards we have set for ourselves. For example, if I wish to be unselfish, I must regularly examine my actions and attitudes and attempt to make corrections when they fall short of this standard. Clearly improvement-oriented self-assessment is of fundamental moral importance and is required of us as moral agents.

In contrast, when we engage in judgment-oriented self-assessment, we examine our past actions and attitudes and sit in judgment of ourselves with regard to our past performance in meeting our standards. In other words, if my past actions and attitudes have been very selfish, I will judge myself to be selfish, unworthy, and a moral failure in this regard. If we look closely, we will see that it is judgment-oriented self-assessment, rather than improvement-oriented self-assessment, that leads to shame, self-reproach, an inability to forgive ourselves, and, in the worst cases, to the kind of integral breakdown described by Harris. Improvement-oriented self-assessment looks to our past failures only to determine how we can do better to meet our moral standards in the future. It does not involve forming a negative judgment about ourselves as persons. I want to suggest that while improvement-oriented assessment is clearly required if we are to respect ourselves as moral agents, judgment-oriented self-assessment is not. Further, judgment-oriented self-assessment has no role to play in recognition self-respect. As I suggested before, sitting in judgment of our past moral track record, or forming more holistic judgments of "who we are as a person" based on this record, as Dillon suggests, is an activity that is devoid of any real value. Instead, it constitutes a distraction from the responsible pursuit of moral growth and contribution to others. If so, it seems that we can abandon judgment-oriented self-assessment, and the shame and self-reproach to which it leads, without loss.

Further, judgment-oriented self-assessment is morally problematic in that it stems from the kind of objectification of persons (in this case, ourselves) that I have identified. Dillon argues that self-forgiveness is *always* concerned with restoring evaluative self-respect but only *sometimes* concerned with restoring recognition self-respect, given that we can reproach ourselves at the same time that we respect ourselves as moral agents. This position follows from her analysis of shame and self-reproach. Regarding shame and self-reproach, she says that "the self-appraisal at its core is that one is seriously flawed as a person. One's moral self-identity and sense of self-worth are called into question...."[22]

[22] *Ibid.*, p. 64.

What we need to recognize once again, however, is that we are not the same thing as our past wrong actions and attitudes. Our past moral track record does not constitute our "moral self-identity," and we cannot regard it as such without wrongfully objectifying ourselves. Rather, our moral identity consists of the fact that we are moral agents with the capacity for moral choice, growth, and awareness.

Dillon's assertion that we can respect ourselves as moral agents at the same time that we regard ourselves with self-reproach is problematic in this respect. When we adopt the morally integrated attitude of genuine self-forgiveness, we of course recognize that we have done wrong. But we also recognize, as a salient feature of ourselves, that we retain the valuable capacity for moral choice, growth, and awareness. This morally significant aspect of ourselves is not called into question by past wrongdoing. Further, in a morally integrated attitude, our feelings will match our cognitive awareness of the value of our moral capacities. We will fully appreciate this feature of ourselves and respond to it in a positive manner. Finally, if we fully appreciate the value of our moral capacities, we will be motivated to put those capacities to good use, and to abandon the fruitless, judgment-oriented dwelling on our past moral errors. It seems, therefore, that when we regard ourselves in light of our wrongdoing, we should not adopt an attitude that involves evaluative self-respect, nor should we adopt an attitude of self-reproach or self-condemnation. Rather, we should abandon judgment-oriented self-assessment and adopt a deep form of recognition self-respect: a true respect for and appreciation of our capacities for moral growth, choice, and awareness. In other words, we should adopt an attitude of genuine self-forgiveness.

Finally, let us consider the three arguments Dillon offers in support of retaining an attitude of self-reproach in some cases, even after we have completed the process of addressing the wrong. First, she cites "considerations of retributive justice," and argues that at times we actually deserve to be punished. We are then justified in punishing ourselves with self-reproach, just as we are sometimes justified in punishing others in other ways. This argument admirably articulates the stance on self-forgiveness inherent in attitudinal retributivism. If my reasoning is correct, however, it commits the moral error of objectification. Again, as Mackie and French pointed out, wrongful actions and attitudes do call for a hostile response from moral agents. But it is only when we conflate ourselves with these actions and attitudes that we extend this attitude of hostility and self-reproach to ourselves as persons. When we look at ourselves as persons, we will see that we warrant respect, compassion, and real goodwill. I will argue in Chapter 7 that retributive theories of punishment should be rejected for these reasons, and others.

Second, Dillon argues that "self-reproach may be necessary to balance a tendency to self-exculpation and so may be necessary to prevent repeated wrong."[23] However, I argued in the last section that the person who has completed the process of addressing the wrong in no sense condones the wrong or exculpates himself. I further argued that self-forgiveness may well be more effective than self-reproach in preventing future wrongdoing.

And third, Dillon argues that "we may need to hold onto self-reproach, especially its emotional dimensions, so that we don't forget what we care about."[24] She considers this argument to be the most important. Clearly it is of the utmost importance to remember what we care about, but again we must consider the relative effectiveness of the attitudes of self-reproach and genuine self-forgiveness in this regard. Whereas self-reproach may remind us of our values, at the same time it draws much of our attention to ourselves and the way in which we assess ourselves in terms of our past moral performance. On the other hand, a person who works through the process of responding to the wrong makes a good faith effort to identify and eliminate the defects of character that led him to commit the wrong, and makes a firm commitment to stay with this effort after forgiving himself. He also makes a firm commitment to make amends to the victim to the extent that he is able to do so. Clearly, then, he is making a strong effort to remember what he cares about. Further, if he forgives himself, this effort is not attenuated by an excessive negative focus on himself. In general, I would argue that a serious program of moral growth accompanied by continual *improvement-oriented self-assessment*, rather than continual *judgment-oriented self-assessment*, will help us most effectively in remembering what we care about. (I am assuming here that we care more about others and about the quality of our moral growth than we care about our past record of moral performance.) Therefore, once again, we have reason to prefer an attitude of self-forgiveness to an attitude of self-reproach.

It seems, then, that an attitude of genuine self-forgiveness is also fully compatible with respect for ourselves as moral agents, whereas an attitude of self-condemnation is not. An attitude of self-condemnation is not fully compatible with respect for ourselves as moral agents in that it

[23] *Ibid.*, p. 79.
[24] *Ibid.*

involves both a morally problematic objectification of ourselves and an excessive and unfruitful focus on the self. It also prevents us from using our moral capacities in a fully responsible manner. If my arguments are correct, then the defense of the attitude of genuine self-forgiveness offered here is uncompromising. It is also articulate. When we replace an attitude of self-condemnation with an attitude of genuine self-forgiveness, our shift in judgment comes with the recognition that although we have done wrong in the past, we are not in any sense the same thing as our past actions and attitudes. Rather, we are persons with the valuable capacity for moral choice, growth, and awareness. Not only do we warrant respect, compassion, and real goodwill as individuals of this sort, we must also use our basic moral capacities in a responsible manner. To dwell on our past record of moral performance with self-contempt is to fail in this responsibility.

We are now in a position to contrast the moral orientation toward ourselves implicit in an attitude of self-condemnation and an attitude of genuine self-forgiveness. In an attitude of self-condemnation, we reify ourselves by conflating ourselves with our past actions and attitudes. Because our past wrongful actions are proper objects of hostility and contempt, we extend these attitudes to ourselves as well. We become alienated from ourselves and dwell in horror on what we have done. An attitude of genuine self-forgiveness embodies a significantly different moral orientation toward ourselves. In adopting an attitude of genuine self-forgiveness, we recognize that we are persons who are not to be conflated with our past actions and attitudes. We do our best to address our wrongs responsibly. When we have done so, we do not forget the wrong and the suffering it inflicted on the victim. But rather than sitting in judgment of ourselves for having committed the offense, we direct our attention to the victim's welfare, to our own moral growth, and to the contribution we can make to others. We recognize that in spite of what we have done, we can still respect ourselves as moral agents and sentient beings.

In this chapter I have defined the attitudes of self-condemnation and genuine self-forgiveness. I have argued that the offender must work through a process of addressing the wrong if he is to honor his moral obligations and reach a state of genuine self-forgiveness. I have also argued that an attitude of genuine self-forgiveness is always appropriate and desirable from a moral point of view for the offender who has sufficiently completed the process of addressing the wrong, regardless of whether he is able to make full restitution for the wrong, regardless of what he has done, and regardless of whether his victim forgives him. In Chapters 3 and 4, I have provided a moral defense of the basic attitudes that ground the paradigm of forgiveness: the attitudes of unconditional genuine forgiveness and genuine self-forgiveness. I have also argued that the attitudes of resentment and self-condemnation endorsed by attitudinal retributivists are ultimately inappropriate from a moral point of view. In the next chapter I will consider the philosophical underpinnings of each of these positions.

5

Philosophical Underpinnings of the Basic Attitudes

We have now examined at some length the moral defensibility of the basic attitudes of forgiveness and resentment, and their self-referential counterparts. Given that basic attitudes ground the unified response to wrongdoing that emerges in the paradigm of forgiveness, it is important to be thorough in examining them. It is only when we have satisfied ourselves that these basic attitudes are both morally and philosophically defensible that we will be able to endorse them without reservation. In this chapter, then, I will complete the initial justification for adopting the basic attitudes that ground the paradigm of forgiveness by attempting to show that these attitudes are compatible with our best philosophical analyses of the nature of persons. (Additional justification for these attitudes will be provided if their practical implications coincide with our considered moral judgments – a question we will consider in Chapters 6 through 8.) Further, I will argue that at least some versions of retributivism will be difficult to reconcile with plausible analyses of the nature of persons. Although there are many questions that could be considered here, I will confine my discussion to three central topics: the equal moral status of persons, personal identity, and moral responsibility.

THE PARADIGM OF FORGIVENESS AND THE
EQUAL MORAL STATUS OF PERSONS

In Chapters 3 and 4, I argued that the basic attitudes of forgiveness and self-forgiveness are always appropriate and desirable from a moral point of view for the person who has worked through the process of responding to the wrong (or in the case of forgiveness, for one who does not need to do so), whereas the basic attitudes of resentment and self-condemnation are not. In arguing for these conclusions, I simply assumed that we all have equal intrinsic worth and an equal moral status as persons. While many readers will accept these claims, others will not. In particular, some retributivists will reject egalitarianism and assert instead that human worth is based on moral merit. John Kekes, George Sher, and Louis Pojman, among others, have defended this latter position.[1] The notion of equality has been notoriously difficult, and a full-scale defense of egalitarianism is obviously impossible here. Nevertheless, because advocates of the paradigm of forgiveness and retributivists may part company on precisely this issue, it is important to give some indication here of how an egalitarian position might be defended.

Those who believe that human worth varies with moral merit often wish to retain some elements of egalitarianism. They often hold that all persons have at least some intrinsic worth and should generally be treated as ends in themselves. Further, they often hold that justice, equality, and rights have some kind of role to play in our moral thinking. For example, Kekes says: "The practical implication of the rejection of egalitarianism is not that we are free to declare open season on evil people."[2] He adds: "Nor do I think that we should get rid of the ideals of justice, equality, and rights. On the contrary, properly interpreted, these ideals are important moral forces."[3] His point is simply that we must ground these claims without reference to the mistaken view that all persons have equal intrinsic worth and moral standing. However, it is not clear exactly how he might defend the aspects of egalitarianism he wishes to retain, especially given his view that the human worth of an evil person is actually negative. It is worth noting that those who reject egalitarianism must either accept the counterintuitive implications of their position (e.g., that an open season on "evil persons" is acceptable if procedural difficulties can be solved) or provide a clear justification *in meritarian terms* of the aspects of egalitarianism that they wish to endorse.

One way to defend egalitarianism, as many authors have pointed out, is to argue that it systematizes our considered moral judgments in wide reflective equilibrium more effectively than any meritarian position.[4] I

[1] See John Kekes, *Facing Evil*; George Sher, *Desert*; and Louis Pojman, "Are Human Rights Based on Equal Human Worth?"
[2] John Kekes, *Facing Evil*, p. 121.
[3] *Ibid.*, p. 122.
[4] For example, see John Rawls, *A Theory of Justice*; Norman Daniels, "Wide Reflective Equilibrium and Theory Acceptance in Ethics;" and Kai Nielsen, "On Not Needing to Justify Equality."

will leave it to the reader to decide at the end of the book how well the egalitarian position proposed here succeeds in explaining our considered moral judgments about response to wrongdoing. Here I will consider only theoretical arguments that bear on the defense of egalitarianism. From a theoretical point of view, the most common objection to egalitarianism is that it is incompatible with any plausible theory of the nature of persons. Pojman puts the objection as follows: "There is good reason to believe that humans are not of equal worth. Given ... empirical observation, it is hard to see that humans are equal in any way at all. We all seem to have vastly different levels of abilities. Some, like Aristotle, Newton, Shakespeare ... and Einstein are geniuses; others are imbeciles and idiots ... Some are wise like Socrates and Abraham Lincoln; others are foolish. Some have great powers of foresight and are able to delay gratification, while others can hardly see their present circumstances, gamble away their futures, [and] succumb to immediate gratification ... Empirically, it looks like Churchill, Gandhi, and Mother Teresa have more value than Jack-the-Ripper or Adolf Hitler."[5]

Pojman is clearly justified in holding that human beings differ significantly from one another in their abilities and character traits. But the critical thing to notice about this argument (and others like it) is the *perspective* from which it addresses the question of human worth. When we look at persons in this manner, we are adopting a *judgmental* perspective. We regard persons in much the same way that we regard prize cows, closely assessing their traits and assigning each of them a value or worth based on this assessment. When we perform such assessments, it seems clear that people have radically different levels of worth, and it is a short step from this conclusion to the claim that they deserve different modes of treatment. We may then arrive at many of the specific conclusions about resentment, blame, and punishment that are endorsed by retributivists. (The reader should bear in mind at this point that many retributivists are egalitarians and do not adopt the reasoning suggested here. I address the views of egalitarian retributivists in other parts of the book.)

Once again, I want to suggest that we wrongfully objectify persons when we look at them in this manner, and that the judgmental perspective that meritarian retributivists adopt here is seriously problematic from both moral and epistemic points of view. Clearly it is sometimes necessary to assess the character traits and abilities that people have when

---

[5] Louis Pojman, "Are Human Rights Based on Equal Human Worth?" p. 621.

we are making specific practical decisions. For example, we would not choose to enter into a long-term romantic relationship with someone who is extremely selfish, arrogant, and abusive. Nor would we select a small, weak, distracted person to play on the offensive line of our football team. But in terms of our fundamental moral orientation toward persons, I believe that the judgmental perspective implicit in Pojman's anti-egalitarian argument must be rejected. Instead, we should adopt the perspective described (or at least partially described) by Bernard Williams in his seminal essay "The Idea of Equality." He suggests that Kant's injunction to treat persons as ends in themselves and never as means only can be at least partially interpreted as an injunction to regard persons from "the human point of view." In explicating the human point of view, Williams points out that there is a significant difference between judging a person in terms of his life and his actions and being primarily concerned "with what it is for *him* to live that life and do these actions...." He says that "each man is owed an effort at identification: he should not be regarded as the surface to which a certain label can be applied, but one should try to see the world (including the label) from his point of view."[6]

I want to suggest that both the paradigm of forgiveness and an egalitarian position on human worth and moral status incorporate what Williams calls the human point of view. When we look at ourselves in terms of what our lives are like for us internally, I think we will encounter the features of persons that are salient in the paradigm of forgiveness. Recall that in the paradigm of forgiveness, the salient features of persons are our capacity to experience happiness or misery; our basic desire for happiness; our capacity for moral choice, growth, and awareness; our status as autonomous beings who can lead meaningful lives only as authors of our own choices and attitudes; and our status as limited beings who are vulnerable to error. These features seem to describe fairly well what it is like to be us, from an internal point of view.

They are also features that we all share, and in terms of which we can be regarded as equals (at least those of us who are moral agents, and therefore possible participants in situations in which wrongdoing occurs and we attempt to respond appropriately). Regardless of our specific abilities and character traits, we all have the capacity to experience happiness and misery, and we all want very much to be happy. Certainly some of us are more intelligent than others. But regardless of whether our IQs are 80, 100, or 180, we all want to make our own moral

---

[6] Both quotations are from Bernard Williams, "The Idea of Equality," p. 236.

decisions and determine our own values. Further, it is important from a moral point of view that we do so. We all view ourselves as responsible for choosing our own actions and attitudes as we progress through our lives. Regardless of whether we are Nobel Prize winners or teenagers with Downs' Syndrome, then, we all have the capacity for moral choice, growth, and awareness that we must develop for ourselves in our own way. The teenager with Downs' Syndrome, like the Nobel Prize winner, can assess the situations she finds herself in and develop morally worthy responses to them. Like anybody else, she can learn to love, to have compassion, to help people as she is able to do so, to be humble, to treat persons fairly and as ends in themselves, and so on. She may not be able to suggest complex economic policies that instantiate the difference principle, but she is capable of moral choice, growth, and awareness nonetheless. Further, although we have radically different abilities and face radically different situations in life, we are all alike in wanting to make our own decisions and to use our own abilities, whatever they are, as we see fit. Finally, it seems clear, as Garrard and McNaughton have argued in some detail, that all of us are vulnerable to error.[7]

It is certainly true that we are not all equally virtuous or responsible, and it is often asked why the mere capacity for a goodwill or moral agency has any significance in determining our moral status as persons. If a goodwill is so important, shouldn't we focus on the actuality of a goodwill rather than on the mere capacity for it? And if we do so, doesn't it seem beyond question that Mother Teresa has more human worth than Adolf Hitler? It is important to notice that this question again shifts us back to the perspective of judgment. In contrast, if we adopt the *human* point of view and *identify* with Hitler as a person with the capacity for moral choice, growth, and awareness (assuming he has this), we will wish for him to recognize this capacity and develop it appropriately. The capacity for moral choice, growth, and awareness is extremely important, and we value it very highly in ourselves. To the extent that we adopt the human perspective and identify with Hitler as a person, we will regard his capacity for moral growth as important as well. Likewise, we know that our own happiness means a great deal to us, and when we identify with other sentient beings and think of what it is like to be them, we will regard their happiness as important. And in the same way, when we identify with others, we will respect their autonomy, just as we put a very high premium on our own. From the human perspective

---

[7] See Eve Garrard and David McNaughton, "In Defense of Unconditional Forgiveness."

we have been describing – from the perspective of internal identification with others, or of thinking what it is like to be them – it seems that one person's happiness, autonomy, and capacity for moral growth is just as important as anyone else's. From this perspective, therefore, it seems that we all have an equal moral status and equal worth as persons in virtue of the basic *capacities* we have been discussing. Further, when we truly identify with others and imagine vividly what it is like to be them, our understanding of the importance of their happiness, autonomy, and moral growth is not just intellectual. Rather, in this case we will respond to persons holistically, with the fully integrated attitudes of caring and respect. Not only will we reject the meritarian demand for the actuality of a goodwill and instead endorse the philosophical position of egalitarianism; we will also genuinely care about others and desire that they grow and flourish as persons.

The human point of view is clearly central to the paradigm of forgiveness, and it is important to recognize that the empirical sciences have a vital contribution to make here as we develop this paradigm more fully. Introspection will take us part of the distance we need to go in adopting the human point of view, but it will certainly not take us all of the way as we attempt to appreciate what it is like internally to be another person. We each have different experiences in life and therefore have limited ability to understand what is going on for others. For example, those of us who do not suffer from addictions such as alcoholism or compulsive gambling may not be able to understand through introspection what life is like from an internal standpoint for those who do. Likewise, those of us who have never suffered from Tourette Syndrome have no idea what this experience is like internally. Our understanding of these matters will be greatly enhanced by psychological and medical research in these areas. Research in neuroscience will be helpful in this regard as well. For example, neuroscientists are currently attempting to find areas of the brain that are involved in some of the Cluster B personality disorders, such as Borderline Personality Disorder and Narcissistic Personality Disorder. As these studies are undertaken, they may well demonstrate that there is a physiological basis in the brain for some of the behaviors that we often judge to be anywhere from annoying to reprehensible. Although these scientific studies will not tell us directly what it is like to be a person who suffers from such disorders, they will improve our understanding that these persons may lack the level of control that the rest of us presumably have over our actions and attitudes. Empirical studies can therefore be expected to enhance the human point of view considerably, and to contribute significantly to our respect and compassion for others.

In sum, it seems that if we adopt Williams's human perspective, we will find some support both for an egalitarian position on human worth and moral status, and for the moral orientation toward persons that is found in the paradigm of forgiveness. From this perspective we will identify with others, see them as equals, and respond to them with respect, compassion, and real goodwill. It is worth noting also that this perspective is diametrically opposed to Strawson's objective attitude, in which we view people as proper subjects of treatment or manipulation as opposed to being persons to whom we can relate as equals. Further, the human perspective has the significant benefit of creating unification among persons at the same time that it maintains a healthy respect for individual autonomy. It draws us together into community with other moral agents and sentient beings, and leads us to mutual caring and commitment to one another.

In contrast, the judgmental perspective implicit in the meritarian position on human worth objectifies us and drives us apart. Rather than looking internally at what it is like for a person to be himself and live his own life, it takes an external perspective on him, assessing his character traits and abilities, and then assigning his worth as a person based on these assessments. Given that these assessments vary widely from one person to another, we are separated and alienated from each other. And, more seriously, when we judge ourselves and find ourselves to be deficient, we are alienated from ourselves. Looking at ourselves and others with an eye toward judgment also leads us to be competitive with one another and excessively focused on our own standing in the community. Thus the perspective of identification seems to be preferable to the perspective of judgment on at least two grounds. First, the perspective of identification avoids the morally inappropriate objectification of persons that inheres in the perspective of judgment. From an epistemic point of view, we might say that it recognizes the morally salient *internal* features of persons that the perspective of judgment overlooks. Second, the perspective of identification draws us together into a strong moral community.

Kekes has raised further objections to the egalitarian position on human worth and moral status in defending his version of meritarianism. One of his central objectives is to discredit what he calls "choice-morality." Choice-morality regards our capacity for choice as our most important characteristic and as the ground of our equal intrinsic worth as persons. It then endorses interpretations of rights, justice, and freedom that are designed to establish conditions in which we can effectively exercise our capacity to choose. One of the devastating results of this way of thinking, according to Kekes, is that it renders us incapable of adequately protecting ourselves from those who are evil and destructive (often through no choice of their own) and who inflict much undeserved harm on us. This argument turns on the practical implications of the egalitarian position – a position that is incorporated in the paradigm of forgiveness. It clearly raises an important concern, and warrants a thorough response. I will address this concern in Chapter 7 when I examine the implications of the paradigm of forgiveness for the public response to wrongdoing.

On the theoretical level, Kekes argues that egalitarianism is based on three beliefs that are generally assumed to be true, but that are actually false. The first of these concerns a distinction between the self and its qualities. The *self* is often thought to be relatively enduring and continuous, and it is viewed as possessing *qualities* that are changeable and contingent. Kekes says that "the heart of the egalitarian case is that human worth attaches to selves, while moral merit depends on qualities."[8] The egalitarian argues that all people have selves, and therefore possess equal worth and moral status. Further, our equal intrinsic worth as persons is prior to any notion of moral merit because "the possession of selves is prior to their development."[9] Against this belief, Kekes argues that we cannot logically view the self as prior to its qualities. If the self were merely a subject of which qualities were predicated, there would be no way to determine if a given self is human. The self abstracted from all of its qualities could just as easily be a ping-pong ball or a cobweb as a human being. Further, Kekes argues that any qualities that we do attribute to the self to distinguish it as human can be viewed as the basis of moral merit.

Kekes suggests that the egalitarian may try to circumvent this difficulty by identifying defining characteristics of *human* selves that are morally neutral. According to Kekes, Rawls adopts this strategy in *A Theory of Justice* when he says that the grounds for human worth are pre-institutional and neutral with regard to various theories of the good, whereas the grounds for moral merit are contingent on social institutions that define the terms in which moral merit is to be assessed in a

---

[8] John Kekes, *Facing Evil*, p. 111.
[9] *Ibid.*

particular society. But here Kekes suggests that Rawls's position on natural duties conflicts with this conclusion. Because we have natural duties
that are prior to institutions (e.g., the duty to be kind rather than cruel),
and because some people comply with these duties whereas others violate them, we have a clear basis for attributing moral merit that is prior
to and independent of social institutions.

The egalitarian need not accept these conclusions. First, it is important to recognize that the egalitarian need not and should not endorse
the view that there is some kind of substantive, enduring self that is logically prior to any qualities it might possess. (I will address this point
further in the next section.) In fact, I have just suggested that both egalitarianism and the paradigm of forgiveness respond to certain enduring
and salient *qualities or characteristics* of persons that are not separate
from or attached to a "transcendental self" of the sort Kekes describes.
More specifically, persons differ from ping-pong balls and cobwebs in
being sentient, in desiring their own happiness, in being moral agents,
in being autonomous, and in being vulnerable to error. Further, I would
not describe these salient qualities as "morally neutral." The egalitarian differs from the meritarian not in viewing the self as prior to any
of its qualities, but rather in the qualities of persons that she regards
as morally significant and in the perspective she takes on these qualities. Egalitarians consider the qualities of the sort listed here to be morally salient, as opposed to past performance in conforming to moral
duties. And rather than judging persons with respect to the qualities they
possess, the egalitarian recognizes that these morally salient qualities
provide a basis for identifying with one another and for regarding each
other with respect, compassion, and real goodwill.

The second belief Kekes identifies that is often presumed to support
egalitarianism is that human worth attaches to universal human qualities such as rationality and the capacity for choice, whereas moral merit
attaches to particular qualities of character that people have but do not
deserve. Here, Kekes refers to Rawls again. Rawls argues that good
character depends to a large extent on natural endowments and social
circumstances, factors over which individuals have little or no control.
Therefore good character is not deserved, and it is unjust to allocate
burdens and benefits according to a conception of desert that is based
on good character or moral performance. A theory of justice should be
based instead on the equal worth and moral status of persons. Against
this position, Kekes argues that the egalitarian and meritarian conceptions of human worth are in exactly the same boat in this regard. If it is

beyond our control as to whether we are given the natural endowments and social circumstances that allow us to develop good character, it is equally beyond our control as to whether we are born with the characteristics that ground human worth for the egalitarian. If we must rule out character and moral merit as bases for allocating burdens and benefits because they are arbitrary from a moral point of view, we must also rule out the traits that ground equal human worth as such bases, for the same reason. Kekes says that "the price we have to pay for giving up the idea that desert ought to be proportional to moral merit is that we also have to give up the idea that desert ought to be based on human worth."[10] In this case Kekes argues that it makes more sense to reject egalitarianism, to regard moral merit as the true measure of human worth, and to adopt the position that moral merit should serve as our basis for allocating burdens and benefits.

Whether or not Kekes' critique of Rawls is successful, he fails here to give us any reason to reject the type of egalitarian position I have outlined above. The egalitarian position I have suggested does not rely on the claim that the characteristics that underlie our moral status must be earned or merited. It seems very reasonable to say that we ought to respond with compassion to all who are capable of experiencing happiness or misery, regardless of whether we have done anything to deserve our status as sentient beings (which presumably we have not). Likewise it seems reasonable to say that we ought to respect the autonomy of all beings who have the capacity for autonomous deliberation and choice, and that we ought to respect the moral agency of all beings who have the capacity for moral choice, growth, and awareness, even though we do nothing to deserve our status as beings with these capacities. No one would say that it is morally acceptable to be cruel to an animal because the animal did nothing to deserve its capacity to feel pain. Likewise, no one would claim that we do not need to respect a person's moral agency because he did nothing to deserve his capacity for moral agency. These salient characteristics of persons may be "morally arbitrary" strictly in the sense that we do not earn them, but they are morally significant nonetheless. Kekes' argument, then, does not show that we should give up the basic egalitarian claims I have endorsed here.

Further, if the position I have developed here is correct, the proposal to allocate burdens and benefits on the basis of moral merit should be rejected. This proposal simply takes the meritarian's judgmental

[10] *Ibid.*, p. 117.

perspective one step further by insisting that after we have assessed peo-ple's character traits and abilities, and assigned their worth based on these assessments, we should go on to allocate burdens and benefits accord-ingly. But if this judgmental perspective itself is morally problematic for the reasons I have suggested, then Kekes' proposal is equally problematic (or more so). It is important to recognize here that this conclusion does not lead to the rejection of all desert claims. I will argue in the next two chapters that we can still retain many of the intuitively plausible claims that we often express in terms of desert in the context of the paradigm of forgiveness and an egalitarian position of human worth.

The third belief that is thought to support egalitarianism and the inde-pendence of human worth from moral merit is that all persons deserve the opportunity to develop their potentialities. Kekes expresses this egal-itarian belief as follows: "We are human, and it is natural for us to wish well for humanity. Justice, equality, and the rights to freedom and welfare protect the conditions in which human potentialities can be developed, and this is the fundamental reason for defending them."[11] According to Kekes, this position is faulty because it presupposes that human nature is primarily good. The egalitarian holds that those who have done wrong continue to have a claim on our moral regard because they are still moral agents and have the potential for reform and improvement. Kekes says that he would regard this position as plausible if we conceived of our-selves as starting at the origin on a graph of our moral performance, and progressing, with various degrees of success, to the right hand or posi-tive side of the graph from there. In reality, however, we have the poten-tial for evil as well as for good, and by developing our potentialities we may range far to the left of the origin on such a graph. Here Kekes says that "if we think about morality and immorality on this model, then the inappropriateness of regarding human worth as necessary becomes apparent. Human worth can be lost because people may have so much demerit as to come to occupy a position on the moral continuum well below the point at which good and evil are equally balanced."[12] Even if we do retain our capacity for moral agency and the potential for moral improvement, these qualities can be overwhelmed by evil potentialities if we go far enough to the left of the origin (whether we chose to do so or are driven there by forces beyond our control). In this case, "human worth may be replaced by its opposite."[13]

[11] *Ibid.*
[12] *Ibid.*, p. 120.
[13] *Ibid.*

The problem with this argument is that Kekes fails to distinguish clearly enough between moral performance and the capacity for moral agency. If we were to graph persons' moral performances, it is abundantly clear that these graphs should extend both to the left and the right of the origin. Some people, on balance, perform in a morally superlative manner (e.g., Mother Teresa) and others, on balance, generate a significant amount of evil (e.g., Adolf Hitler). Both the egalitarian and the meritarian can accept this conclusion. Further, both the egalitarian and the meritarian can agree that we all have the potential for both good and evil, and the potential to inflict undeserved harm on one another. In fact, I have the potential to be cruel this afternoon, to a student who disturbs me, to a family member who irritates me, and so on. I also have the potential to fail to pay sufficient attention driving home from work and to kill someone. It is even possible that I have the potential, if I get to be under prolonged pressure that is extremely severe, to go on a shooting spree or something of the sort. But these potentials do not defeat my basic status as a moral agent; nor do they impugn the egalitarian position on human worth.

The idea that our accumulated moral demerit could overwhelm or outbalance our basic human worth is flawed – first, because it presupposes the perspective of judgment as opposed to the perspective of identification; second, because it commits the moral error of objectifying persons by conflating them with their actions and attitudes; and third, because it fails to recognize the intrinsic importance of the capacity for moral agency that persists (barring some kind of neurological damage) through any wrongdoing we may engage in. Kekes is of course correct that some people are very destructive and dangerous and that we need protection from people of this sort. He is also correct in asserting that we may need to limit the opportunities that people of this sort have to exercise their potential for destructive behavior. But it does not follow that these persons have no human worth and deserve no respect or compassion. In sum, it seems that Kekes has failed to offer us any plausible grounds for rejecting an egalitarian position on human worth and moral status, or for adopting the view that human worth varies with moral merit.

If my arguments in this section have been correct, we have at least some additional support for the paradigm of forgiveness and the egalitarian position on human worth and moral status that this paradigm incorporates. I have also raised some questions about the feasibility of defending a retributivist position that is based on the claim that human worth varies with moral merit. (Of course, an *egalitarian* defense of retributivism is still a possibility, and the plausibility of this approach must be assessed in light of arguments developed in other parts of the book.)

THE PARADIGM OF FORGIVENESS AND PERSONAL IDENTITY

Let us now turn to an examination of the compatibility of the paradigm of forgiveness with plausible theories of personal identity. Derek Parfit distinguishes between two types of conceptions of the self: nonreductionist and reductionist. A nonreductionist conception holds that the self is some kind of entity that persists through time and is not reducible to a body, brain, or series of mental and physical events. We might think of this entity as a soul, a Cartesian ego, or simply a "deep further fact about the person." On the other hand, a reductionist conception holds that the self is not some metaphysical entity that exists beyond the body, brain, and series of mental and physical events. Reductionists regard X and Y as the same person if there is a sufficient number of direct psychological connections of memory, desire, intention, belief, and so on, between them (psychological connectedness); if there is a sufficient number of overlapping chains of direct psychological connections between them (psychological continuity); and if this relationship is unique (e.g., X has this relationship with Y, but not with some other person, Z, as well).

It seems that a nonreductionist view of the self would be clearly compatible with the paradigm of forgiveness. We could hold that we have an enduring transcendental self that is both a subject of experience and an autonomous moral agent. We could hold that we all have equal human worth and moral status in virtue of having (or being) this kind of self. And given that the self is viewed as an entity that transcends series of mental events, we could easily hold that the self retains its worth and warrants respect and compassion regardless of the offender's wrongful actions and attitudes. It may be more difficult for a retributivist to argue that her position is compatible with a nonreductionist view of the self. If the self is transcendent, it seems that we would have a clear basis for separating the sin from the sinner, and resentment would then be more difficult to justify. The retributivist might attempt to argue that the transcendental self is enhanced by virtuous actions and attitudes and damaged by vicious ones. She could then hold that we ought to withdraw our goodwill from significantly damaged selves. However, a position of this sort would be difficult to defend, and I will not pursue it further here. Most philosophers will wish to avoid the metaphysical complexities of a nonreductionist view of the self, and will opt for reductionism instead.

It seems that the paradigm of forgiveness can also be reconciled with a reductionist view of the self, thanks to recent work on personal identity. My defense of the basic attitudes of forgiveness and self-forgiveness requires that we regard persons both as sentient beings (or the subjects of experience) and as autonomous moral agents. As Christine Korsgaard has pointed out, Parfit recognizes the need to look at persons in this manner and argues that this perspective can be accommodated within the reductionist framework. He addresses this point in the following passage, quoted by Korsgaard: "Even Reductionists do not deny that people exist. And on our concept of a person, people are not thoughts and acts. They are thinkers and agents. I am not a series of experiences, but the person who *has* these experiences, or the *subject* of experiences. This is true because of the way we talk. What a Reductionist denies is that the subject of experiences is a separately existing entity, distinct from a brain and body, and a series of mental and physical events."[14]

Korsgaard argues that Parfit focuses primarily on persons as subjects of experiences, and that shifting our focus to persons as agents will necessarily strengthen our notions of personal identity. When we function as agents we adopt a practical perspective, from which we deliberate about both ends and means and make decisions based on these deliberations. The deliberative or practical perspective is very different from the theoretical perspective, which we adopt when we are concerned to study and explain various aspects of ourselves and our behaviors, and it imposes different constraints on the way in which we regard ourselves as persons. From the deliberative perspective, we have no choice but to view ourselves as *agents* who make *choices*. But Korsgaard also argues that this perspective is fully compatible with a reductionist view of the self. She writes: "From a theoretical standpoint, an action may be viewed as just another experience and the assertion that it has a subject may be, as Parfit says, 'because of the way we talk.' But from the practical point of view, actions and choices must be viewed as having agents and choosers. This is what *makes* them, in our eyes, our actions and choices rather than events that befall us... This does not mean that our existence as agents is asserted as some further fact, or requires a separately existing

---

[14] Derek Parfit, *Reasons and Persons*, p. 223. Quoted in Christine Korsgaard, "Personal Identity and Unity of Agency," p. 368.

entity. It is rather that from a practical point of view our relationship to our actions and choices is *authorial*."[15] Further, although it would be possible from the theoretical perspective to view our "choices" as determined, when we deliberate and make choices we must regard ourselves, as Kant suggests, as free, autonomous, and responsible. And although it would be possible from a theoretical point of view to view ourselves as a series of persons or person stages, from a practical point of view, in order to make plans and decisions and carry them out over the course of our lives, we must regard ourselves as unified agents who persist through time.

Parfit suggests that reductionism supports a utilitarian perspective. Given that we are not enduring, transcendental selves but merely person stages connected in various ways, there is less basis for regarding ourselves as persons who are separate from one another, and less basis for objecting to utilitarianism on the grounds that it may impose undue burdens on some persons in order to maximize good consequences overall. However, Korsgaard argues to the contrary that we will see things differently when we adopt the practical point of view. From the practical point of view we form intentions, make plans, and enter into relationships over the course of a lifetime, and because we expend resources and energy in pursuit of these goals, we must regard ourselves as separate individuals throughout our lives.

If Korsgaard's reasoning is correct, and I think it is, then the paradigm of forgiveness is compatible with a reductionist view of the self. We can view ourselves as moral agents who are subject to moral obligations and who are responsible for our past and present actions and attitudes. We can also regard ourselves as sentient beings who very much want to be happy; as individuals who possess the valuable capacity for moral choice, growth, and awareness; and as autonomous individuals who can lead meaningful lives only as authors of our own choices and attitudes. And, significantly, we can view ourselves as separate individuals who persist through time, who are responsible for making amends for wrongs we have committed in the past, and who can, over time, develop and inculcate morally appropriate attitudes in ourselves. Further, the practical perspective that Korsgaard describes here can be incorporated into or seen as a part of the perspective of identification articulated in the last section. When we adopt the practical perspective or the perspective of deliberation, we are specifically looking internally at what it is like to

[15] Christine Korsgaard, "Personal Identity and the Unity of Agency," p. 378.

be us as we make choices. We view ourselves, internally, as agents and choosers, and we view our choices as our own, as opposed to "events that befall us." Likewise, we can view others in the same manner, and identify with and respect them as fellow moral agents.

A retributivist who endorses a reductionist view of the self can draw on these arguments as well. Retributivists also view persons as moral agents who are responsible for their actions and attitudes, and who are unified and persist through time. They can also incorporate Korsgaard's practical perspective into the perspective of judgment. Rather than looking at what it is like internally to be an agent of choice, and using this perspective to identify with others, they can take the constraints of the practical perspective as a reason to view persons as responsible for their own actions and attitudes. They can then assert that persons are properly subject to judgment on the grounds that they have made wrongful choices. However, there are additional challenges that will face those who attempt to defend retributivism in the context of a reductionist view of the self. In general, the enduring attitudes of resentment and self-condemnation endorsed by retributivists seem to require a thicker conception of the self than the basic attitudes endorsed in the paradigm of forgiveness. At least as they have been defended in the literature, enduring attitudes of resentment and self-condemnation seem to require judgment of a "self" thick enough that it can be worthy of contempt or self-contempt in view of wrongful past actions. For example, Dillon is careful to point out that an attitude of self-reproach attaches not merely to our past actions and attitudes, but also, more fundamentally, to our selves. But whereas the perspective of deliberation requires us to view ourselves as free, responsible, autonomous choosers who persist in a unified state through time, it does not seem to require us to think of ourselves as a thing or entity that can be the subject of such a judgment. In this case it seems that a retributivist view may require us to go beyond a reductionist conception of the self.

More specifically, as we have seen, many retributivists argue that we cannot legitimately separate the sin from the sinner, and that the offender who fails to repent or who is guilty of very serious wrongdoing remains in some way identified with the offense. But this position seems to require a view of the self in which our actions and attitudes are in some way an integral part of ourselves. Both Michael Sandel and George Sher have argued that claims of desert, on which many attitudinal retributivists rely, require a conception of the self as "thickly-constituted." Sandel says that "claims of desert presuppose thickly-constituted selves" whose identity is determined, in part, by their aims and preferences.[16] Sher, who defends a meritarian version of retributivism, expresses this point as follows: "When we say that persons deserve things because of their current abilities, character traits, or actions, we clearly draw ... on the assumption that persons are constituted by their present traits."[17] He attempts to defend this position in the context of a reductionist view of the self, asserting that the deliberative perspective "compels us to view ourselves as both constituted by our preferences and abilities and extended over time."[18] He adds that theoretical coherence requires us to extend this view to others. To show that we must view ourselves as constituted by our preferences and abilities, Sher argues as follows: "Because deliberation aims at decisions about which act(s) to perform, the prospective agent's preferences, values, skills, and abilities are never themselves its primary subjects. To deliberate is precisely to look *through* one's preferences, abilities, and related traits to the available actions themselves." From the perspective of the deliberating agent, then, "preferences, abilities, and the self are merged."[19] Clearly some people have preferences, values, and abilities that are superior to others, so given that we are at least partially constituted by these traits, we can conclude that some people have more human worth than others, and deserve to be treated accordingly.

Sometimes it does seem that we "look through" our preferences, values, and abilities to the actions available to us. For example, when we act in a purely spontaneous manner, it seems clear that we do so. When we act in a nonreflective or habitual manner, our thought processes might be described in this way as well. However, Sher's claim seems to break down at exactly the point at which it becomes significant – when we deliberate and make choices, or when we ought to do so: in other words, when we function as moral agents.[20] For example, when I do my financial work on the first of the month, I must make decisions about whether I will contribute to the causes I find worthwhile, and if so, how much money I will send to each. Here I do not look through my preferences and abilities. Instead, I carefully examine both my ability to contribute

---

[16] Michael Sandel, *Liberalism and the Limits of Justice*, p. 178.

[17] George Sher, *Desert*, p. 174.

[18] *Ibid.*, p. 171.

[19] *Ibid.*, p. 161.

[20] In cases of negligence, of course, we do not deliberate, although we could have and should have done so. In cases of this sort, there is thus no necessity that we "look through" our abilities and preferences.

and my preferences as to the disposition of my available funds in making my decision. Likewise, I might prefer to cancel my classes on a beautiful afternoon, but I can't just "look through" that preference and act accordingly. Instead, I must examine the preference to see if it is justified. And if I were unable to do so, there would be no grounds for holding me responsible for failing to meet my classes. Contrary to what Sher says, therefore, it seems that from the *deliberative* perspective I am *not* constituted by my preferences and abilities. Rather, as a moral agent and autonomous decision-maker, I examine my preferences to see if they are justified and I examine my abilities to see how they can best be used in service of my chosen aims. The capacity to examine our preferences in this manner, and to reject some and affirm others, seems to imply a gap between ourselves and our preferences rather than a constitutive relationship between them.

Sher recognizes that we can dissociate ourselves from particular preferences and refuse to act on them. However, he says that "the mere possibility of disavowal does not yet seem to defeat the implication that one is constituted by a preference or ability. The more pertinent question is whether, in any given situation, one actually has dissociated oneself; and to that question, the answer is often 'no.' Moreover, even when we do disavow a preference or ability, our disavowal must itself be grounded in some higher-order preference or value, and must draw on some further ability. Hence we cannot possibly disavow all of our preferences, values, or abilities. And any preference or ability that is *not* explicitly disavowed will automatically enter into any deliberation to which it pertains."[21]

But this argument is highly problematic. First, it seems to me that the mere possibility of disavowing a preference *is* sufficient to show that we are not *constituted by* our preferences. To say that an individual is constituted by X seems to imply that X is an integral part of that individual. I am not constituted by my sweatshirt, which I am now wearing, because I can take it off later and remain myself. (For the purposes of this discussion, I will interpret "remaining myself" as remaining the same unified agent persisting through time that I identify when I look at myself from Korsgaard's practical perspective.) Likewise, an individual is not constituted by a preference she holds now if she can disavow it later and remain herself. In this case the preference is not an integral part of her. Further, consider carefully what happens when we disavow a preference. Like Korsgaard, Sher argues effectively that from the deliberative perspective,

[21] George Sher, *Desert*, p. 160.

we must regard ourselves as unified agents who persist through time. But if I am constituted by my preference P_1, it is not clear how I could evaluate it and disavow it. If my current self, S_1, is constituted by P_1, then it seems that another self, S_2, would be required to step in and evaluate P_1 (or, more accurately, the set (S_1,P_1)), and to choose to disavow it. But this picture conflicts directly with the view of ourselves as agents who persist through time.

It may be true that when we disavow a preference or ability, we do so in reference to some higher-order preference or ability. (Coherentists may object here, but I will set this objection aside.) However, this point also fails to show that we are constituted by our current preferences and abilities, because as moral agents we must often evaluate our higher-order preferences as well. Let us return to the decision about canceling classes. Suppose that it is not just a beautiful day, but a beautiful day when the river near my house is running at the perfect level to offer the most superb whitewater kayaking experience. As I make the decision about canceling my classes, I may well have to look at very high-order preferences. I may place a very high value both on communing with nature and on meeting my moral obligations to my students, and I must assess these preferences to determine which is most important under the circumstances. But if I am constituted by my higher-order preferences, it seems that I would not be able to evaluate them, assess their relative levels of importance, or disavow them in particular circumstances. In other words, in this case I could not function as a moral agent. Because all of our preferences are subject to moral evaluation, it seems that there must be a gap between us and each one of our preferences.

It is also probably true that although we can disavow any one of our preferences at a given point in time, we could not possibly disavow all of our preferences at once. But again, this point does not imply that we are constituted by our preferences. The fact that I cannot take off my sweatshirt, my shoes, and my socks all at the same time does not show that I am constituted by these things. Rather, the fact that I can take off any one of them and remain myself suggests that I am actually not constituted by any articles of clothing. Likewise, the fact that I can disavow any one of my preferences suggests that I am not constituted by my preferences. Rather than being (in part) a set of preferences, I am an *agent* who has the capacity to assess preferences, and to choose to retain or adopt some and disavow others.

But perhaps Sher's argument is not that we cannot disavow all of our preferences at once, but rather that we cannot disavow all of our preferences even over the course of our entire lives. We may then be constituted by the preferences that we never disavow. It is true that there are some preferences, and perhaps many preferences, that we will continue to hold throughout our lives. However, in response to this argument, we can point out that even if we do not disavow a given set of our preferences throughout our entire lives, we hope, as moral agents, that we will at some point evaluate or assess those preferences to determine that they are worth retaining. And if we do so, we must be agents, distinct from these preferences, who have the capacity to assess them. Further, the fact that it is at least *in principle* possible to assess and disavow any one of our preferences suggests that we are simply not constituted by our preferences. If a woman decides that she will never remove a particular piece of jewelry throughout her life, and sticks to that decision, we would not say that she is constituted by this piece of jewelry, because it is in principle possible that she can take it off and remain herself.

Finally, it seems problematic to claim that any preference that has not been explicitly disavowed will automatically enter into any deliberation to which it pertains. Again, this claim seems to conflict with the claim that we have the capacity to function as moral agents. Suppose that I am inclined to be judgmental, and so far I have not disavowed this preference. I then encounter a situation in which my close friend does something wrong, and I start to deliberate about how I will regard him in light of his offense. In this case, my preference for judgment does not *automatically* enter into my deliberation about how to regard my friend. Instead, as a moral agent, I will examine this preference at this time and *choose* whether or not it will enter into my deliberation, and if so, what role it will play. It is very possible at this point that I will recognize my tendency to be judgmental as a fault and attempt to correct it. Further, if my preferences did automatically enter into my deliberations, it is not clear how I could ever disavow any one of them. And again it is not clear in this case how I could function as a moral agent.

It might be objected at this point that at least some of our preferences really do define who we are, in that we can't imagine the person without the preference. In light of this point, we might think that although we are not constituted by our preferences in general, we may well be constituted by the values to which we are most deeply committed. For example, it may be impossible to imagine Martin Luther King as a bigot, or Mahatma Gandhi as a warmonger. And if King were to become a bigot or Gandhi a warmonger, we might say that they are simply no longer the same person. These claims sound plausible. However, I think they simply exhibit a way of talking that emphasizes (and perhaps dramatizes) the strength and importance of some of our central moral commitments. It is important to notice that if we are to have strong moral commitments, we must be moral *agents* who have the capacity to examine various values and preferences and to *choose* to commit ourselves strongly to some while we reject others. Presumably we admire Gandhi in part because he *chose* to commit himself so strongly to his moral principles. If so, then if Gandhi were to become a warmonger (as ludicrous as this scenario seems), in order to respect him as a moral agent we would have to say that he once held an excellent set of values with real conviction, and then *he chose* to abandon those values and replace them with values that are unworthy. Likewise, if an individual holds wrongful values, commits an offense, and then rejects those values and repents, if we are to respect him as a moral agent we must say that *he chose* to reject his former preferences.

Notice that if we actually regard the changed individual as a different person in either of these cases, we lose any robust understanding of the notions of moral choice and moral agency. If our hypothetical Gandhi is P_1 when he is committed to nonviolence and P_2 when he is a warmonger, or if the person who repents his former wrong action is P_1 when he commits the offense and P_2 when he repents, then who is it who makes the *choice* to reject one set of values and adopt the other? Perhaps we could say that P_2 somehow comes into existence and makes this choice. But in this case we would encounter serious difficulties with the notions of forgiveness, self-forgiveness, repentance, and perhaps most significantly, moral responsibility for our past actions. If P_1 wrongfully harms me and then actually becomes a different person, P_2, with a different set of core values such that he abhors P_1's offense, it would seem to make no sense for me to forgive P_2 for P_1's offense. And how could P_2 forgive himself for something that another person, P_1, did? Further, while P_2 might regret that P_1's victim was injured, how could he *repent* for something that he did not do? And if P_1 and P_2 are actually different people, why would we regard P_2 as responsible for P_1's act? And on what grounds could we argue that P_2 is responsible for making amends for what P_1 did? It seems, then, that the claim that we actually become a different person when we disavow one preference and adopt another creates more problems than it solves. In sum, it seems clear that we are not actually constituted by our preferences and values and, further, that we do not and could not coherently regard ourselves as being constituted in this way. Rather, we do (and must) regard ourselves as unified agents who persist through time and who make various *choices* about the values and preferences we wish to hold over the course of our lives.

It might also be objected that if we reject the view that the self is constituted by its preferences and values, we will be left, as Michael Sandel suggests, with the highly questionable notion of a radically disembodied self that makes choices independently of any values and preferences, in a way that can only be described as arbitrary.[22] However, I do not think that we will be forced to adopt any such conclusion. Sandel's critique may be effective against Rawls's theory of justice, but I do not believe the concerns he develops in that context will plague us here. First, in the context of the position developed here, if we reject the claim that we are constituted by our preferences and values, we need not hold that our commitments to certain values and preferences are arbitrary. It seems clear that there are good *reasons* for rejecting some preferences and values and endorsing others (at least outside of the original position) – reasons that, as moral agents, we are fully capable of grasping. In this case, our choices concerning preferences and values need not and should not be arbitrary.

Further, if we reject the claim that we are constituted by our preferences and values, we need not deny that we are socially situated. It seems very clear that the preferences, values, and beliefs that we acquire are extensively influenced by the social contexts in which we are born and raised, and in which we continue to live our lives. Much has been written about the strong influences extended on us by our families, cultures, social and economic structures, peer groups, racial and gender stereotypes, local communities, and so on. We need not deny any of these obvious facts in order to reject the claim that we are constituted by our preferences and values. Nor need we deny these obvious facts in order to assert that we are autonomous moral agents who are separable from our current attitudes and preferences, as is required if we are to separate the sinner from the sin, or the unrepentant offender from his wrongful actions and attitudes. We need only assert that however we have acquired our current values, as moral agents we have the valuable capacity for moral choice, growth, and awareness. In other words, there is a gap between ourselves as agents on the one hand, and our preferences and values on the other hand, such that we are capable of stepping back and assessing the values we have acquired in various ways, and of choosing

---

[22] Michael Sandel develops this critique of John Rawls's theory of justice in *Liberalism and the Limits of Justice.*

to reject, accept, or modify them over time. Arguably, from the practical or deliberative perspective, there *must* be a gap of this sort. There is simply no other way to make sense of moral deliberation and moral choice. If the arguments in this section are correct, the paradigm of forgiveness seems to be compatible with a plausible reductionist account of personal identity and the self (or for that matter, with a nonreductionist account as well). Further, there are serious questions as to whether the retributivist positions that incorporate the claim that the offender is in some sense constituted by his wrongful actions or attitudes can be made compatible with any plausible position on personal identity.

In developing the argument in this section so far, I have asserted, with Korsgaard, that from the practical perspective, we must view ourselves as separate, unified individuals who persist through time. If we do not view ourselves in this manner, but instead see ourselves as different person-stages, we will have great difficulty in making sense of the notions of forgiveness, self-forgiveness, moral responsibility, and moral agency. However, it is important to recognize that viewing ourselves as separate individuals who persist through time need not conflict with the view endorsed by many feminist philosophers that the self can be described as fragmented as well. For example, Norlock writes that "when I describe the self as fragmented, I intend to refer to the structure or composition of the self as well as the multiplicities of self-perceptions and social perceptions. I take recognition of the existence of fragmented selves to be compatible with projects of integrity; descriptions of our inward multiplicity are not intended as arguments against the value of integrating our self-perceptions."[23]

In addition to endorsing a reductionist conception of the self in which person-stages can be unified with psychological connections and psychological continuity, Norlock views the self as fragmented in the sense that our self-perceptions can and do change in important ways over time, and sometimes over very short periods of time. This claim is exceedingly plausible. As Norlock points out, self-forgiveness sometimes involves adopting a conception of the self that is closely identified with the victim and that rejects part of an earlier self-conception as unworthy. Further, our self-conception can change dramatically with severe trauma, as Susan Brison describes from first-hand experience in her book *Aftermath*. As Brison says, our self-conceptions can be shattered by severe trauma, and then must, in an important sense, be recreated. Further, self-conceptions

---

[23] Kathryn Norlock, *Forgiveness from a Feminist Perspective*, p. 139.

can change dramatically in cases of significant moral growth. There is no question that we are versatile and capable of renouncing, generating, regenerating, integrating, and significantly modifying large parts of various conceptions of ourselves. But as Norlock correctly recognizes, none of this implies that we cannot or should not undertake projects of integrity that require us to view ourselves as agents who persist through time, and who are, in an important sense, integrated. More specifically, it does not prevent us from regarding ourselves as responsible for our past actions, however different we may be at present. Nor does it prevent us from undertaking a sustained program of moral development. And, significantly, to recognize the self as fragmented in these respects does not imply that we must view ourselves as in some way fused or conflated with our past or current actions and attitudes. Rather, we can and should regard ourselves as agents who are distinguishable from our past and current actions and attitudes, and who have the basic capacity to evaluate those actions and attitudes over time.

It is important to recognize as well that there are some extreme forms of fragmentation that do raise questions about our moral responsibility. For example, dissociative identity disorder or schizophrenia may at times render us incapable of fully responsible thought and action in certain areas. Norlock provides an interesting discussion of extreme fragmentation, and points out, correctly, that fragmentation is properly seen as a matter of degree. However, fragmentation that is so severe as to preclude responsibility for some of our actions and attitudes is clearly the exception rather than the rule, and thus does not undermine the basic structure of the paradigm of forgiveness. Rather, cases of extreme fragmentation will be identified as exculpating excuses in the cases in which they occur, in either the private or public domain. Let us now turn to the question of whether the paradigm of forgiveness is compatible with a robust conception of moral responsibility.

THE PARADIGM OF FORGIVENESS AND MORAL RESPONSIBILITY

As we can see from the extensive discussion in the literature on freedom, determinism, and moral responsibility, it is extremely difficult to construct an adequate philosophical account of moral responsibility. Utilitarians avoid this problem with a compatibilist position on response to wrongdoing, but as we have noted, serious objections have been raised to the utilitarian position. Erin Kelly has argued that we can resolve the issue of freedom, determinism, and moral responsibility with a nonutilitarian compatibilist position that rejects retributivist reactive attitudes.[24] However, while she argues effectively against retributive reactive attitudes, I believe that her argument fails to provide a satisfactory account of punishment and other legal practices that respond to serious wrongs. I will consider her position on punishment in Chapter 7, given that part of her position converges with the paradigm of forgiveness. Many other compatibilist accounts have been proposed, but space does not permit me to examine them here. Rather than examining the extensive debate on freedom, determinism, and moral responsibility any further, at this point I will simply rely on Korsgaard's Kantian position outlined earlier. This position holds that although determinism may seem correct from the theoretical perspective, from the *deliberative* perspective we *must* regard ourselves as autonomous and as responsible moral agents. Korsgaard's position will suffice to support the outline of the paradigm of forgiveness that I will develop here. It will also suffice to defend the paradigm of forgiveness against most retributive arguments, given that retributivists also typically assume that we are autonomous and responsible moral agents. Obviously a complete defense of the paradigm of forgiveness (or of any retributivist position, for that matter) would require a much more thoroughly defended stance on the issue of freedom, determinism, and moral responsibility.

The question I will examine here is whether retributivists or advocates of the paradigm of forgiveness encounter special difficulties with the notion of moral responsibility within the framework Korsgaard has developed. It is sometimes thought that when we endorse the attitudes of forgiveness and self-forgiveness, we move away from a robust conception of moral responsibility. When we forgive an unrepentant offender, we may let him off the hook too soon, and fail to hold him accountable both for his offense and for his failure to renounce it. And when we forgive ourselves, we may let ourselves off the hook too easily, or as Griswold suggests, degenerate into "self-interested ... excuse making."[25] Retributivist positions, on the other hand, may seem to incorporate a strong position on moral responsibility and to hold persons more fully accountable for their actions and attitudes.

In response to this objection, the first point to notice is that both retributivists and advocates of the paradigm of forgiveness assign a

---

[24] See Erin Kelly, "Doing Without Desert."
[25] Charles Griswold, *Forgiveness*, p. 122.

central role to the concept of moral responsibility in developing their respective positions on response to wrongdoing. Both positions hold that there are moral standards that govern our actions and attitudes, and that as moral agents we are responsible for complying with these standards. Further, both positions hold that we are properly regarded as morally responsible for any failure to do so. In addition, both positions outline moral responsibilities that apply to us in responding to wrongdoing, although the responsibilities that emerge in each of these positions diverge to some extent from one another. Retributivists hold unrepentant *offenders* accountable for past wrongdoing by maintaining an attitude of resentment toward them. On the other hand, advocates of the paradigm of forgiveness hold *themselves* responsible for recognizing the offender as a sentient being and moral agent in spite of his wrongdoing, and for responding to him accordingly. Likewise, retributivists who endorse an attitude of self-condemnation hold themselves responsible by subjecting themselves to self-reproach, and sometimes even lifelong punishing self-reproach, for their past wrongs. But when we endorse an attitude of genuine self-forgiveness, we hold ourselves responsible in another way. In this case we hold ourselves responsible for addressing the wrong to the best of our ability, transcending the egocentric focus on ourselves, and then using our moral and personal capabilities in a constructive manner. Further, both types of theorists will hold wrongdoers responsible for completing the process of addressing the wrongs they have committed, as outlined in Chapter 4. It seems, therefore, that there is a strong sense of responsibility both in the paradigm of forgiveness and in retributive positions, and that the difference between them lies in their different positions on what we are responsible for. If the arguments in Chapters 3 and 4 are correct, we have reason to endorse the view of our moral responsibilities embodied in the paradigm of forgiveness.

A second point to notice here is that the paradigm of forgiveness incorporates a recognition of the offender as a moral agent who is, in many cases, properly held accountable for redressing his wrong. As we will see in Chapter 7, advocates of the paradigm of forgiveness will endorse legal practices that require those who have wrongfully harmed others to make restitution for that harm, within reasonable limits of sacrifice. In the context of the paradigm of forgiveness, we will impose this requirement without malice and with an attitude of respect, compassion, and real goodwill for the offender, but we will impose it nonetheless.

It seems, therefore, that the paradigm of forgiveness incorporates a clear and robust conception of moral responsibility. However, it is important to notice that *retributivists* may encounter two additional problems in articulating an adequate conception of moral responsibility – problems that do not arise in the context of the paradigm of forgiveness. The first problem is the one we alluded to in Chapter 3, and are now in a position to articulate more fully in light of our examination of Sher's position. As we saw in Chapter 3, many attitudinal retributivists hold that we cannot legitimately separate the sinner from the sin, or the offender from his wrongful actions and attitudes, when the offender has yet to repent or is guilty of very serious wrongdoing. These retributivists typically argue that the offender is in some sense identified with his wrongful actions and attitudes. As noted, if we cannot separate the offender from his wrongful actions and attitudes, then judging him and withdrawing our goodwill from him does make sense. As moral agents, we must judge wrongful actions and attitudes to be wrong. Further, wrongful actions and attitudes call for a hostile response from members of the moral community.

However, it seems that attitudinal retributivists who make this kind of claim, or who hold that unrepentant perpetrators of serious wrongs deserve retributive reactive attitudes, face the following dilemma. They must either assert or deny that the offender, as he persists through time, is in some sense partially constituted by his wrong actions and attitudes. If they assert that the offender is in some way constituted by his actions and attitudes, then, as I argued in examining Sher's reasoning, they will lack any coherent account of how the offender can be responsible for those actions and attitudes. If we hold that we are in some way *constituted by* our preferences, we will lack a plausible account of how it is possible for us to examine these preferences and choose to disavow them, or to prioritize them if they come into conflict with one another in a particular situation. And if we are unable to perform these tasks, then we cannot rightly be considered moral agents, nor can we properly be considered morally responsible for our actions and attitudes. In this case we cannot rightly be regarded as responsible for repenting of or making amends for our wrongful actions and attitudes. Further, it will not help retributivists at this point to shift to a position in which we regard ourselves as sequential persons rather than as unified agents who persist through time. Resorting to a position of this sort *also precludes* a clear and coherent conception of moral responsibility, because we cannot rightly hold one person responsible for what another person has chosen to do. Further, we cannot hold one person responsible for repenting of or making amends for another person's actions and attitudes.

On the other hand, if the retributivist chooses the second horn of the dilemma and denies that we are in some sense constituted by our actions and attitudes, her position becomes much more difficult to defend on moral grounds. Here she denies that the offender is in any way the same thing as his actions and attitudes, and in doing so, she at least implicitly recognizes a gap or separation between them. It is possible for the retributivist to hold that we can separate the sinner from the sin, and then to insist that instead of loving the sinner and hating the sin, we should hate them both. But this position seems both mean-spirited and difficult to defend. Apart from the offender's wrongful actions and attitudes, what is there to hate about him? It seems that there are four possible answers here, none of which is plausible. First, we might hate the offender because he constitutes some kind of threat to us, or to someone or something we hold dear. However, we can take whatever steps are possible to protect ourselves and others (or whatever it is that we hold dear) from this threat without hating the offender, and at the same time that we regard him with respect, compassion, and real goodwill. It seems, therefore, that this reason for hating the offender is bound to fail. Given that the offender remains a sentient being and moral agent, we have a fundamental reason to regard him with respect, compassion, and real goodwill while we take the steps necessary to secure what we value.

Second, we may hate the offender, because by doing so we believe that we can get him to repent, to make amends to his victim, and to reform his wrongful attitudes and behavior patterns. However, once again, we can wish for him to do these things, and we can do what we can (without resorting to morally objectionable manipulation) to get him to do these things, at the same time that we regard him with respect, compassion, and real goodwill. In this case we again lack any reason for hating him, or for holding a retributive reactive attitude toward him. (The reader should recall at this point the distinction between holding and expressing a retributive reactive attitude, as developed in Chapter 3.)

Third, we may hate the offender because we recognize that he *ought* to repent, make amends, and reform his wrongful attitudes and behavior patterns, and because he has not yet done so. But, as before, we can recognize that the offender has these moral obligations and that he has failed to meet them at the same time that we extend to him an attitude of (recognition) respect, compassion, and real goodwill. We can recognize that he has these moral obligations, and we can hope that he will acknowledge and comply with them in the near future. Once again, it seems that we lack any viable reason for hating him. Although we do not

have evaluative respect for the unrepentant offender in view of his failure to meet his moral obligations, we can and should recognize that he
is a moral agent and sentient being who, as such, warrants recognition
respect, compassion, and real goodwill.

Finally, we may hate or resent the offender because we believe that
this is an appropriate way to respect his capacity for moral choice, which
he has failed to exercise properly. But here again we can respect the
offender and his valuable capacity for moral choice without hating or
resenting him, and at the same time that we regard him with respect,
compassion, and real goodwill. Rather than resenting him, we can simply hope that he learns to exercise his valuable capacity for moral choice
in a responsible manner in the near future. Thus it seems, all things considered, that the second horn of the dilemma is no more attractive than
the first.

A second problem that may arise for the retributivist, but not for
those who endorse an attitude of unconditional genuine forgiveness,
stems from the need to assess *degrees* of moral responsibility in particular cases. As I have argued, when we forgive the offender we do not sit
in judgment of him for committing the offense or for holding wrongful
attitudes. Instead, we simply recognize that whatever wrong choices he
has made, he remains a valuable human being who is capable of moral
choice, growth, and awareness. Korsgaard's position, outlined earlier,
suffices to ground this view of the offender. However, as Erin Kelly has
pointed out, when we sit in judgment of the offender, we need a much
more complex account of the degree of moral responsibility that this individual bears for his wrong choices. She says that "we think such an agent
deserves the sanction of our reactive attitudes and behavior and, generally, we think that it is a good thing if people get what they deserve. But
why shouldn't we worry, then, about what caused the agent's defect ...?
The concern to justify our reactive attitudes may lead us to look at the
psychological history and social context of the agent's defective choice,
and then to be skeptical about whether we can pin down a notion of
reflexive self-control that is suitably robust to support judgments about
desert."[26] It seems, therefore, that in order to justify holding an attitude
of resentment toward an offender, we would need a full understanding
of the extent to which the offender is responsible for the wrong – an

---

[26] Erin Kelly, "Doing Without Desert," p. 186. Here Kelly refers to the notion of reflective
self-control as the basis of responsibility, developed by R.J. Wallace in *Responsibility
and the Moral Sentiments*.

understanding that takes account of the myriad of complex challenges he has faced throughout his life that bear on his commission of the wrong. And we may legitimately wonder whether we are ever epistemically situated in such a way that we can make judgments of this sort. Given the two problems I have outlined in this section, it seems that it is actually the retributivist, rather than the advocate of the paradigm of forgiveness, who will face special difficulties in articulating a clear, coherent, robust conception of moral responsibility in the context of her position on response to wrongdoing.

If my arguments in this chapter are correct, the paradigm of forgiveness incorporates a defensible position on equal human worth and moral status. Further, it is compatible with plausible positions on personal identity, and it incorporates a clear and robust conception of moral responsibility. I have also suggested that serious difficulties may arise for various versions of retributivism in each of these areas. At this point I have concluded the defense of the basic attitudes that ground the paradigm of forgiveness. In the next chapter I will turn to the implications of these basic attitudes for the structure of our moral theories.

6

Moral Theory: Justice and Desert

Up to this point, I have examined the basic attitudes of forgiveness and resentment, and their self-referential counterparts. In addition to defining these attitudes, I have provided both a moral and philosophical assessment of them. My discussion so far has focused on the attitudes we might adopt in the personal domain – in response to wrongs inflicted on us personally, or in response to our own wrongdoing. We are now in a position to turn to the public domain and to consider what a properly forgiving society would look like. A broad account of response to wrongdoing will tell us not only how to respond to personal wrongs, but also which laws, policies, and social practices we ought to adopt as a public response to wrongdoing.

In this chapter I first examine the connection between basic moral attitudes and moral theories that can be used to justify laws, policies, and social practices. Specifically, I argue that the basic moral attitudes incorporated in the paradigm of forgiveness lead to at least the broad outlines of a moral theory structured in terms of justice. I will then draw on this theory in the remaining chapters of the book to develop the public response to wrongdoing embedded in the paradigm of forgiveness. It is important to recognize that the kind of moral theory that emerges in the paradigm of forgiveness does not constitute a departure from the virtue-ethical approach to response to wrongdoing developed in this book, and I explain why this is the case.

Retributivists believe that legal punishment is the intrinsically appropriate public response to serious wrongdoing. Whether or not they believe that a desert-based moral theory emerges from retributive reactive attitudes, many retributivists believe that the justification for inflicting legal punishment as a public response to wrongdoing rests, at least in part, on the claim that the offender *deserves* the punishment given the nature of his offense. (Other retributivists offer more specific justifications of punishment than this, and I will examine some of their arguments in Chapter 7.) Russ Shafer-Landau explains the retributive position on punishment as follows: "Retributivists claim that the point of legal punishment, and the standard that ought to govern the construction of penal institutions, practices and rules, is that the guilty must be given their just deserts. Punishment must be commensurate with moral desert."[1] For retributivists of this sort, desert is a fundamental moral concept, and any adequate moral theory will be structured, at least in part, in terms of desert. Advocates of the paradigm of forgiveness and these retributivists will therefore be centrally divided on the question of whether we should adopt a justice-based moral theory or a desert-based moral theory, and it is therefore important that we examine this question in some depth. In this chapter I argue that we have reason to prefer a moral theory structured in terms of justice to a moral theory structured in terms of desert. I argue that desert-based moral theories will encounter significant structural problems when we attempt to justify desert claims, to determine how much of a given burden or benefit is deserved, and to balance considerations of desert against other moral considerations such as needs, rights, or utility. Further, I show that many of these structural problems can be avoided if we adopt the justice-based moral theory that emerges in the paradigm of forgiveness.

However, as noted in Chapter 1, one reason that retributivism has been enjoying a recent resurgence in popularity is that it seems to explain some of our most deeply held moral intuitions about response to wrongdoing, which are commonly expressed in terms of desert. Samuel Scheffler has argued that both political and philosophical liberalism may be subject to attack on the grounds that liberals have failed to accord a significant *preinstitutional* role to desert, or to incorporate a substantial conception of desert in their moral theories.[2] Institutional conceptions of desert are always possible. Given the rules of any social institution, if these rules assign a benefit to persons in virtue of a positive characteristic they possess, or a burden to individuals in virtue of a negative characteristic, we might say that individuals with the relevant characteristic

[1] Russ Shafer-Landau, "Retributivism and Desert," p. 189.
[2] See Samuel Scheffler, "Responsibility, Reactive Attitudes, and Liberalism in Philosophy and Politics."

deserve the burden or benefit in question. But the concern is that liberal theories fail to recognize a *fundamental* or *preinstitutional* conception of desert, in which desert is *first* regarded as a fundamental concept in our moral reasoning, and *then* the rules of our social institutions are formulated in such a way that they assign to persons the burdens and benefits they actually deserve (as specified in our moral theories). Further, a moral analysis of how we ought to structure our social institutions that fails to account for desert in this fundamental or preinstitutional manner may conflict significantly with our considered moral judgments, given that we often criticize our public institutions on the grounds that they fail to give persons the benefits or burdens they deserve.

It seems, therefore that we are faced with a choice between endorsing a (structurally flawed) moral theory formulated in terms of desert, as has been advocated by retributivists, or endorsing a moral theory formulated in terms of justice that fails to accord with our deep moral intuitions commonly expressed in terms of desert. I suggest in this chapter that this is a false dilemma, and that there is a middle ground between these two positions. The justice-based moral theory that emerges in the paradigm of forgiveness is actually capable of explaining many of the considered moral judgments that we often express in terms of desert. It can therefore account for many of our considered moral judgments about desert and personal responsibility at a fundamental or preinstitutional level. In this chapter I begin the explanation of how our justice-based moral theory can account for the moral convictions that we often express in terms of desert by briefly outlining how this theory can systematize our intuitions about desert in the domain of distributive justice. I will then complete this explanation in Chapter 7 by showing how it accounts for our plausible intuitions about desert and personal responsibility in the domain of retributive justice, or public response to wrongdoing. Let us begin, then, by examining the connection between basic moral attitudes and moral theories.

BASIC ATTITUDES AND MORAL THEORIES

The virtue-ethical response to wrongdoing that I am developing in this book begins with basic attitudes. My position on response to wrongdoing, as it has been developed so far, rests on the claim that the basic attitudes of unconditional genuine forgiveness and genuine self-forgiveness are always appropriate and desirable from a moral point of view, and that we should attempt to inculcate these attitudes in ourselves as regular responses to wrongdoing. I have explained how this approach to response to wrongdoing applies in the personal domain, and I must now extend these attitudes to the public sphere.

A connection between the basic moral attitudes we adopt toward one another and the laws and social practices we consider to be justified has already been suggested by some retributivists, although, in my view, both aspects of their position are mistaken. Attitudinal retributivists hold that a basic attitude of resentment is called for toward an unrepentant offender or toward an offender who is guilty of very serious wrongdoing. As we saw, the perspective from which the offender is regarded by attitudinal retributivists is one of judgment, and the attitude of resentment extended toward the offender embodies an element of hostility, or at least a partial withdrawal of goodwill. In Hieronymi's terms, this attitude embodies a form of protest. It seems clear that for many retirbutivists, a theory of punishment follows naturally from attitudinal retributivism. For example, John Kleinig and Edmund Pincoffs have each argued that we can regard desert claims as appraisals, or judgments. When we determine that an individual who has committed a serious wrong deserves punishment, we appraise his wrong actions and attitudes. Then, based on this appraisal, we match the severity of the punishment to the gravity of the offense.[3] Here we judge the offender and his offense, and inflict punishment as a measure of the wrongfulness of the offender's violation. Whereas an attitude of resentment extends hostility or withdrawal of goodwill to the offender based on an appraisal of his offense, a practice of legal punishment extends to the offender a more substantial and serious response, based on the same kind of judgment. The justification for inflicting the punishment thus rests, at least in part, on the claim that the offender *deserves* the punishment in view of the nature of his offense, just as we might say that the unrepentant offender *deserves* the attitudinal response of resentment.

The basic moral attitudes that ground the paradigm of forgiveness also lead to a moral theory in reference to which we can justify laws and social practices. As I have argued, an attitude of unconditional genuine forgiveness incorporates an attitude of respect, compassion, and real goodwill for all persons regardless of what they have done or suffered

---

[3] See John Kleinig, *Punishment and Desert*, and Edmund Pincoffs, "Are Questions of Desert Decidable?" In his article, Pincoffs only explores the rationality of desert claims and a retributive theory of punishment based on desert. He does not endorse retributivism.

and regardless of whether they have acknowledged the wrongs they have committed. I have also argued that if we adopt Williams's human perspective and *identify* with persons (as opposed to judging them), we will have reason to extend these attitudes to all persons equally. If we extend the attitudes of respect, compassion, and real goodwill to all persons equally, we will want each person's life to be as fulfilling as it can be. We will want each individual to have all of his or her needs met, to have extensive opportunities for personal and moral growth, and in general, to have a life that is as rich, rewarding, and meaningful as possible. In this case there is only one set of circumstances in which we will have reason to limit an individual's well-being or to impose a burden on her, and that is when our commitment to secure a good life for this individual infringes in an equal or more significant manner on our commitment to secure a good life for others. In other words, from the basic attitudes of respect, compassion, and real goodwill, extended to all persons equally, we can derive the following moral principle: Each individual ought to be secured the most fundamental benefits in life compatible with like benefits for all, and no individual ought to be required to sacrifice a significant interest so that others can benefit in less important ways. This moral principle can then be viewed as the basic principle in a moral theory structured in terms of justice, in reference to which we can justify our laws, policies, and social practices.

It is important to understand that I am not abandoning a virtue-ethical approach to response to wrongdoing by adopting a moral theory. The first point to recognize here is that in the context of the paradigm of forgiveness, our moral theory is derived from and can be seen as an extension of the attitudes of respect, compassion, and real goodwill for all individuals. Accordingly, our moral principle may be viewed as a heuristic device that helps us to determine whether a given law, policy, or social practice actually extends our attitudes of respect, compassion, and real goodwill to all persons equally. Given that laws and social practices can be highly complex, especially in societies with large populations and advanced technologies, it is important that we have a heuristic device of this sort.

Second, I am not suggesting that we abandon our basic attitudes and rely exclusively on moral theory when we move from the personal domain to the public domain. Rather, I believe that it is of the utmost importance for those of us who are involved in the public domain to retain the attitudes of respect, compassion, and real goodwill, extended to all persons equally, in every aspect of our work. It is important for police officers, judges, prison officials, members of Congress, members of the Supreme Court, and so on to maintain these attitudes as they perform their respective tasks. Holding these attitudes consistently is important for a number of reasons. For one thing, as John Stuart Mill and others have pointed out, it is easy to distort the application of a moral principle in making decisions that involve our self-interest or implicate our own biases. If we cultivate in ourselves the morally integrated attitudes of respect, compassion, and real goodwill for all persons, we will be consistently motivated to ensure that each person is secured the most fundamental benefits in life compatible with like benefits for all.

As I argued in Chapter 2, morally integrated attitudes also have a significant and continuous impact on the quality of our lives. We can easily imagine the difference between a community in which police officers, prison officials, judges, and so on regard each person with respect, compassion, and real goodwill, and a community in which these officials simply attempt to apply the dictates of a particular moral theory. We can also easily imagine the difference between a community in which those who work in the public sphere genuinely respect and care about all persons, and a community in which they adopt a perspective of judgment and withhold goodwill from those who they believe deserve harsh treatment.

Further, as Alastair MacIntyre has argued, the application of any theory, principle, or rule will at some point require the use of judgment (and it is important to recognize here that this kind of judgment has nothing to do with being judgmental or adopting a retributive perspective of judgment). It is impossible to articulate rules that will dictate precisely how we ought to make every decision with which we are faced.[4] If we have cultivated in ourselves the morally integrated attitudes of respect, compassion, and real goodwill for all persons, then the judgments we are required to make are likely to be morally appropriate. In this case we will have the understanding, affect, and motive to exercise our judgment in a manner that is respectful, compassionate, and beneficial for all who are affected by our decisions.

It might be asked at this point whether justice is an attitude as well as a concept in a moral theory. In the context of the virtue-ethical position I am proposing here, it is.[5] The cognitive component of this attitude includes a recognition of the salient features of persons that I have

[4] Alastair MacIntyre, *After Virtue*, pp. 143–145.
[5] I owe this point to Christianna White.

described earlier: our capacity to experience happiness and misery; our basic desire for happiness; our capacity for moral choice, growth, and awareness; our status as autonomous beings who can lead meaningful lives only as the authors of our own choices and attitudes; and our status as limited beings who are vulnerable to error. It also includes a salient recognition that it is morally appropriate to identify with persons (as opposed to judging them), that each person has an equal moral status from this perspective, and that each person ought to be secured the most fundamental benefits in life compatible with like benefits for all. Finally, it includes an acute awareness of how cruel and damaging it is for any person to be left out as we attempt to secure good lives for persons, or worse, to be used as a mere means to the ends of others. The affective component of the attitude of justice, as I believe it should be understood, is a feeling of great sympathy for anyone who is left out or used in these ways, and a feeling of urgent concern for his well-being.[6] And the motivational component consists of a desire to secure for each individual the most fundamental benefits at stake in the situation at issue, compatible with like benefits for all. Thus an attitude of justice incorporates an attitude of respect, compassion, and real goodwill extended to all persons equally. If my reasoning in this section has been correct, then, we can maintain a virtue-ethical approach to response to wrongdoing and at the same time extend the paradigm of forgiveness to include a moral theory structured in terms of the principle of justice cited here. And we can refer to this moral theory as we attempt to determine how our laws, policies, and social practices ought to be articulated. Let us now consider the relative merits of a moral theory structured in terms of justice and a moral theory structured, at least in part, in terms of desert.

MORAL THEORIES STRUCTURED IN TERMS OF DESERT

Much has been done in recent literature to clarify the concept of desert. There is now a general consensus that desert is a triadic relation between

---

[6] Here I follow John Stuart Mill in viewing sympathy as a central part of the affective component of justice, but depart from his analysis in omitting anger. The arguments in this book suggest that anger is an inappropriate response to wrongdoing (at least for someone who has completed the process of addressing the wrong). I see no reason why we should not replace anger with an urgent concern for the welfare of the person being treated unjustly. Some have argued that anger motivates us to do something about the injustice, but the same can be said about a genuine, urgent concern for the victim's welfare.

a person (P), a mode of treatment (T), and a basis (B) in virtue of which P deserves T. The desert basis (B) is generally thought to be in some sense revelatory of the agent. Concerning desert bases, Schmidtz writes: "It is not necessary, and may not be feasible, to produce a complete catalog of all possible desert bases. Suffice it to say, the standard bases on which people are commonly said to be deserving include character, effort, and achievement."[7] When we make a desert claim, we assert either that it is morally fitting for a person who possesses a desirable characteristic to receive a desirable mode of treatment, or that it is morally fitting for a person who possesses an undesirable characteristic to receive an undesirable mode of treatment. For our purposes here, I will also consider desert to be preinstitutional, or in other words, prior to and independent of the rules of social practices. Rather than referring to these rules to determine what people deserve, we refer to considerations of desert to determine how social practices ought to be structured. (In contrast, I will refer to the burdens and benefits allocated to persons by the rules of social practices as liabilities and entitlements.)

There is a long-standing philosophical tradition that holds that desert is a fundamental and irreducible component of morality. Although specific desert claims may be derived from more general ones, desert claims in the final analysis cannot be derived from principles formulated in terms of other moral concepts such as utility, justice, or rights. Because desert is an irreducible component of morality, we must consider which modes of treatment persons deserve when we determine how we ought to respond to them in either the personal or public domain. I will refer to moral theories that incorporate this position on the status of desert claims as moral theories structured in terms of desert, or alternatively, as desert-based moral theories.[8]

As I have noted, many of the moral convictions that we express in terms of desert seem quite plausible. For example, it seems plausible (although it is not uncontroversial) to say that at least some criminal offenders deserve punishment, that persons who work hard deserve more pay than those who do not, and that veterans deserve special benefits. An adequate moral theory will either have to incorporate these claims or provide a very persuasive reason for rejecting them. The question I want

---

[7] David Schmidtz, *Elements of Justice*, p. 34.
[8] In using these terms, I do not mean to imply that the theory in question is based exclusively on desert, but only that desert is regarded as an irreducible component of the theory.

to ask in this section is whether desert-based moral theories can provide adequate *justification* for these claims.

The most fundamental question that arises when we attempt to justify desert claims is *why* persons who possess characteristic B ought to receive mode of treatment T. This question may be asked from two perspectives. First, we can ask why persons who possess characteristic B ought to receive T, as opposed to some other mode of treatment. For example, we can ask why criminal offenders deserve punishment, as opposed, say, to rehabilitation, or another chance to do the right thing. Second, we can ask which desert basis (if any) should be used in allocating a given mode of treatment. For example, we can ask whether the appropriate desert basis for student grades is effort, mastery of the subject matter, raw ability in the field, originality of thought, and so on. And we can ask whether the appropriate desert basis for criminal punishment (if criminal punishment is justified at all) is the wrongfulness of the offender's intention, the extent of the harm he inflicted on others, the extent to which he has undermined the community, and so on.

It is important to recognize that the proponent of a desert-based theory cannot answer these questions simply by referring to another type of moral consideration, such that the appeal to desert is superfluous. For example, the proponent of a desert-based theory cannot say that persons who work hard should receive more pay than those who do not, because this arrangement will maximize utility by giving everyone an incentive to be productive. The desert-based theorist holds that desert is irreducible, and therefore that desert claims cannot be derived from moral principles formulated in terms of other moral concepts. Thus there seem to be two basic strategies open to the desert-based theorist when he is asked to justify his claim that a particular mode of treatment ought to be matched to a particular desert basis.

First, he might respond that the desert claim he is asked to justify constitutes a fundamental principle in his moral theory – one that cannot be derived from or explained in terms of a principle that is even more fundamental. Every moral theory must include some claims of this sort, from which more specific conclusions can be derived. These fundamental principles can then be justified by showing that they explain our considered moral judgments and cohere well with relevant background theories. The problem with this strategy is that desert claims that link a particular mode of treatment with a particular desert basis have a limited degree of explanatory power. For example, the claim that persons who are guilty of serious moral wrongdoing deserve punishment explains our conviction that it is morally legitimate to punish criminals, as well as some of our convictions about the way in which a practice of punishment ought to be structured. However, few (if any) additional beliefs can be explained in reference to this principle. And the claim that students deserve to be graded on the basis of originality of thought explains an even more limited range of our considered moral judgments.

As David Schmidtz points out, a theory composed of a plurality of principles is not necessarily inferior to a monistic theory. He reminds us that astronomers tried for a long time to construe planetary orbits as circular, with a single focus, and finally concluded that they were actually elliptical, with two foci, in spite of the fact that circular orbits are simpler. And a theory that reduces the periodic table to 4 elements, or even to one, will not be preferable to the periodic table that we currently accept, with 115 elements. Schmidtz concludes: "So simplicity is a theoretical virtue, but when a phenomenon looks complex ... the simplest explanation may be that it looks complex because it is."[9] Schmidtz is of course correct in thinking that we do not want our theories to be simpler than reality, or simpler than is required to adequately explain the subject matter under investigation. However, it also seems clear that we have reason to prefer moral principles that explain a greater range of our considered moral judgments, provided that they adequately systematize those judgments. The less explanatory power a principle has, the greater the risk that it is ad hoc, or that it constitutes an accidental generalization of our considered moral judgments. If we had a great deal of confidence in all of our considered moral judgments, we would have no need to construct moral theories at all. The basic assumption that underlies the process of theory construction is that some of these judgments are unreliable as they stand. By attempting to systematize them under broader moral considerations or principles, and by examining the way in which these principles cohere with relevant background theories, we can gain insight into which of our intuitive beliefs are reliable and which are in need of revision. When we merely restate one of our intuitions, then, or formulate a generalization on the basis of a small range of them, we make little progress toward this goal. Therefore a desert-based moral theory that incorporates several fundamental principles that have a limited degree of explanatory power will be weak in this regard.

Of course it may be possible to offer *arguments* for specific desert claims at the same time that we claim that they are fundamental and

[9] David Schmidtz, *Elements of Justice*, p. 4.

cannot be derived from a more basic moral principle. George Sher has developed a pluralistic analysis of desert, in which he offers independent arguments to show that autonomous action, diligence, virtue, and merit should be seen as desert bases.[10] In the case of autonomous action, Sher argues that because autonomous action itself has value, it enhances the value of a state of affairs in which the agent receives a predictable outcome of his choice. He suggests, for example, that if Jones chooses to leave his house without an umbrella when he knows it might rain, we can say that the state of affairs in which Jones is drenched in a rain shower is good, and that Jones got what he deserved. But this claim seems highly implausible. Even if Jones knows that it might rain, and leaves home without his umbrella anyway, it does not seem "good" that he gets drenched. Nor does a state of affairs in which a mountaineer gets killed in an avalanche seem "good" or "valuable," even when the climber knows in advance there could be an avalanche and that it is possible that she will be killed. Further, it is far from clear how the value of an autonomous choice could enhance the value of a particular state of affairs.

Sher's justification of virtue as a desert basis is no more convincing. He says: "But if a virtuous person does have greater worth than others, then his desires and sustained effort will be able to confer correspondingly more value on their objects."[11] Therefore a state of affairs in which a virtuous person succeeds will have more value than a state of affairs in which an ordinary person succeeds. But I have argued in Chapter 5 that the meritarian position on which this argument relies should be rejected. There is an important difference between the claim that we ought to strive to cultivate morally worthy attitudes or virtues in ourselves and the claim that success in this regard increases our intrinsic worth as a person and gives us a moral status that is superior to that of other persons. I have argued that a virtuous person will adopt the perspective of identification, which responds to the most morally salient features of persons, and that from this perspective she will regard persons as equals. Further, the way in which Sher believes the virtuous person transfers his extra value to the object of his desires is obscure, as is the way in which he believes that an ordinary person transfers value to the objects of his desires through diligent effort. It seems, then, that Sher fails to offer clear and convincing arguments for the desert bases he recognizes.

---

[10] George Sher, *Desert*.

[11] *Ibid.*, p. 144.

Finally, Sher acknowledges that on his analysis, "most ... significant desert claims are grounded not in anyone's obligations, but rather in the value of the person's coming to have what they deserve."[12] And although desert claims may have influence on our obligations, "there is no reason to expect that influence to be straightforward or direct."[13] In response to the question of whether we can explain how desert influences our obligations, Sher says that "clearly we cannot do so in any detail; for the degree to which a potential outcome's value affects any person's obligations depends on too many factors."[14] Thus it seems that even if Sher's arguments were plausible, his analysis of desert would not be of much help to us in the context of constructing a moral theory to which we can refer in justifying our laws and social practices.

The second general strategy the desert-based theorist might adopt when he is asked to justify his claim that a particular mode of treatment ought to be matched to a particular desert basis is to derive this claim from a broader and more fundamental moral principle formulated in terms of desert. A principle of this sort will have more explanatory power than a particular desert claim, if it succeeds in adequately systematizing the considered moral judgments that we generally express in terms of desert. Joel Feinberg suggests a general analysis of desert in the following passage, when he says that personal desert might be "likened to, or even identified with, a kind of 'fittingness' between one person's actions or qualities and another person's responsive attitudes. This view suggests in turn that responsive attitudes are the basic things persons deserve and that 'modes of treatment' are deserved only in a derivative way, insofar perhaps as they are natural or conventional means of expressing the morally fitting attitudes. Thus punishment ... might be deserved by the criminal only because it is the customary way of expressing the resentment or reprobation he 'has coming.'"[15]

This analysis of desert seems to suggest a moral principle that could have a great deal of explanatory power – roughly, the principle that we ought to allocate burdens to those who deserve retributive reactive attitudes, in proportion to the strength of these attitudes, and benefits to those who deserve positive reactive attitudes, again in proportion to the strength of those attitudes. Feinberg's position here does seem

---

[12] *Ibid.*, p. 195.
[13] *Ibid.*, p. 202.
[14] *Ibid.*, p. 203.
[15] Joel Feinberg, *Doing and Deserving*, p. 82. J.R. Lucas proposes a similar analysis in *On Justice*, p. 209ff.

natural and intuitive. However, it is problematic in at least two respects. First, I have argued in the first part of this book that retributive reactive attitudes are *not* morally appropriate, at least for someone who has completed the process of addressing the wrong. Second, even if these attitudes were justified, it would not follow directly that we would be justified in punishing criminal offenders. We can resent an offender for an offense he has committed without imprisoning him or fining him, and we can also *express* our resentment, if we feel justified in doing so, without imposing these substantial burdens on him. Additional justification is clearly required, for the choice to express our resentment is a manner that is so detrimental to the offender. Likewise we can express our approval of persons who have good characteristics without offering these persons high salaries, providing them with special opportunities, or giving them benefits of other sorts. In the public sphere, justification is required for expressing our positive reactive attitudes in these ways as well, given that our resources are finite, and that by providing extra benefits for one person we may adversely affect someone else. The fact that certain modes of treatment are the "natural" or "customary" methods of expressing our reactive attitudes is hardly sufficient justification for allocating substantive burdens and benefits in a particular manner.

It will be instructive to consider at this point why retributivists may encounter special difficulties in making the transition from retributive reactive attitudes to a moral theory in reference to which we can justify laws and social practices. As we have seen, retributive reactive attitudes take a judgmental perspective toward the offender. However, once an accurate judgment is formulated, the task of judging has been completed. Any further step we take beyond mere judgment must be in service of some further end, and requires additional justification. Expression of the judgment may seem to be a natural subsequent step, but then the manner of expression requires justification, especially when it inflicts serious harm on the recipient. On the other hand, if we adopt perspective of identification, and the attitudes of respect, compassion, and real goodwill that emerge from this perspective, we clearly have much to do beyond simply expressing our attitudes. In this case we have both reason and motive to do everything we can to secure for everyone the most fundamental benefits in life compatible for like benefits for all. Thus we have reason to expect that the attitudes that ground the paradigm of forgiveness will lead to a robust and coherent moral theory that can justify laws and social practices, whereas we have at least some reason to doubt that the basic attitudes endorsed by the retributivist will suffice to do so.

Eric Moore has also proposed an analysis of desert that is based on a broad principle capable of explaining a wide range of desert claims. He says: "My view is, roughly, that all desert is based upon the possession of virtues and vices, the fit between one's previous deserts and receipts, and one's potential for developing virtues in the future."[16] The central belief that underlies his position is that virtuous persons and persons who perform virtuous actions deserve to fare well, and vicious persons and persons who perform vicious actions deserve to fare poorly. However, Moore claims that in applying this basic idea, we must take account of what has happened in the past. For example, if a man's daughter was murdered in the past, he has suffered a substantial burden that he did not deserve. Even if he has done nothing especially virtuous, then, he may deserve a substantial benefit now, in compensation for this undeserved suffering. Further, we must take account of the fact that very young children have had no opportunity to cultivate either virtue or vice. Instead of saying that they deserve nothing, as we would have to say if the only desert bases we recognize are actual virtue and vice, we should say that they deserve an opportunity to develop their virtues. This reasoning can be extended to adults as well, provided that it is through no fault of their own that they have not yet developed their virtues. Here Moore construes virtues very broadly, to include things such as musical talent and the ability to run well. Interestingly, and unlike Sher, Moore does not provide an argument for his analysis of desert, but tells us that we must simply regard it as fundamental. He says: "I do think that virtue is a desert base, but I cannot provide a direct argument to show this. The connection between what is deserved and the reason for that desert – the desert base – must be taken as primitive. There is no reason why (for instance) the virtuous are deserving *beyond* the fact that they are virtuous."[17]

Moore's position is admirable in that it seems to subsume desert claims under an overarching principle of desert that would have a significant amount of explanatory power. However, an account of this sort will face significant challenges. First, a major task facing anyone who adopts this position is to explain how we are to assess the relative worth of the various actions and characteristics that constitute desert bases. We will not be able to apply Moore's principle successfully unless we are able to make at least rough assessments of this sort. For example, in

---

[16] Eric Moore, "Desert, Virtue, and Justice," p. 421.
[17] *Ibid.*

order to allocate benefits properly, we will have to know who ought to receive a greater increase in welfare – the worker who has made a diligent effort all year, perhaps without much success; the mother who has exhibited exceptional patience and compassion for her children; the individual who has made a great contribution to society by inventing a new product, perhaps without much effort or concern for others; a person who has performed one heroic deed, such as diving into an icy river to save someone from drowning; a poor person who has donated her time and some of the little money she has to the local animal shelter, and so on. While we may be able to agree that all of these people are virtuous, we would need a much more detailed, lexically ordered conception of virtue and vice in order to construct a moral theory in reference to which we can justify our laws and social practices. When we consider seriously what would be required here, we can begin to understand why philosophical liberals have not, so far, adopted a preinstitutional conception of desert.[18] Further, as Jeffrie Murphy has pointed out, even if we could agree on a detailed, lexically ordered conception of desert (so defined) in a democratic society, we would then have to assert that the government should be assigned that task of determining how much virtue and vice each of us possesses in order to determine what we deserve.[19] This latter claim raises a host of obvious difficulties.

[18] An anonymous reader for Cambridge University Press has raised the question of whether a virtue-theorist will face a similar problem in having to rank the virtues. This is a serious issue that warrants a clear response. The response I am inclined to give involves a thesis about the unity of the virtues, which would take some time to develop. Given the limitations of space here, I will reserve this project for a future occasion. Briefly, however, I do not think a ranking of the virtues will be necessary. On the virtue-ethical approach adopted here, our goal is not to judge persons according to the virtues that they have managed to develop, as would be required in the context of a desert-based moral theory. Rather, our goal is to cultivate morally worthy attitudes in ourselves. Morally worthy attitudes respond to the features of persons (and of the situations we face) that are most salient from a moral point of view. Any attitude that is fully worthy from a moral point of view will then involve a correct recognition of the most morally salient features of persons and situations, and the affective and motivational components will respond appropriately as well. Any virtues we develop, therefore, should be based on the same cognitive recognition of the most morally salient features in question, and so should not conflict with one another. Of course we must then be able to recognize the morally salient features of persons and situations. I have suggested here five morally salient features of persons in developing the paradigm of forgiveness. If the reader finds the paradigm of forgiveness to be reasonably coherent, she has at least one small reason to believe that the virtue-ethical approach adopted here can be worked out in a coherent manner. Of course, many other issues would have to be addressed to defend this claim more fully.

[19] See Jeffrie Murphy, "The State's Interest in Culpability."

These problems alone are daunting. Unfortunately, further problems will arise as well. It is important to recognize that there are several areas in which we believe that a person's interests ought to be secured without reference to the worth of his character or deeds. For example, we hold that all citizens ought to have freedom of speech and freedom of religion. We do not say that only virtuous persons should have these freedoms, or that the extent of each person's opportunities to speak or to choose his own religion should be proportional to the extent of his virtue. Unless the desert-based theorist wants to propose that we should revise several of our basic beliefs, he must explain why his basic principle of desert does not apply in these cases.

Further, in order to apply moral principles formulated in terms of desert, we must have a method for determining *how much* of a given mode of treatment is deserved. It will be useful here to distinguish between two types of desert claims: *evaluative* desert claims, which assert that an agent deserves a particular evaluation, and *allocative* desert claims, which assert that an agent deserves to be allocated a particular burden or benefit on the basis of our evaluation of him. Although it may be difficult to make judgments in borderline cases, no special theoretical difficulties arise in determining the degree of desert when we are dealing with evaluative desert claims, after the appropriate desert bases have been specified. For example, in a diving competition, we know how to determine whether a diver deserves a 9.85 or a 9.90, once we have decided upon the criteria to use in judging dives. The deserved mode of treatment in this case is simply an accurate description of the relevant characteristics of the agent's dive, as they compare with the characteristics of the performances of other divers. Here we are still working within the confines of the perspective of judgment. However, the situation changes when we move beyond the context of judgment to the allocation of substantive burdens and benefits.

There is one type of situation in which we can determine without difficulty the extent of the burdens or benefits an individual deserves, and that is a situation in which we have a fixed quantity of burdens or benefits to allocate among a definite number of individuals, in reference to a clearly defined desert base. For example, suppose that two persons, Jane and John, have worked together to complete a job. Both of them worked at approximately the same level of efficiency, but Jane worked fifteen hours while John worked only ten hours. When they get paid a fixed amount for the job, it is easy to calculate how much money each of them deserves.

However, some of the most significant allocative desert claims we make address situations in which we do *not* have a fixed quantity of burdens and benefits to allocate among individuals who possess a given characteristic. In this type of situation, it seems that we have no theoretical basis for determining how much of the given burden or benefit the individual deserves to receive. John Kleinig proposes a solution to this kind of problem in connection with his desert-based analysis of punishment. He suggests that we can construct an ordinal scale of crimes, ranked from the least serious to the most serious, and a cardinal scale of punishments, ranked from the least severe to the most severe. We can then convert the ordinal scale of crimes into a cardinal scale by making reasonable judgments concerning how much more serious one crime is than the next. The problem that remains is to anchor the two scales together in such a way that we can assign a punishment to each crime. In order to anchor the scales, at least two points of contact must be established, and Kleinig suggests the following procedure for identifying them: "Our human condition places certain limits, upper and lower, on both the wrongs we can commit and the penalties we can inflict.... In relating punishments to offenses, we simply reserve the mildest punishment we can reasonably give for the least serious wrong, the most severe punishment for the most wicked deed."[20]

The problem with this solution is that it seems completely arbitrary. The most (or least) serious crime could be matched with any point on the scale of punishments, and there seems to be no way to determine, within the context of the kind of desert-based theory we are considering, which point represents *the* punishment that is *truly deserved*.[21] For example, it is not clear how we could determine whether a convicted serial killer deserves forty years of imprisonment, eighty years of imprisonment, capital punishment, or two years of torture followed by capital punishment. Of course, the desert-based theorist can propose other more specific arguments to establish how much punishment an offender deserves. We will consider some of these arguments in Chapter 7. (I do not believe that any of the proposed arguments succeed, and will refer the reader at this point to Russ Shafer-Landau's excellent article, "Retributivism and Desert," which argues systematically that they do not.) In general,

[20] John Kleinig, *Punishment and Desert*, p. 123–124.
[21] I make this argument in my article, "Justifying Desert Claims: Desert and Opportunity." Russ Shafer-Landau presents a similar critique of Kleinig in his "Retributivism and Desert."

however, unless the desert-based theorist can identify two points of contact between a cardinal scale of a given desert basis and a corresponding
cardinal scale of the mode of treatment with which it is to be correlated,
he will lack any justifiable method for determining how much of that
mode of treatment is deserved. And considering the extent of the impact
that allocations of burdens and benefits often have on individuals' lives,
this is an important shortcoming.

Again, it is important to recognize that this problem arises for the
retributivist because she adopts the perspective of judgment. As I have
suggested, desert claims are made from the perspective of judgment, and
after an adequate judgment has been formulated, the task of judging is
complete. The task of judgment itself is not concerned with human welfare. When we judge how wrong an individual's actions or attitudes are,
we do not concern ourselves with any other practical end. Thus there
is no criterion available, internal to the task of judging, in reference to
which we can determine how much of a given mode of treatment someone truly deserves. On the other hand, when we adopt the perspective
of identification and extend an attitude of respect, compassion, and real
goodwill to all persons, we are directly concerned with each person's
welfare. In this case, we will have a criterion for determining the quantity of burdens and benefits that individuals ought to receive. We will
secure for each person the most fundamental interests in life, compatible
with like benefits for all.

Finally, regardless of the way in which a desert-based moral theory
is formulated, it seems that it will be necessary to weigh desert against
other types of moral considerations, such as needs, rights, and utility.
For example, we will encounter situations in which one person deserves
to have the money he has earned, but another person desperately needs
some of that money; situations in which one person is given property
and seems to have a right to keep it, in spite of the fact that he has done
nothing to deserve it; or situations in which one individual has worked
hard for a position and perhaps deserves it, but many people would
benefit if it were given to someone else. Unless the desert-based theorist claims that desert is always the overriding consideration (and this
claim would be implausible), he will be forced to weigh considerations
of desert against other moral factors such as needs, rights, and utility.
Although some proponents of desert-based moral theories embrace this
conclusion, it presents obvious difficulties when we attempt to justify
our social practices. In the context of this type of analysis, the structure of several of these practices will depend on highly specific intuitive

judgments about the relative weighting of moral factors that appear to be incommensurable. To summarize, then, it seems that desert-based moral theories will encounter significant structural difficulties when we attempt to justify desert claims, to determine how much of a given mode of treatment is deserved, and to weigh considerations of desert against other kinds of moral considerations.

THE PARADIGM OF FORGIVENESS, JUSTICE, AND DESERT

In the previous section, I suggested that significant structural problems will arise in desert-based moral theories. Further, as noted in Chapter 5, Sher and Sandel (among others) hold that a desert-based moral theory requires a conception of the self as "thickly constituted," or as partially constituted by values, preferences, and abilities, and I have argued that this conception of the self is problematic. If Sher and Sandel are correct, and if my arguments in Chapter 5 were successful, then we also have reason to question whether a desert-based moral theory will be compatible with a plausible theory of the person. It seems, then, that we now have at least some reason to question whether a desert-based moral theory can provide an adequate reference point for justifying our laws and social practices. On the other hand, I have acknowledged that many of the moral convictions that we express in terms of desert are plausible and deeply held, and that any adequate moral theory should be able to account for them. Further, it seems that an adequate moral theory must account for these moral convictions in a preinstitutional manner, given that we often criticize laws and social institutions on the grounds that they fail to give persons what they deserve.

In this section, I argue that the justice-based moral theory that emerges in the paradigm of forgiveness will allow us to avoid some of the most serious structural problems that arise in a desert-based moral theory. I then go on to suggest that it will also allow us to account for many of the moral convictions we express in terms of desert, in a preinstitutional manner. Here I provide only a brief indication of how this moral theory can account for our central desert claims in the domain of distributive justice. An analysis of how this theory explains plausible desert claims in the domain of retributive justice will be reserved for Chapter 7, in which I provide a more detailed account of the laws and social practices that will be endorsed as public responses to wrongdoing in the paradigm of forgiveness.

At this point in our discussion, a utilitarian might interject that her moral theory allows us to avoid the structural problems that arise in a desert-based moral theory, and it seems clear that this claim would be correct. The principle of utility is obviously a broad moral principle that would have a great deal of explanatory power if it succeeded in adequately systematizing our considered moral judgments. It also provides us with an intelligible method for determining the quantity of burdens and benefits that individuals ought to receive. Finally, in the context of the utilitarian moral theory, we are not required to weigh incommensurable moral factors against one another. Retributivists have objected, however, that utilitarianism does not succeed in adequately systematizing our considered moral judgments expressed in terms of desert, for reasons that have been thoroughly discussed in the literature. George Sher articulates this objection as follows: "As long as the utilitarian's basic tenet is that the rightness of acts depends on their consequences, he must still maintain that punishing and rewarding in accordance with desert is wrong whenever its costs outweigh its benefits. However, it is central to our beliefs about desert that a person may deserve reward or punishment ... even if his receiving it will not maximize overall utility."[22] Further, as retributivists have noted, utilitarianism seems to embody Strawson's objective attitude toward persons, and it lacks an argument to show that we are not using persons as mere means to obtain social benefits. Of course, utilitarians have responded in various ways to these objections, but an examination of their responses would divert us from the primary purpose of this book, which is to develop the paradigm of forgiveness and argue that it is preferable to retributivism. For our purposes here, I will simply assume that retributivists are correct in suggesting that we have reason to question the adequacy of the utilitarian position.

However, it seems that some retributivists overstate their case against the utilitarian analysis of response to wrongdoing. Utilitarians have also raised an important objection to those retributive justifications of punishment that the claim that persons who are guilty of criminal wrongdoing deserve to suffer punishment regardless of whether the punishment would result in any benefits for anyone. More specifically, utilitarians have famously objected that this position is no more than a glorified form of revenge, and that it is wrong to inflict punishment on the offender merely for the sake of making him suffer. They hold that any

[22] George Sher, *Desert*, p. 12.

moral analysis that is not tied in some way to concrete human interests has no rational foundation, and must be rejected. Although this objection does not obviate the difficulties that retributivists have identified with the utilitarian position, I believe that the utilitarians are correct on this point. Like utilitarianism, the moral theory that emerges in the paradigm of forgiveness rejects retributive desert claims that are not tied to concrete human interests and that insist that it is morally appropriate to make persons suffer when there are no benefits to be derived from their suffering. If we hold an attitude of respect, compassion, and real goodwill toward all persons, we will always be concerned to provide benefits for persons – the most fundamental benefits in life compatible with like benefits for all. And we will never have reason or motive to inflict suffering on anyone unless we must do so to prevent greater or equal harm to others.

The justice-based moral theory that emerges in the paradigm of forgiveness avoids some of the central problems that retributivists have identified in the utilitarian analysis of response to wrongdoing. Our equal, fundamental concern for each individual ensures that we will not use persons as mere means to obtain social benefits. We will always be concerned to secure the most fundamental interests for each person, compatible with securing like benefits for all. Thus, our response to wrongdoing will not be dictated by whatever course of action happens to maximize utility, nor will it be unfair to individuals. Further, as we have seen, the perspective of identification that underlies the paradigm of forgiveness is diametrically opposed to Strawson's objective attitude. In the context of the paradigm of forgiveness, we avoid not only Strawson's objective attitude toward persons, but also the morally problematic objectification of persons that occurs when we conflate them with their actions and attitudes. Further, as I will argue in the remainder of this chapter and in Chapter 7, we will be able to account for many of the considered moral judgments that we express in terms of desert in the context of the justice-based moral theory that emerges in the paradigm of forgiveness.

Moreover, the justice-based moral theory that emerges in the paradigm of forgiveness allows us to avoid some of the serious structural difficulties that arise in a desert-based moral theory. The moral principle we have articulated is very broad and will have a great deal of explanatory power if it adequately systematizes our plausible moral convictions. Our justice-based moral theory also provides a theoretical framework for determining the quantity of burdens and benefits that each person should receive. Again, the guiding concern in reference to which we can make determinations of this sort is to secure for each individual the most fundamental benefits in life compatible with like benefits for all. Further, this theory provides us with a theoretical framework for adjudicating between many of the conflicts that commonly arise between different kinds of moral considerations.[23] For example, suppose that I know of a highly sensitive military secret concerning a planned movement of troops, and that if I revealed this secret I would endanger the lives of thousands of soldiers. Here there may appear to be a conflict between utility and my "right" to freedom of speech. The moral principle we have articulated will resolve this conflict when we recognize that the interest that any given soldier has at stake in this situation is much more fundamental than the interest I have in speaking in such a way that I reveal this information to the public. There will of course be borderline cases in which it is difficult to determine which of the interests at stake in a conflict situation is more fundamental. And in very complex situations (such as in a collapse of the global financial markets), it may be difficult even to identify which aspects of our lives will be affected by various courses of action. Nevertheless, the guiding concern of securing for each person the most fundamental benefits in life compatible with like benefits for all will determine what kind of information we should attempt to obtain and how we should use it in making our decisions. Finally, by deriving our principle of justice from the basic attitudes that respond to morally salient features of persons, and by arguing that these attitudes are compatible with a plausible philosophical position on the nature of persons, we have provided additional reasons to accept it.

It might be objected at this point that some of the interests we would like to have secured for us in life are incommensurable, and that from the point of view of public policy, we have no objective method for determining when one interest is more fundamental than another. A full discussion of these points would again divert us from the primary aim of this book, and I will not undertake it here. However, it is worth noting that as we move from abstract claims about desert to claims about concrete human interest, we enter into a domain in which we have a

---

[23] I do not claim completeness here, and it is obviously impossible in this context to develop a justice-based moral theory in sufficient detail to explain how all such conflicts could be resolved. In particular, I think that conflicts between justice and utility will still be an issue. For example, if interest X is regarded as slightly more fundamental than interest Y, and we have a choice between securing interest X for one person or interest Y for 1,000 persons, we may have to weigh considerations of justice against considerations of utility.

great deal of experience. Value pluralists have made a strong case for the incommensurability of values.[24] But even value pluralists generally acknowledge that we are actually very well versed in weighing the different interests we have in life against one another, and that we engage in this activity on a daily basis. Our choices about our daily activities, our careers, our family life, our relationships, our vacations, and a host of other things require us to weigh our different interests against each other. It would be implausible to suggest that these choices are arbitrary, and that we have no rational grounds for making them.

Further, if these choices were arbitrary and irrational, our conception of moral agency would be greatly impoverished, if not rendered completely meaningless. An important part of what we do as moral agents is to determine which ends in life are significant (in our own lives and in the lives of others), and how these ends should be prioritized when they cannot all be realized. As Korsgaard suggests, from the deliberative perspective we must see ourselves as agents who are capable of making judgments of this sort. It seems, then, that any plausible moral theory (including a desert-based moral theory) would have to include the evaluative assessment of the various ends and interests that we have in our lives. It is important to notice that the same point cannot be made about the assessments of desert. Utilitarians and persons who adopt justice-based moral theories of the sort described here must weigh interests (their own and others') against one another to function as moral agents, but their moral outlooks do not require them to weigh desert claims against each other and against other kinds of moral considerations.

With regard to public policy, we may have no objective formula for determining whether one interest is more fundamental than another, but we can certainly make plausible judgments of this sort. In addition, the salient features of persons outlined here will provide us with some guidance as to which interests are the most fundamental for us. For example, given that we are autonomous and can live meaningful lives only as the authors of our own choices and attitudes, we have a significant interest in individual liberty. And given that we are sentient beings who are capable of happiness and misery, and who very much want to be happy, we have a fundamental interest in the basic necessities of life that are indispensable for our happiness. We might also draw on Rawls's notion of primary goods in making these determinations. And empirical data can be collected about which interests the people in a given society consider

---

[24] For example, see John Kekes, "Pluralism and the Value of Life."

to be the most important to them. Of course, if we wish to construct a liberal theory of justice using this moral principle, there will be certain constraints on how these determinations can be made. However, I will not pursue these matters further here. At this point, I am only providing a very broad outline of the kind of theory of justice that will emerge in the paradigm of forgiveness – an outline that should suffice to ground the public response to wrongdoing that will be developed in the remaining two chapters. At this point I will simply note that there are several different directions we can take in fleshing out the type of justice-based moral theory I have suggested here.

It seems, then, that the kind of justice-based moral theory that emerges in the paradigm of forgiveness avoids some of the structural problems that will be encountered in a desert-based moral theory. It remains to be seen if our justice-based theory can adequately account for the plausible moral intuitions that we commonly express in terms of desert. The first point to note in this regard is that the moral theory I have articulated easily accommodates many of our evaluative desert claims. To return to our earlier example, we can say that a diver deserves a 9.85 on her dive if this number accurately reflects the extent to which her performance matches the accepted criteria of judgment. Any evaluative desert claim can be accommodated in the context of this theory, *provided that* the activity in which the judgment takes place is sanctioned by our basic moral principle. Arguably, athletic competitions secure important interests for everyone, and will be supported by this principle. On the other hand, if a group of students gets together to judge who of all the persons on campus is the ugliest, we would not say that person P *deserves* to be recognized as the ugliest person on campus, even if the judgment is accurate and P is in fact the ugliest. This activity would be ruled out by the moral principle I have cited, as it imposes a cruel burden on those being judged, without securing a significant interest for anyone.

Let us now turn to allocative desert claims in the domain of distributive justice. In this domain, some of our most deeply held moral convictions expressed in terms of desert concern allocations of burdens and benefits based either on our own past choices and efforts, or on merit. I want to suggest that plausible claims about burdens and benefits owed to individuals based on their past choices and efforts can be derived from the moral theory that emerges in the paradigm of forgiveness, once we recognize that we all have a fundamental interest in being able to make the most of our lives through our own choices and efforts. Let us turn first to the distribution of wealth and income. If we were to distribute wealth and income equally, we would each have a certain amount of money with which to pursue our life plans. But consider the individual, Smith, who wishes to develop his life or undertake projects in a manner that requires more financial resources than he has been allocated. If wealth and income are distributed equally, then Smith will have virtually no opportunity to pursue these goals. Working extra hours, working more efficiently, inventing new products or processes, and so on are all to no avail. Whenever he manages to generate more resources, they will be distributed equally among the members of his society, and the returns he gets on his efforts will be negligible.

Now, if every member of society were putting forth his best effort, this state of affairs would not be objectionable. In this case, if Smith's opportunity to improve his life were enhanced, another person's opportunity to do so would be diminished. However, when others are not working to capacity, Smith, under an equal distribution of income and wealth, is denied a fundamental benefit that could be secured for him compatible with like benefits for all. He is denied the opportunity to make the most of his own life through his own efforts, without being bogged down by others who are not doing their best. Given that our moral principle requires that we secure the most fundamental benefits in life compatible with like benefits for all, and given that the opportunity to make the most of our lives through our own choices and efforts is a fundamental benefit, we must allocate a greater share of financial resources, everything else being equal, to those who make a consistent effort to do their best work. Therefore, one of the convictions we often express in terms of desert – specifically, that those who make a consistent effort to do their best work deserve more in return than those who do not – can be derived from our moral principle. (It is important to notice here that a lazy worker, Jones, cannot legitimately wait until Smith has worked very hard while she (Jones) has done very little, and then argue that she has exactly the same interest as Smith in receiving a particular increase in salary. If the competing interests are assessed in this manner, we will all be deprived of the fundamental interest of making the most of our lives through our own efforts.)

On the analysis I have suggested, the opportunity to make the most of our lives through our own choices and efforts will be secured for everyone, *except* when it can only be secured at the expense of another interest that is even more fundamental. It should be recognized that situations of the latter sort will occur on a regular basis. For example, we cannot plausibly claim that the interest we have in the opportunity to advance by our own efforts is as important as the disabled person's interest in a guaranteed decent level of subsistence. Thus we can legitimately limit the opportunity individuals have to advance their own life plans by taxing citizens in order to provide a decent level of subsistence for those who cannot provide for themselves.

A similar line of reasoning allows us to derive from this moral principle claims that jobs and positions should be allocated on the basis of merit. Jobs, positions, and special opportunities are often allocated on the basis of the skills and abilities we possess. To the extent that persons have control over the development of their skills and abilities, social practices structured in this way also secure for each of us the opportunity to pursue our life plans through our own choices and efforts. To some extent, though, the skills and abilities we possess are beyond our control. Many people simply lack the potential to develop the skills required to become a neural surgeon, a professor of relativity physics, the conductor of a symphony orchestra, or the quarterback of a professional football team. Nevertheless, these positions are given to those who possess the required skills because *other persons* have an important interest in having competent people fill these positions. Thus we can derive from our moral principle the claim that merit should be the basis for allocating jobs and positions, a claim that we often express by saying that the most qualified person deserves to be chosen for the position at issue. Again, it is important to recognize that this line of reasoning is not absolute. For example, affirmative action programs may constrain purely merit-based systems of allocation if we can plausibly claim that persons who are members of groups that have suffered discrimination have a more fundamental interest at stake than those who would sacrifice another interest if we chose someone slightly less qualified to fill a particular position.[25]

David Schmidtz has pointed out that we also sometimes make promissory desert claims: claims that persons deserve an opportunity of a given sort, even if they have not made the choices or efforts that we generally take to establish positive desert. For example, we might claim that a promising student deserves a scholarship, that every child (who has a certain threshold level of ability) deserves an education, or, following

---

[25] There may be some residual resentment on the part of white males if affirmative action programs are adopted, but if these programs can be justified, all things considered, to those who are involved, then *a fortiori* this resentment is not justifiable, even for an attitudinal retributivist. The most we can ask of anyone on either the individual level or the level of social policy is that they do the right thing, all things considered.

Moore, that every child deserves an opportunity to develop his virtues.[26] Claims of this sort are also easily justified in the context of the justice-based moral theory that emerges in the paradigm of forgiveness. The opportunities to get an education and to develop one's virtues are of fundamental importance in life, and thus will be secured for each individual who might benefit from them on the moral principle I have proposed. Persons who have special abilities that may result in significant benefits for others will also be given the opportunity to develop those abilities.

It seems, then, that the justice-based moral theory suggested here clearly explains some of the central moral convictions that we express in terms of desert in the domain of distributive justice. Further, it does so in a preinstitutional manner, given that our moral theory dictates how our laws, social practices, and social institutions *ought* to be structured. In Chapter 7 I will go on to argue that many of the central desert claims we make in the domain of retributive justice, or public response to wrongdoing, can also be explained in terms of the interest we have in making the most of our lives through our own choices and efforts, and can therefore be derived from the justice-based moral theory we have proposed. If so, it seems that we will have substantial reason to prefer the justice-based moral theory proposed here to the kind of desert-based moral theories endorsed by many retributivists.

Before we close this chapter, let us return to Scheffler's thesis that both philosophical and political liberalism have been subject to attack because liberals have failed to accord a significant preinstitutional role to desert. If the arguments in this chapter (and the next) are correct, then the justice-based moral theory that emerges in the paradigm of forgiveness actually does explain many of our intuitions about personal responsibility and desert at a preinstitutional level. Further, the paradigm of forgiveness is egalitarian, and it incorporates a fundamental respect for individual autonomy. These points taken together raise the question of whether parts of the paradigm of forgiveness could be defended in the context of a liberal position, and could perhaps strengthen this position against the central objection that Scheffler has identified.

As Scheffler points out, philosophical liberals are often accused of bad faith because they claim to remain neutral among various conceptions of the good life, when in fact they do not. He says: "To its critics, the liberal framework itself seems to incorporate an understanding of what it is to be a human individual that is highly contentious, and that

---

[26] David Schmidtz, *Elements of Justice*, Chapter 8.

leads inevitably to the design of institutions and the creation of conditions that are far more hospitable to some ways of life than others."[27] Further, John Rawls argues in *Political Liberalism* that due to the complexity of our experiences and the inevitable variation in experiences from one individual to another, we cannot expect persons in a modern pluralistic society to reach an agreement on any particular philosophical theory (liberal or otherwise) or on any religious view. He therefore casts his theory of justice as a freestanding *political* conception of justice (political liberalism) that may be widely accepted by citizens with diverse views because it is part of an overlapping consensus. In other words, persons who adopt different philosophical or religious positions may be able to agree on central features of a *political* conception of justice, although they endorse these central features for very different reasons that are specific to their own philosophical or religious convictions. An anonymous reader for Cambridge University Press expresses the general requirements of a political conception of justice in a pluralistic society as follows: "It is simply a fact about modern pluralistic societies that they require forms of government that are sufficiently neutral between conflicting moral (and religious) traditions to provide stability and basic unity to a pluralistic society. No matter how 'objectively true' … any moral theory might be, citizens who endorse these theories are simply advocates of one moral tradition alongside others."

To show that parts of the paradigm of forgiveness could be defended in the context of political liberalism, then, it seems that we would have to argue that some components of it could reasonably be expected to be part of an overlapping consensus broad enough to provide stability and unity in a pluralistic society. Although I cannot undertake a detailed discussion of this question here, there are two points that should be emphasized. The first is that this is an empirical question, and therefore a full development of the paradigm of forgiveness will rely heavily on the empirical sciences at this juncture. Research in political science, sociology, and religious studies will be of central importance in answering this question. There are a few points to be made in favor of the empirical position that some components of the paradigm of forgiveness could be part of a broad overlapping consensus. First, if Scheffler is correct in thinking that philosophical and political liberalism have come under attack primarily because they fail to account for our intuitions about

---

[27] Samuel Scheffler, "Responsibility, Reactive Attitudes, and Liberalism in Philosophy and Politics," p. 317.

desert and personal responsibility at a preinstitutional level, then we have some reason to believe that components of the paradigm of forgiveness could be part of an overlapping consensus if this paradigm succeeds in accounting for these intuitions at a preinstitutional level. Second, I will argue in Chapter 8 that the paradigm of forgiveness incorporates the central tenets of the restorative justice movement (although perhaps with some modifications). Given that the restorative justice movement is making substantial inroads into the practice of criminal justice here and in many jurisdictions around the world, we may again have some reason to believe that components of the paradigm of forgiveness could be a part of a broad overlapping consensus. Finally, it is worth noting that the basic attitudes of respect, compassion, and real goodwill that ground the paradigm of forgiveness are endorsed at least to some extent in a wide variety of philosophical and religious views.

The second point to be emphasized is that if a relatively complete empirical analysis were to show that the paradigm of forgiveness could not be part of a sufficiently broad overlapping consensus, the principle of justice that emerges in the paradigm of forgiveness would itself dictate that the laws and public policies endorsed in the paradigm of forgiveness should be modified. This principle of justice requires that we secure for each individual the most fundamental benefits in life compatible with like benefits for all. Given that our interest in social stability is quite significant, our principle of justice will require us to secure this benefit for citizens whenever it conflicts with interests that are less fundamental. Let us now turn to the laws and social policies that will be endorsed in the paradigm of forgiveness, assuming for the sake of argument that this paradigm will not have to be modified in order to create social stability and unity.

7

The Public Response to Wrongdoing

In Chapter 6 I suggested that the basic attitudes of respect, compassion, and real goodwill that ground the paradigm of forgiveness, extended to all persons equally, lead to a moral theory structured in reference to a central principle of justice. This principle is that all persons ought to be secured the most fundamental interests in life compatible with like benefits for all, and that no individual ought to be required to sacrifice an important interest so that others can benefit in less important ways. I also argued that a moral theory based on this central principle will avoid some of the serious structural difficulties that arise in desert-based moral theories endorsed by some retributivists. Finally, I explained briefly how the justice-based moral theory that emerges in the paradigm of forgiveness can account for some of the central moral convictions in the domain of distributive justice that we often express in terms of desert. Our central concern in this book is, of course, with the domain of retributive justice.

We are now in a position to consider the implications of the paradigm of forgiveness, as I have developed it so far, for the laws and social practices that we ought to adopt as a public response to wrongdoing. In other words, we are ready to ask what kinds of laws and social policies a properly forgiving society would endorse. In this chapter I argue that the basic attitudes that ground the paradigm of forgiveness and the moral theory that they entail lead to a public response to wrongdoing that has three central components: prevention of wrongdoing, restitution for primary harm, and restitution for secondary harm. If certain conditions are met, the third component will include a practice of legal punishment. (Refinements of the second two components will be considered in Chapter 8.)

I also argue that the moral analysis of the public response to wrongdoing that emerges in the paradigm of forgiveness explains many of the central moral convictions that we often express in terms of desert in the domain of retributive justice. This analysis will complete the argument that the justice-based moral theory embedded in the paradigm of forgiveness offers a *preinstitutional* account of a wide range of the moral convictions that we often express in terms of desert at the same time that it avoids the structural difficulties that arise in desert-based moral theories.

Retributivists endorse a practice of legal punishment as an appropriate public response to criminal wrongdoing, and they have offered a variety of moral arguments to justify this practice. Although advocates of the paradigm of forgiveness also endorse a practice of legal punishment under certain circumstances, they do so for reasons that are very different from those advanced by retributivists. It is important to recognize that different justifications of punishment have different implications for the way in which a practice of punishment ought to be structured. Therefore I will examine some of the central justifications of punishment that have been proposed by retributivists (and others), and argue that we have reason to prefer the justification of this practice that emerges in the paradigm of forgiveness, along with its implications for the structure of our system of criminal justice.

A further concern of this chapter is to address John Kekes' important claim (cited in Chapter 5) that what he refers to as "choice-morality" fails to respond adequately to the evil we find in the world. Kekes distinguishes between two types of moral theories, which he calls "choice-morality" and "character-morality," and argues that only character-morality provides us with adequate conceptual resources to face evil and protect innocent persons from undeserved harm. Briefly, moral theories that fall under the heading of choice-morality share two central characteristics. First, they are egalitarian. They hold that all persons have equal intrinsic worth and ought to have equal rights to develop their various potentials. Second, these theories hold that persons can legitimately be held accountable only for the wrong actions that they have chosen to commit. Theories that fall under the heading of choice-morality adopt what Kekes calls the "soft reaction" to evil. The problem with the soft reaction to evil, according to Kekes, is that much of the evil in the world is unchosen, and therefore choice-morality leaves a wide range of harmful behavior unchecked. Further, by insisting that we all be granted equal rights to develop our potentials, choice-morality actually *promotes* evil by guaranteeing to those who produce it the opportunity to act on their vices. Choice-morality also devotes considerable attention to the sympathetic understanding of wrongdoers, because it insists that we attempt to determine whether they *chose* to commit their wrong acts and are therefore properly held accountable. But in doing so, Kekes contends, it does "not give sufficient weight to the fundamental moral fact that great evil has been done. *That* should occupy the center of our moral attention; *that* is what it is the task of morality to prevent from happening."[1]

Kekes argues that because of these failings, we should reject choice-morality and replace it with character-morality. Character-morality holds that persons have different degrees of intrinsic worth, based on their moral merit. Moral merit is the basis for desert, and to a large extent, burdens and benefits should be allocated according to desert. Because so much evil is unchosen, character-morality holds that we should not focus so much on determining whether wrong acts were chosen, but rather on whether the perpetrators of wrong acts have flawed characters, or enduring dispositions to act in ways that are destructive to others. Kekes argues that persons should be held accountable for both chosen and unchosen wrongs although they deserve a greater degree of censure for violations they have chosen to commit. Accordingly, he redefines moral agency simply as the capacity of normal human beings to cause good and evil. The type of accountability for wrong actions endorsed by character-morality constitutes the "hard reaction" to evil. Kekes says that "from a moral point of view, the salient fact is that there are many people who cause simple evil because their characters are flawed. If we want to minimize evil, we must be concerned with that. We must want to curtail their activities, to hold them up as examples to avoid, and to use our influence to stop others from becoming like them. Moral censure is the clearest expression of our wanting all this."[2] Finally, he underscores the importance of the distinction between the soft and hard reactions to evil by saying that "the disagreement between them discloses one of the deepest moral divisions of our age."[3]

Given that the paradigm of forgiveness is egalitarian, encourages us to have understanding and compassion for offenders, and holds that we are morally accountable only for those actions that we have chosen (or ought to have chosen) to perform, it constitutes a version of choice-morality and incorporates the soft reaction to evil. It is therefore

[1] John Kekes, *Facing Evil*, p. 98.
[2] *Ibid.*, p. 101.
[3] *Ibid.*, p. 85.

important that we respond to Kekes' challenge here, and address the
question of whether the paradigm of forgiveness adequately protects persons from evil, or, in the terminology I will adopt here, from unnecessary
harm. In general, it seems natural to wonder whether the paradigm of
forgiveness, as desirable as it sounds, is strong enough or tough enough
to address the serious and extensive damaging behavior that we find in
the world. Throughout this chapter and the next, I argue that not only
does the paradigm of forgiveness do a reasonably good job of responding
to offenders and protecting innocent persons from wrongfully inflicted
harm, we also have some reason to believe that it will be more effective
than retributive positions in this regard.

PREVENTION OF WRONGDOING AND OTHER KINDS OF DAMAGING BEHAVIOR

Given that the paradigm of forgiveness is based on the attitudes of
respect, compassion, and real goodwill extended to all persons equally,
in the context of this paradigm we will be fundamentally concerned to
prevent unnecessary harm for all persons. We will be concerned to protect innocent persons from unnecessary harm, and we will be concerned
to protect both actual and potential offenders from unnecessary suffering as well. Because punishment and moral censure are generally very
painful for those who are forced to endure them, we will be motivated
to avoid these responses to the extent that we are able to do so without incurring equal or more serious burdens for others. Therefore we
will not endorse Kekes' hard reaction to evil. Punishing and censuring
offenders arguably is one way in which we can help to protect innocent
persons from harm, and many discussions of response to wrongdoing
have been centrally focused on this technique. However, in the context
of the paradigm of forgiveness, the ideal response to the wrongdoing
and damaging behaviors that we know may occur is to try to *prevent*
them from ever taking place. To the extent that we can prevent damaging behavior from occurring, we can improve the lives of both those
who would have been victims of this kind of behavior and those who
would have perpetrated it. While utilitarians share this primary interest
in preventing damaging behavior, many utilitarians have focused on preventing criminal violations through a practice of legal punishment.[4] In

[4] Of course, some utilitarians have focused on preventing damaging behavior primarily through a practice of rehabilitation, but our discussion of prevention will be more
extensive and diverse than these discussions as well.

the context of the paradigm of forgiveness, however, *nonpunitive* means of preventing wrongdoing and other forms of damaging behavior will be a central concern. We will therefore have both reason and motive to devote far more time and energy than we have to date to examining and instituting nonpunitive methods for preventing harmful behavior.

Kekes is careful to distinguish between harm *simpliciter* and "undeserved harm." He points out that the suffering we take on voluntarily to achieve some further end, such as the discomfort we endure at the dentist's office, is not undeserved harm. He also argues that proportional harm inflicted on those who exhibit morally flawed characters through harmful action is deserved harm, and is therefore a good thing rather than something to be avoided. In contrast, in the context of the paradigm of forgiveness we will not regard *any* suffering as intrinsically deserved harm, and we will regret all forms of suffering that sentient beings experience – whether those beings are victims of wrongdoing, perpetrators of wrongdoing, or simply unlucky beings who happen to be in harm's way. However, we will recognize that it is sometimes necessary to allocate burdens to persons in order to prevent greater or equal suffering for others. (I will argue shortly that in order to achieve this end, we must often allocate unavoidable suffering on the basis of fault.) We will also, of course, accept forms of suffering that persons take on voluntarily as necessary or expedient means to the ends they are seeking. In all other cases, we will have both reason and motive to prevent harm from falling on anyone. I will refer to any harm that is not undertaken voluntarily to secure a further end, that is not necessary to prevent greater or equal harm to others, and that can be controlled in some way by human agency as "unnecessary harm." Specifically, it is unnecessary harm that we will be concerned to prevent in the context of the paradigm of forgiveness.

In thinking about nonpunitive methods of preventing unnecessary harm, it will be helpful to consider some of the causal factors that contribute to wrongful or damaging behavior. Sadly, one of the reasons that persons sometimes harm one another is that they lack the material resources to maintain a minimally decent standard of living. At times, persons take the possessions of others by stealth or by force simply to meet their basic needs.[5] This kind of activity occurs from the local level

---

[5] There was recently a case in Iowa of a woman who was caught breaking into houses, and when questioned, she said "Well what was I supposed to do?" She had been laid off from her job and had been so far unsuccessful in obtaining any kind of social assistance.

(through individual acts of theft) to the international level (through acts of warfare). In some cases, actions of this sort are justified, and in other cases they involve various sorts of wrongdoing, but wrongdoing that is mitigated by the offender's state of desperation. In any case, harmful behavior of this sort can be prevented if we take global, national, and local action to provide all persons with at least a minimally decent standard of living. If we hold the morally integrated attitudes of respect, compassion, and real goodwill for all persons, we will have reason and motive to do what we can in this regard. It is also worth noting that effective global action to mitigate climate change is one step that we must take immediately if we are to avoid widespread human desperation.

Continuing with this line of discussion, persons sometimes engage in destructive behavior as a result of genetic or congenital mental illness, whether the illness renders them incapable of conforming to moral requirements or results only in a diminished capacity to do so. In either case, we can limit unnecessary harm of this sort if we regard mental illnesses in the same way that we regard physical illnesses. Here we must eliminate the stigma that we attach to mental illness, and regard the persons who suffer from it with more respect and compassion. By doing so we can be more effective in encouraging these persons to seek help. We can also devote more effort and resources to researching medical, pharmacological, and therapeutic methods for alleviating these illnesses, and to developing techniques for supervising the mentally ill that maximize their freedoms and opportunities but at the same time protect innocent persons from unreasonable risks of harm.

Third, damaging behavior often results from mental or emotional difficulties caused by environmental sources of stress. Abusive or stressful situations in persons' lives can lead them to inflict unnecessary harm on others. As before, these situations may provide exculpating excuses for harmful actions or they may simply result in diminished capacity to conform to moral standards. In any case, there is much we can do in this area to prevent unnecessary harm. Again, we can take mental and emotional difficulties as seriously as we take physical difficulties. We can ensure that all persons have access to adequate health care for both mental and physical complaints, and we can devote resources to researching methods for alleviating both of these kinds of suffering. Further, we can attempt to ensure that there is as little stigma attached to seeing a therapist or entering a mental health program as there is to seeing a physician. Providing high-quality care to those who are experiencing mental and emotional difficulties will reduce instances in which these persons harm others.

We can also work to prevent the stressful environmental conditions that cause persons to experience mental and emotional difficulties. Children are particularly vulnerable to environmental sources of stress because they lack the resources to deal with them effectively. It is therefore especially important that we work to improve conditions in our families and school systems. We can find ways to educate current and prospective parents about the substantial, lasting damage that physical, sexual, verbal, and emotional abuse inflicts on their children. At the same time, in the context of the paradigm of forgiveness we will have compassion for parents who are abusing their children, and we will respect them as valuable moral agents who are capable of change. Rather than judging and condemning them and thereby giving them motivation to hide their behavior, we will provide them with easily accessible sources of help. If persons who are engaging in abusive behavior are regarded with respect, compassion, and real goodwill, they will be encouraged to take advantage of opportunities of this sort. Clearly we must also have effective programs in place that allow us to intervene compassionately in situations in which parents are seriously damaging or endangering their children.

In the schools, we must educate faculty and staff to have respect and compassion for each student. Teachers set an example for students, and teachers who are encouraging, kind, and respectful toward students can have a significant impact in improving their lives. In addition, some schools have already adopted programs that are effective in preventing bullying behaviors among students, and we can make sure that other schools follow suit. Recent school shootings are a dramatic demonstration of the unnecessary harm that can result from this kind of stress. Further, we can ensure that schools provide nonjudgmental drug and alcohol rehabilitation programs for students who have problems of this sort. And we can reduce negative pressures on students by ensuring that our schools have effective counseling programs to help all students find career paths that are well suited to their interests and abilities and to address other kinds of difficulties that students may be experiencing.

Both children and adults can suffer significant stress from neighborhood environments in which poverty, racial tensions, widespread unemployment, drug and alcohol abuse, and violence are prevalent. Again, if we have respect, compassion, and real goodwill for all persons, we will attempt to alleviate these conditions. We can start to clean up these neighborhoods, improve their schools, offer significant tax breaks to companies that locate in these areas and employ the residents, establish drug and alcohol rehabilitation centers, offer athletic and artistic programs for children and adults, and so on. Rather than orienting ourselves toward judging and condemning persons from these areas who engage in wrongful behaviors, we can first attempt to prevent moral violations by taking the kinds of actions that emerge from the morally integrated attitudes of respect, compassion, and real goodwill extended to all persons equally.

Adults are also often subjected to environmental sources of stress in their work environments, and there is much we can do to eliminate this source of stress. As a matter of common decency, as well as a means of alleviating this kind of stress, workers must be treated with the kind of concern and respect that is endorsed in the paradigm of forgiveness. Providing workers with reasonable expectations, fair pay for their work, reasonable benefits, and general respect for their abilities and contributions will go a long way in this regard.

Persons who are members of groups that are subject to discrimination, persons who are disabled or disfigured in some way, and persons who simply lack the ability or opportunity to succeed in our society may also be subject to the significant stress that results from being shunned or held in contempt by others. It is important to notice that persons who hold these scornful attitudes are adopting the perspective of judgment. We can help to alleviate this source of stress by combating various forms of discrimination and also, significantly, by encouraging persons to adopt the perspective of identification and the attitudes of respect, compassion, and real goodwill embodied in the paradigm of forgiveness.

In his discussion of unchosen evil, Kekes offers a very insightful analysis of how malevolence can emerge in persons who have experienced environmental sources of stress. He says of these persons that "they may realistically view the past as an unrelieved stretch of humiliation and the future as the continuation of the same," and that "they are handicapped in various ways ... [and] forced to face it in their constant and inevitable contacts with the defenders of the standards of which they fall short." He acknowledges that there are a limited number of ways in which they can cope with this situation, one of which is by developing malevolence. He then describes malevolence as follows: "It involves saying no to life – to their own, to the lives of people like them, and certainly to the lives of those who adversely judge them. It is not a resigned no but a hate-filled, resentful, enraged no."[6] Persons who have been abused as children,

---

[6] John Kekes, *Facing Evil*, p. 80.

bullied at school, humiliated in their social or work environments, or generally subjected to the rejection and contempt of others may well react in this way, and there is no question that such malevolence often results in very damaging behavior. But what is puzzling about Kekes' position is that after developing this sensitive and compelling analysis of malevolence, he proposes to respond to it with more public condemnation and censure. Heaping additional humiliation and contempt on those who have already had to endure these things to the extent that they maliciously harm others seems only to add fuel to the fire. It seems that it would be more compassionate and respectful, and also much more effective in preventing unnecessary harm, to make a sustained and diligent effort to alleviate the sources of stress that lead to malevolence in the first place. The Allies recognized this point as they responded to Germany and Japan after World War II, and to good effect. Many historians have argued that the utter humiliation of Germany after World War I was a major causal factor in the malevolence that this nation unleashed during the Nazi era.

Finally, and perhaps most fundamentally, wrongful behavior is often caused by a simple failure to take our moral standards seriously enough, or to devote sufficient attention to cultivating morally worthy attitudes in ourselves. Whether our wrongful behavior is a form of negligence, weakness of will, or intentional violation, sufficient attention to the fundamental importance of our moral standards would prevent us from committing the wrong. As we have noted, many retributivists hold that a strong moral community will adopt retributive reactive attitudes and retributive punishment as an expression of its opposition to wrongdoing and its strong commitment to its moral standards. It is undeniably important for the moral community to maintain a strong commitment to its moral standards and to those who are harmed by moral violations. However, it is important to recognize that a genuine concern for the victims of wrongful behavior will lead to a strenuous effort to prevent violations from occurring in the first place.

A deep and abiding concern for those who will be hurt by moral violations will lead us to work diligently to cultivate morally worthy attitudes in ourselves so that we do not harm others. By inculcating the morally integrated attitudes of respect, compassion, and real goodwill in ourselves, we not only reduce the risk that we will harm others, we also go some distance toward improving the lives of others and setting a good example for everyone to follow. Meditation techniques for inculcating compassionate attitudes have been practiced for centuries to excellent effect in Eastern cultures, and are currently being made available to Westerners.[7] A genuine concern for those who will be hurt by moral violations will also lead us to articulate our moral standards clearly, and to be vigorous in expressing our commitment to them on a regular basis. We can articulate our moral standards and the great importance we attach to them in a variety of ways, ranging from ratifying political documents that express these standards to discussing our moral commitments with other individuals. It is important to recognize that we need not resort to resenting and condemning persons in order to express these commitments. We can always articulate them in a constructive, respectful, and compassionate manner, and in the context of the paradigm of forgiveness, we will be enjoined to do so. A sincere desire to protect persons from unnecessary harm will also lead us to express our concern for those who may be harmed by moral violations – clearly, often, and *before* the violations have taken place. And it will lead us to develop clear, readily accessible regulations, policies, and procedures to prevent harmful behavior. Regulation is damaging when it encumbers our freedom to act in ways that do not produce a significant risk of harm, but it is needed for activities that bear a serious risk of harm to others.

We can illustrate these points by considering examples on the local, national, and international levels. First, consider a case in which a professor significantly impedes the progress of one of his graduate students who has filed a grievance against him for discrimination and harassment, simply because he resents his student for embarrassing him in this manner. While this act would clearly be wrong, resentment and moral censure of the professor will be of limited use to the student, as the damage to her career path has already been done. In a moral community that is truly concerned about the welfare of its members, we will see a disciplined effort to prevent these kinds of harm. The college or university will institute mandatory training programs for faculty concerning issues of discrimination, harassment, and retaliation. Deans and department chairs will find natural opportunities to remind faculty of the importance of keeping students' career paths on track, and faculty members will remind each other of these points when they suspect that a situation of this sort is arising. There will also be clear regulations, policies, and procedures in place to help prevent the occurrence of such actions.

---

[7] A highly effective technique for beginners is the practice of *tonglen*, or sending and receiving. A clear description of this practice can be found in Yongey Mingyur Rinpoche's *Joyful Wisdom*, pp. 196–197, as well as in several other Buddhist texts.

Likewise, when we consider the collapse of the U.S. financial markets in 2008, we can see that a genuine concern for the victims of wrongful behavior requires, at a fundamental level, a diligent and continuous effort to prevent wrongful behavior. Arguably, the deregulation of these markets and the unbridled greed of big business executives were major causal factors in the collapse of these markets. This collapse resulted in widespread, serious harm, not only to U.S. citizens, but also to people all over the world. Individuals lost their jobs, their homes, significant proportions of the savings they worked to accumulate over the course of their lives, their ability to educate their children or to retire, and so on. Further, the enormous government bailout package will burden taxpayers for generations to come. However, at this point, resentment and moral censure of government and business leaders will do a limited amount of good. A healthy moral community would have been much more focused on prevention, insisting on regulation of the markets; expressing serious concern for those who could be hurt; reminding executives of the need to limit their own salaries and to be more generous with their employees, shareholders, and customers; passing legislation requiring them to do so; and so on. When we are genuinely concerned about the potential victims of immoral behavior, we will watch very carefully and continuously for ways to prevent the wrongful behavior from occurring in the first place.

On the international level, let us look briefly at the global war on terror. When terrorist attacks such as the destruction of the World Trade Center are committed, we tend to react with intense moral anger and a strong desire to retaliate. But again, a real concern for potential victims of such horrendous acts will lead, fundamentally, to a concerted and sustained effort to prevent them. It will lead to much more extensive efforts at international cooperation than we have made to date – efforts to understand the needs, feelings, and concerns of persons of other cultures; efforts to help the peoples of other nations and to form bonds of friendships with them; efforts to learn from other cultures and to engage with them in mutually beneficial projects; and so on. If we, as a nation, can cultivate the morally worthy attitudes of respect, compassion, and real goodwill for all persons, we will naturally take actions of this sort, and I think we can reasonably expect that they will help to prevent war and terrorism. On the other hand, responses of judgment, hatred, and retaliation are not only of limited use, they also often tend to escalate the tensions that already exist and therefore to result in further harm. Thus it seems that on the local, national, and international levels, a moral community is best maintained, at least primarily, not through the negative reactions of resentment and retributive punishment, but rather through the positive attitudes and preventive measures endorsed by the paradigm of forgiveness.

Finally, civil commitment is a measure of the last resort that we can use to prevent individuals from inflicting unnecessary harm on persons. If there is strong evidence that an individual poses a clear and present danger to himself or others, we can legitimately confine him to prevent the harm from occurring. The paradigm of forgiveness will endorse civil commitment when it is really necessary, provided that it is carried out with respect and compassion for the person who is confined and with the least possible infringement on his legitimate interests.

Clearly we should not assume that this discussion of nonpunitive methods of preventing unnecessary harm has been exhaustive. Rather, in the context of the paradigm of forgiveness we will want to give this matter much more thought. We will have reason and motive to pursue local, national, and global initiatives to study further the causal conditions that contribute to wrongful or damaging behavior, and to determine effective means of mitigating these conditions. The contributions that the empirical sciences have to make to this endeavor cannot be overstated. Research in economics, criminology, sociology, psychology, psychiatry, social work, political science, and many other areas will be critically important as we develop this component of the paradigm of forgiveness more fully.

To summarize, then, in the context of the paradigm of forgiveness, the first component of the public response to wrongdoing is prevention. Kekes is correct in suggesting that morality is fundamentally concerned with preventing harm to those who should not have to bear it. However, if my reasoning here has been correct, he is mistaken in believing that "moral censure is the clearest expression of our wanting all of this." A genuine concern to protect persons from unnecessary harm will not lead us directly to resentment, moral censure, and retributive punishment. Instead, it will lead us at a very basic level to take the kinds of nonpunitive steps listed here to prevent this type of harm. Further, as I have suggested in our discussion of retributive reactive attitudes, and as I will argue in the remainder of this book, *retributive responses to wrongdoing themselves* inflict unnecessary harm on persons. We can protect persons from unnecessary harm *without* the additional layer of suffering that accompanies resentment, self-condemnation, moral censure, and retributive punishment. Thus, retributivism is part of the problem rather than part of the solution when we address our fundamental concern of protecting persons from unnecessary harm.

The preventive measures suggested here should go some distance toward meeting Kekes' concern that we will not be able to face evil adequately in the context of choice-morality. Of course, we cannot expect that our nonpunitive efforts to prevent wrongful behavior will be completely effective. We must therefore go on to determine which laws and social policies we ought to adopt in response to the wrongful behavior that will certainly take place. I will turn to this task in the remainder of this chapter.

RESTITUTION FOR PRIMARY HARM

Let us now consider the laws and social policies we ought to adopt when persons have engaged in wrongful or damaging behavior and inflicted unnecessary harm on others as a result. First, let us recall from the discussion in Chapter 2 that resentment and forgiveness are generally responses to wrongs done to us personally, or to others with whom we have some kind of personal connection. The public response to wrongful behavior that emerges in the paradigm of forgiveness, therefore, does not involve forgiveness per se. As I have argued, it is the injured person's prerogative to determine for herself whether or not she will forgive her offender. But as I also noted in Chapter 2, governments as well as individuals are responsible for endorsing and adopting morally worthy attitudes. Our laws and social policies should uniformly evince morally worthy attitudes, and those who carry out our laws and social practices should adopt these attitudes as well. As we develop a public response to situations in which persons wrongfully inflict harm on one another in the context of the paradigm of forgiveness, we must clearly regard the person who inflicts the harm with respect, compassion, and real goodwill. However, as I have argued, the attitudes of respect, compassion, and real goodwill must be extended not only to the offender, but to all persons equally. In determining the morally appropriate response to wrongful or damaging behavior, then, we must invoke our principle of justice, which states that each individual ought to be secured the most fundamental interests in life compatible with like benefits for all, and that no individual ought to be required to sacrifice a significant interest so that others can benefit in less important ways.

In *An Introduction to the Principles of Morals and Legislation*, Jeremy Bentham distinguishes between primary harm, which is harm to the immediate victim(s) of the act in question and to those who have a specific connection with her, and secondary harm, which is harm that befalls the members of the victim's community, whether or not they have any specific connection with her. In this section I will consider how we ought to respond to the fact that an individual has inflicted primary harm on another (or others), and in the final section of this chapter I will consider how we ought to respond to the fact that an individual has inflicted secondary harm on the members of his community.

Although primary harm comes in many different varieties, we are generally familiar with this type of harm. Some forms of primary harm are relatively trivial, involving small financial losses or minor damage to property. Others, of course, are much more serious. Persons may assault, rape, or murder each other; injure each other severely through various kinds of reckless or negligent behavior; steal or embezzle large amounts of money; negligently cause one another large financial losses; and so on. Victims of seriously damaging acts are likely to endure various forms of emotional suffering, which may extend well beyond the time required to recover from their physical injuries and material setbacks. Further, as Bentham points out, when serious harm is inflicted on one individual, indirect or derivative forms of harm are often inflicted on others as well. To return to a case considered in Chapter 2, the father of a child who is paralyzed by a drunk driver is likely to experience two kinds of derivative harm. First, he will be emotionally devastated by the damage that has been done to his child. Second, his own interests will be adversely affected as he must now sacrifice much more of his time, money, and attention to meet his child's additional needs. Primary harm, as Bentham understands it, and as I will understand it here, incorporates all of these kinds of harm.

In our legal system we address situations in which one person inflicts primary harm on another through the law of torts. The paradigm of forgiveness requires that we respond to this kind of situation in a manner that overlaps considerably with our current system of tort law. In the context of the paradigm of forgiveness, the appropriate response to situations in which one person inflicts primary harm on another will depend on the circumstances. In many cases, persons who inflict primary harm on others do so wrongfully. They *ought not* to have performed (or have failed to perform) the act that resulted in harm to the injured party, whether they did so purposefully, knowingly, recklessly, or negligently. In this type of situation it seems clear that the person who wrongfully inflicts harm on another ought to compensate the victim for her loss, at least to the extent that he is reasonably able to do so. Here we encounter one of our central moral convictions in the domain of retributive justice that we often express in terms of desert.[8] As Joel Feinberg writes, "We say that persons deserve compensation for harm wrongfully inflicted by others" and that "the wrongdoer deserves to be held liable for the harm that he has caused; he deserves to be forced to compensate his innocent (or relatively innocent) victim."[9]

The justice-based moral theory embodied in the paradigm of forgiveness also yields the conclusion that our laws ought to require those who wrongfully inflict primary harm on others to compensate them for their losses. As we saw with some of our most central desert claims in the domain of distributive justice, this conclusion is easily reached when we recognize that each of us has a significant interest in having the opportunity to make the most of our own lives through our own choices and efforts. Consider a situation in which A has unjustly inflicted primary harm on B. Once this act has been committed, someone must make a sacrifice. Either B must absorb the loss, or A or an innocent third party must take on the burden of making the loss good. If we institute a practice in which those who are responsible for bringing about the loss are required to make restitution for that harm, we create a situation in which each person has the opportunity to avoid making extensive sacrifices in this regard. We thereby secure for each of us the opportunity to make the most of our own lives simply by making good choices. On the other hand, if we adopt a practice in which B or an innocent third party is required to absorb the loss, we deny persons the opportunity to make the most of their own lives through their own choices and efforts. This latter practice gives us no opportunity to avoid the harm that results from wrongdoing, and we are likely to be extensively hindered in the pursuit of our own life plans by other persons' wrong choices.[10] (Again we should notice here that A cannot rightfully wait until after he has made his wrong choice, and then argue that he has the same interest in keeping whatever would be offered as restitution as B has in receiving it. In this case, we could never secure for persons the fundamental interest in being able to make the most of our lives through our own choices and

---

[8] Here I am using the term "retributive justice" broadly, to refer to response to wrongdoing in general, rather than simply in the context of the criminal law.

[9] Joel Feinberg, *Doing and Deserving*. The first part of the quotation is from p. 74, the second part from p. 75.

[10] For a similar analysis of restitution, see Edmund Pincoffs, "Does Responsibility Have a Future?"

efforts.) Thus the justice-based moral theory embedded in the paradigm of forgiveness holds that those who wrongfully inflict primary harm on others ought to be required to make restitution for that harm, subject to reasonable limits of sacrifice, as I will argue later. It therefore explains, at a preinstitutional level, a central intuition in the domain of retributive justice that we often express in terms of desert.

It is important to recognize, however, that in the context of the paradigm of forgiveness, we do not hold that the offender intrinsically deserves to suffer, or that his suffering is desirable or good. Rather, we impose this burden on him regretfully, in order to prevent others from suffering in a more fundamental manner. It is also important to recognize that when we require the offender to make restitution, we do not adopt the perspective of judgment. We do not judge him to be bad, wicked, deficient in moral character, and so on, as we may do if we adopt a traditional retributive approach. Instead we adopt the perspective of identification and regard him with respect, compassion, and real goodwill.

As with the central desert claims we considered in the domain of distributive justice, the requirement that the offender make restitution for wrongfully inflicted primary harm is not absolute. Sometimes when we require an individual to make full restitution for harm that he has wrongfully inflicted on another, we actually impose on him a greater burden than we would impose on others by requiring them to absorb their loss, over which they have no control. For example, suppose that a very poor person, A, becomes intoxicated and crashes his car in such a way that he damages B's expensive sports car. Suppose also that B is a billionaire and that A would have to work overtime continuously for the rest of his life to fully repay the loss. In this case it seems clear that the interest that A has at stake in being released at some point from his obligation to make full restitution for this loss is more fundamental that B's interest in being fully compensated, although some restitution is certainly in order. Thus there is a limit of sacrifice that can legitimately be required of the offender. Further, we can conclude that this limit is relational: it depends not only on the situation of the offender, but also on the situation of the injured person. Although it may be difficult to determine exactly what the limit of sacrifice is in a given situation, our guiding concern of securing for each individual the most fundamental interests in life compatible with like benefits for all provides us with a theoretical framework for making judgments of this sort.

Although the central concern of this book is response to wrongdoing, and I have derived from the paradigm of forgiveness the social practice that responds to wrongfully inflicted primary harm, let us extend our discussion of tort law a bit further at this point. The justice-based moral theory embedded in the paradigm of forgiveness, again coupled with the recognition that we each have a significant interest in having the opportunity to make the most of our lives through our own choices and efforts, leads to a justification of another principle of liability in the law of torts – that of strict liability in cases of nonreciprocal risks. Jules Coleman explains the difference between strict liability and liability for wrongfully inflicted harm as follows: "In fault liability, the costs of accidents that are no one's fault are the burden of victims; in strict liability, they are the burden of injurers."[11] In some situations, we allow, and ought to allow, the pursuit of activities that carry a risk of significant harm to others *even after* all justly required precautions have been taken. The justice-based moral theory in the paradigm of forgiveness yields the conclusion that strict liability is sometimes morally appropriate in this type of case. If we impose strict liability on those who pursue, for their own profit or enjoyment, activities that create a nonreciprocal risk of harm to others, then we secure for all of us the opportunity to make the most of our lives through our own choices and efforts. By requiring those who pursue these risky activities for their own profit or enjoyment to bear the associated costs, we provide for each person the opportunity to avoid these costs if he wishes to do so.

Of course, harm may occur in situations in which there is no wrongdoing and in which there are no nonreciprocal risks. In cases of this sort, in the context of the paradigm of forgiveness we have no reason to require restitution. Perhaps the injured person will incur losses that are more than he can reasonably be expected to bear on his own, but the person who inflicts the harm has no special obligation to make good the injured person's losses in this case. Rather, society as a whole has a responsibility to ensure that the injured person does not fall below a minimally decent standard of living.

Again, we have reason to believe that the practice of requiring restitution for primary harm that we have outlined in this section will go some distance toward protecting persons from unnecessary harm. It will therefore help to alleviate Kekes' concern that choice-morality will be

---

[11] Jules Coleman, "Theories of Tort Law," p. 10.

inadequate in preventing unnecessary or undeserved harm. Let us now leave the law of torts and turn to the more difficult and controversial arena of the criminal law.

RETRIBUTIVE THEORIES OF PUNISHMENT

In the first two sections of this chapter, I outlined the first two components of the public response to wrongdoing that emerges in the paradigm of forgiveness. The first of these components is prevention. The second is restitution for primary harm, which we address through the law of torts. Retributivists may find themselves in agreement with many of my conclusions about the law of torts, although they may arrive at these conclusions by a different line of reasoning. However, the paradigm of forgiveness will diverge more significantly from retributivist positions on the question of how we ought to respond to the kinds of offenses that are generally addressed in our system of criminal law. For retributivists, legal punishment is the appropriate response to criminal wrongdoing, and the arguments they offer to justify legal punishment have important implications for the way in which this practice ought to be structured. In this section I examine some of the most prominent arguments that retributivists have advanced to justify punishment, and I argue that they are all seriously flawed. In the next section I will develop and defend the response to criminal wrongdoing that emerges in the paradigm of forgiveness.

The definition of legal punishment has been the subject of much discussion, but for our purposes here, the definition offered by R.A. Duff will suffice. He says that "legal punishment involves the imposition of something that is intended to be burdensome or painful, on a supposed offender for a supposed crime, by a person or body who claims the authority to do so."[12] As noted in Chapter 1, one of the most striking developments in the recent philosophical analysis of punishment has been the resurgence of "strong" or "positive" retributivism in the past four decades. I cannot undertake a complete survey here of all of the retributive theories that have been proposed in this time frame. However, it will be important for our purposes to understand both the reasons for the resurgence of strong retributivism and the basic problems that arise in the best known versions of this position.

Let us begin with the evolution of theorizing about punishment in the past few decades, and the reasons for the resurgence of strong

[12] R.A. Duff, "Legal Punishment," p. 2.

retributivism.[13] Bentham's utilitarian theory of punishment clearly had a major impact on the systems of criminal law both in the United Kingdom and the United States, but critics also found serious problems with his theory. Initially the objections that were generally regarded as most troubling were that under certain circumstances, utilitarianism could sanction punishment of the innocent, severe punishment for minor crimes, and the abolition of well-accepted excusing conditions (such as the insanity defense). The early forms of "weak" or "negative" retributivism were specifically designed to correct for these defects. Perhaps the most notable proponent of weak retributivism was H.L.A. Hart. Hart argued that the *general justifying aim* of punishment is utilitarian (preventing future violations and maintaining respect for the law), but our pursuit of this aim must be constrained by distributional principles, or principles of fairness. These principles, which function as side-constraints on the general justifying aim of punishment, provide the (weakly) retributive content of Hart's theory. They assert that we must never knowingly punish the innocent, that the severity of the punishment must be (at most) proportional to the gravity of the offense, and that we must recognize standard excusing conditions in the criminal law in order to give each citizen a fair opportunity to comply with the requirements of law.

While these principles of fairness initially seemed to correct for the defects of the utilitarian analysis, theorists on further reflection began to notice problems with weak retributivism as well. As Duff points out, we can raise questions both about side-constraints and about the general justifying aim of punishment.[14] Although Hart's side-constraints seem plausible, we can and should ask how they are to be justified. It seems that there are two general approaches we could take here: we could attempt to derive the side-constraints from a more basic principle of justice, or we could attempt to account for them in terms of desert. In either case, the justification of the side-constraints requires a more fully developed theory (of justice or desert), which, in turn, may well diverge from the utilitarian moral theory in its implications for the general justifying aim of the practice of legal punishment.

Further, and more seriously, the utilitarian argument for the general justifying aim of punishment can also be called into question. As we

---

[13] For two excellent discussions of this point, See R.A. Duff, "Legal Punishment," and Anthony Ellis, "Critical Study: Recent Work on Punishment." I draw heavily on both of these accounts in what follows.

[14] R.A. Duff, "Legal Punishment," pp. 8–10.

have seen, some authors hold that we have a deep-seated moral intuition that punishment for serious offenses is deserved independently of considerations of maximizing utility. Also in the context of the utilitarian justification of punishment, even with the addition of side-constraints, we may be using those who are punished as mere means to our own ends. Imagine a practice of slavery carefully constrained by principles of fairness that govern the distribution of burdensome roles – perhaps we will draw lots to determine who is to be a slave. Such a practice would still be seriously objectionable from a moral point of view. In Kantian terms, we would be violating the human dignity of the slaves and using them as mere means to our own ends of generating social benefits. In general, if a social practice is to be justified, an argument is required to show that we can legitimately pursue the desired social benefits via this practice, however fairly it is constrained in its implementation.

In addition, as I have noted, the utilitarian justification of punishment, even coupled with side-constraints, seems to adopt Strawson's objective attitude toward offenders. It seems to take the position that we must train, manage, cure, or take precautionary account of offenders, in much the same way that we would respond to a dog that is exhibiting problematic behavior. What is missing here is a genuine respect for offenders as autonomous moral agents, or as members of the moral community with a status equal to our own.

In light of objections of this sort, many theorists have abandoned both the utilitarian analysis of punishment and weak retributivism, and turned instead to strong or positive versions of retributivism. Duff defines this position as follows: "'Positive' retributivism holds not merely that we must not punish the innocent, or punish the guilty more than they deserve, but that we should punish the guilty to the extent that they deserve: penal desert constitutes not just a necessary, but an in-principle sufficient reason for punishment..."[15] The idea here is that it is in some sense intrinsically appropriate from a moral point of view to inflict suffering on those who have committed serious violations without justification or exculpating excuse. From the perspective of the paradigm of forgiveness, we can anticipate that these theories will be unsuccessful. If we recognize that the offender remains a valuable human being in spite of his offense, we will hold that the morally appropriate attitudes to adopt toward the offender are respect, compassion, and real goodwill. In this case, we will not claim that the offender *deserves* punishment, or

---

[15] *Ibid.*, p. 10.

that it is intrinsically appropriate from a moral point of view for the state to inflict suffering on him. I will argue here that the most prominent versions of strong retributivism are in fact unsuccessful. Many versions of strong retributivism have been proposed. For our purposes it will be useful to divide them into three categories: simple desert-based theories, reciprocity theories, and communicative or expressive theories.

Some persons endorse versions of strong retributivism that are simple desert-based theories. Here I am not using the term "simple" in a pejorative sense, but rather to indicate that in these theories, desert is a fundamental or primitive moral concept.[16] Simple desert-based theories are grounded in the kind of desert-based moral theories that we considered in Chapter 6. They hold that persons who are guilty of serious wrongdoing deserve to suffer punishment, and that this claim is either a fundamental desert claim or derivable from a more fundamental desert claim. Therefore we are justified in structuring the state in such a way that it includes a system of criminal law and a practice of legal punishment. The paradigm of forgiveness, of course, rejects both the perspective of judgment adopted in these desert-based theories and the notion that it is morally appropriate to harm persons as we mete out their just deserts. The paradigm of forgiveness insists instead that we adopt the perspective of identification and extend to all persons an attitude of respect, compassion, and real goodwill.

Simple desert-based theories will encounter the types of problems we outlined in Chapter 6. To review, someone wishing to claim that persons who are guilty of serious wrongdoing deserve to suffer punishment may either assert that this claim is basic and cannot be derived from another moral principle, or she may attempt to derive this specific desert claim from a broader moral principle formulated in terms of desert. In either case, difficulties will arise. If we adopt the first strategy and regard this specific desert claim as basic, the claim will lack explanatory power. We will be left wondering why offenders deserve punishment, as opposed, say, to rehabilitation or some other response, and we will wonder if our specific desert claim is mistaken, ad hoc, or an accidental generalization of our considered moral judgments. If we adopt the second strategy, we must provide a plausible, general principle of desert, and it is very difficult to do so. The most plausible proposal to date seems to be that desert is based on the possession of virtue

---

[16] For a prominent and relatively recent example of this kind of retributivist theory, see Michael Moore, "The Moral Worth of Retribution."

and vice. However, in order to employ this principle to justify a practice of legal punishment, we would have to argue, implausibly, that the state ought to adopt a specific, lexically ordered account of virtue and vice, and allocate to its citizens the burdens and benefits they deserve according to the state's assessment of how they rate against this framework. Further, whichever of these strategies we adopt, we will lack a plausible method for determining how much punishment is deserved. Finally, any broader moral theory in which such an analysis of punishment is situated will require us to weigh considerations of desert against other types of moral considerations (e.g., needs, rights, and utility) that appear to be incommensurable.

Problems of this sort have led many strong retributivists to move beyond simple desert-based theories to more complex analyses of punishment. Kant famously provides us with one such theory. He argues that in order to respect the criminal as an autonomous moral agent, we must punish him in accordance with the maxim that he freely chose to adopt in committing his offense.[17] This line of reasoning yields the *lex talionis* – the principle that the state must respond to the criminal in the same manner that the criminal chose to respond to his victim, or at least by imposing on the criminal the same quantity of harm that he imposed on his victim. However, this argument has generally been regarded as problematic as well. As I argued in Chapter 3, and as Kant himself argues in other contexts, respecting persons as autonomous moral agents entails recognizing their intrinsic worth as persons and being committed to their moral development and personal flourishing.[18] This vitally important component of respect for persons seems to conflict directly with the claim that we respect offenders by making them suffer in the same way that they have chosen to make their victims suffer. Further, as Scarre and others have argued, Kant does not seem to endorse his own reasoning whole-heartedly. Scarre comments, "Kant appears ambivalent about the conditions for respect. If he is unprepared for a murderer who tortures his victim to death to be executed with the same degree of cruelty as he inflicted on his victim, then he cannot be fully committed to the principle of proportionality. Further, by refusing to countenance savage punishments for savage crimes, he compromises his claim that we show respect for people by holding them wholly responsible for their

---

[17] For a clear discussion of this interpretation of Kant's position, see Edmund Pincoffs, *The Rationale of Legal Punishment.*
[18] See especially the second chapter of Kant's *Groundwork of the Metaphysic of Morals.*

acts."[19] Given that we ought not countenance savage punishments for savage crimes, it seems mistaken to hold that we respect offenders as autonomous moral agents by doing to them what they freely chose to do to their victims.

Several strong retributivists have therefore turned to a different strategy for explaining why it is intrinsically appropriate to punish offenders: an argument from reciprocity. Essentially these theorists argue that it is a legitimate function of the state to maintain a fair distribution of burdens and benefits among citizens, and that those who commit criminal violations gain an unfair advantage over those who comply with the law. Therefore the state may impose punishment on the criminal to negate this unfair advantage and restore a balance of burdens and benefits that is equitable. Perhaps the most notable proponent of this view is Herbert Morris. He argues that the criminal law provides each of us with an extremely important benefit – a "sphere of noninterference" from assault, murder, theft, and so on, which allows us to pursue our positive life plans. However, we can obtain this crucial benefit only if we assume the corresponding burden of restraining ourselves from violating the law. Morris then argues that "a person who violates the law has something the others have – the benefits of the system – but by renouncing the burden of self-restraint, he has acquired an unfair advantage. Matters are not even until this advantage is in some way erased. Another way of putting it is that he owes something to the others, for he has something that does not rightfully belong to him."[20]

It is plausible to claim that the state ought to maintain a fair distribution of burdens and benefits among citizens, and that criminal violations disrupt such a distribution, thereby bringing about the need for corrective measures. It is also plausible to claim that criminal offenders owe a debt to society. In the next section I will defend an analysis of the public response to criminal wrongdoing that incorporates these claims. As he presents it, however, Morris's analysis must be rejected in the context of the paradigm of forgiveness. I have argued that the appropriate attitudes to extend toward all offenders are respect, compassion, and real goodwill. If we hold these attitudes toward the offender, we will not wish to inflict harm on him if no concrete benefit can be produced for others in this manner. We will inflict suffering on him only if we must do so to

---

[19] Geoffrey Scarre, *After Evil*, p. 118. See also Margaret Falls, "Retribution, Reciprocity, and Respect for Persons."

[20] Herbert Morris, "Persons and Punishment," p. 34.

prevent an equal or greater loss for others. Thus we will not punish him simply to "make matters even" or to "erase the unfair advantage" he has gained over law-abiding citizens.

Critics have also developed at least three other compelling objections to this kind of retributivist theory. First, as Shafer-Landau argues, reciprocity theories (or "unfair advantage" theories) seriously misrepresent the kind of harm that is involved in criminal violations. He writes that "it is a mistake to think that the fundamental wrong associated with most crimes against persons is a kind of free-riding offense. Rape isn't wrong because of the advantage the rapist enjoys with regard to all other law-abiding citizens, but because of the harm imposed on the victim."[21] Even if we were justified in inflicting punishment as retribution, it seems that we should inflict it as retribution for the wrong that the offender has perpetrated against the victim, rather than for the unfair advantage he has gained over law-abiding citizens.

Second, as Margaret Falls points out, it is far from clear that we should regard the offender as having an unfair advantage over law-abiding citizens. If we accept the Socratic claim that losing our moral integrity is the worst harm we can suffer, then the offender is actually *worse off* than the rest of us. Falls writes that "the theory of reciprocity does not work within the tradition that says willing the moral good is the highest human good and therefore doing evil harms the evildoer."[22] While this point may seem idealistic, it also seems correct. Few of us would willingly trade places with the murderer, rapist, or kidnapper, even if we knew that we would never be apprehended for our offense. Nor would we ever say (even to ourselves), "That's not fair! He got to commit a murder, and I did not!"

A third reason to doubt the adequacy of Morris's position is that it fails to yield a plausible method for determining the severity of the punishment. As many authors have argued, on Morris's analysis it seems that the severity of the punishment should be proportional to the extent of the burden that law-abiding citizens bear in restraining themselves from violating the law that the offender has violated. However, most of us experience little or no inclination to commit very serious crimes such as murder, mayhem, rape, or kidnapping, while many of us struggle on a daily basis (often unsuccessfully) to prevent ourselves from committing minor violations such as speeding or jaywalking. It seems, then, that

---

[21] Russ Shafer-Landau, "Retributivism and Desert," p. 205.
[22] Margaret Falls, "Retribution, Reciprocity, and Respect for Persons," p. 31.

this analysis would require serious punishments for trivial offenses and minor punishments for the worst kinds of crimes.[23]

George Sher recognizes this last difficulty in Morris's position and attempts to restructure the reciprocity argument so as to avoid it. Sher suggests that the offender's unfair advantage over law-abiding citizens should be calibrated not by "the strength of one's inclination to transgress," but rather by "the strength of the moral prohibition he has violated." In this way we could ensure that the severity of the punishment would be proportional to the gravity of the offense. To obtain this result, Sher reformulates the argument as follows: "A person who acts wrongly does gain a significant measure of extra liberty: what he gains is freedom from the demands of the prohibition he violates. Because others take that prohibition seriously, they lack a similar liberty. And as the strength of the prohibition increases, so too does the freedom from it which its violation entails."[24]

However, this position also seems unsatisfactory, as it is difficult to understand exactly how the offender gains extra liberty by comparison with law-abiding citizens. The most straightforward interpretation of this claim seems to be that the offender gains extra liberty simply by allowing himself to commit the violation, whereas law-abiding citizens assume the burden of restraining themselves from doing so. But this interpretation seems to return us directly to Morris's position, with its attendant difficulties. Alternatively, we might say that the offender gains extra liberty, or "freedom from the prohibition he violates," in that he is not bound by the prohibition whereas law-abiding citizens are bound by it. But as David Dolinko points out, this claim is implausible because both the offender and law-abiding citizens seem to be in the same position with respect to the prohibition. Both are morally and legally required not to commit the offense and both are "free" or able to commit the offense if they wrongfully choose to do so.[25] As a third attempt to interpret Sher's claim, we might say that the offender actually gains extra liberty *as a result* of committing his offense. For example, a bank robber may have more money to work with in pursuing his own life plans as a result of his offense, or a murderer may gain extra freedom by eliminating an individual who was encumbering his life in some

---

[23] See, for example, Richard Burgh, "Do the Guilty Deserve Punishment?" George Sher, *Desert*, pp. 80–81, and David Dolinko, "Some Thoughts about Ritributivism."

[24] George Sher, *Desert*, pp. 81–82.

[25] David Dolinko, "Some Thoughts about Retributivism," pp. 547–548.

way. On this interpretation of the argument, however, it seems that the severity of the punishment may also diverge significantly from the gravity of the offense. The bank robber may lose his ill-gotten gains, and therefore his extra liberty, very quickly, or the murderer may believe that he will be freed of an encumbrance by killing his victim, only to realize afterward that he was mistaken. If the punishment is supposed to counterbalance the extra liberty the offender gained from his offense, then it seems that under circumstances of this sort, the punishment would have to be greatly reduced.

Finally, Michael Davis has developed a proposal for determining how much of an unfair advantage, or how much extra liberty, the offender has gained. He argues that this determination should be made by estimating the amount that an ordinary person would pay in a free market economy for the prerogative of committing the type of violation in question without being punished.[26] Unfortunately, this interesting suggestion is problematic as well, as the amount that persons would pay for the prerogative of committing an offense is not directly tied to the gravity of the offense. As Shafer-Landau remarks, "it may be ... that being excused for a multimillion dollar robbery would net a higher bid than an excuse for murder."[27] Further, given Davis's proposal, it seems that if a society were to enter a prolonged economic depression, punishments would be significantly reduced, and in a time of great prosperity they would escalate dramatically, and this result is counterintuitive.

Let us now turn to the third category of retributive theories of punishment. Communicative and expressive theories are especially interesting in that they mirror most closely the arguments offered by attitudinal retributivists to justify retributive reactive attitudes. Communicative theories of punishment are based on the claim that the state has a duty to communicate to the offender a moral message regarding his offense. Further, this act of communication has a purpose, such as educating the offender about the wrongfulness of his act, or inducing him to repent, atone for the wrong, and reform his moral personality.

R.A. Duff has developed a communicative theory of punishment in some detail. He insists, first and foremost, that we must always respect the offender as an autonomous moral agent. For Duff, this requirement

---

[26] Michael Davis, "How to Make the Punishment Fit the Crime," "Criminal Desert and Unfair Advantage: What's the Connection?" and *To Make the Punishment Fit the Crime.*

[27] Russ Shafer-Landau, "Retributivism and Desert," p. 206.

rules out deterrence as a legitimate aim of punishment, as any attempt to punish as a deterrent will involve manipulation of the offender rather than rational communication with him. (I will have more to say about this claim in the next section.) Duff argues that law differs from mere tyranny in that law involves claims of obligation and authority, which in turn must be justified to those who are subject to them. Thus, law addresses the citizen as "a rational and responsible agent," and "seeks her voluntary acceptance of and obedience to requirements which themselves can be justified to her."[28] Duff then argues that the criminal trial can best be understood in light of these objectives. The criminal trial is a rational dialogue with the offender, designed both to reach an accurate judgment of her past action and to communicate and justify that judgment to her. A verdict of "guilty" serves to condemn the offender's wrong act and constitutes a symbolic punishment. In addition, the hard treatment that is involved in punishment can be justified as a kind of compulsory "secular penance." According to Duff, compulsory penance is fully continuous with the proper aims of the criminal law. It serves "to make our communicative endeavor more effective, forcing the criminal's attention onto the implications of his crime." Further, "the pain or suffering which begins as a coercive attempt to attract and direct the unrepentant criminal's attention should become the penitential pain which the repentant criminal accepts for himself."[29] According to Duff, although punishment so understood is coercive, it does not require us to abandon respect for the offender's autonomy. We are simply forcing the offender to do something that he is morally obligated to do: to consider and repent of his offense. Throughout the process, we respond to him as a rational being and an autonomous moral agent.

This line of reasoning is interesting, but it is also open to a number of serious objections. Von Hirsch has pointed out that the kind of response to wrongdoing that Duff advocates is very intrusive. He remarks: "Someone has acted inconsiderately toward me, and I respond in a critical manner. How far I may properly go in trying to elicit the morally appropriate response from him depends on the character of our relationship."[30] Von Hirsch's point here is that it is inappropriate, at least among strangers, for one person to attempt to intervene in another's inner life in order to

---

[28] R.A. Duff, *Trials and Punishments*, p. 97.
[29] *Ibid.*, p. 261. Duff's reasoning about punishment seems to me to be expressed as well here as anywhere. For further development of his thought, see his *Punishment, Communication and Community*.
[30] Andrew Von Hirsch, "Punishment, Penance, and the State," p. 72.

ensure that the latter repents and atones for a transgression that he has committed. And if it is wrong for strangers to respond to one another in this way, then it is surely wrong for the state (especially the liberal state) to do so. If anything, it actually seems that von Hirsch is being too generous here. Even in the context of very close personal relationships, it would often seem to be inappropriate to intervene in another person's inner moral life in this manner unless we have made a specific agreement in advance with that person to improve our moral characters by holding one another accountable in this way.

Reflection on the invasiveness of this response to wrongdoing leads to a further problem with the type of justification of punishment that Duff proposes. It seems odd that Duff arrives at his theory of punishment in an attempt to avoid manipulating the offender by punishing him in order to create a deterrent. Whether or not it is manipulative to impose punishment as a deterrent, it seems *clearly manipulative* to impose hard treatment on an offender in order to get him to respond to his offense internally in a morally appropriate manner. While Duff specifically rejects the utilitarian analysis of punishment on the grounds that it fails to respect persons as autonomous moral agents, in some respects he actually shows less respect for individual autonomy than John Stuart Mill. In *On Liberty,* Mill insists that we preserve for each individual complete freedom of conscience, thought, opinion, and public expression of opinion, at least in the domain of self-regarding behavior. (Note here that although the criminal offense lies in the domain of other-regarding behavior, the offender's own internal response to the crime is self-regarding.) Here again, the paradigm of forgiveness agrees with Mill, although in the context of this paradigm we arrive at this conclusion through a different line of reasoning. It seems that if respect for persons as autonomous moral agents means anything at all, it means that we must respect each (adult) individual's right to determine his own beliefs and attitudes, and to direct his own internal moral development. As I have noted, in the context of the paradigm of forgiveness it is a morally salient feature of persons that we can lead meaningful lives only as authors of our own choices and attitudes.

Duff points out correctly that the offender is morally obligated to consider and repent of his wrong. Nevertheless, we cannot infer from this fact that we are justified in using coercion to get him to do so. Presumably we are justified in using (some) coercion to get people to comply with their moral obligations when, by violating those obligations, they would cause significant harm to others. However, there is a wide range of moral obligations that are not properly enforced by coercion. For example, no one may appropriately use force to get us to develop various virtues in ourselves, to hold a particular set of moral beliefs even if they happen to be true, to be ideally honest about our thoughts and feelings in our interpersonal relationships, to develop our talents, or to do our share of the housework. It is far from clear, then, that the state is justified in using force to get offenders to adopt appropriate attitudes toward their own violations.

Finally, even if these problems could be solved (and I do not believe they can be), we can question whether undertaking a penance, understood as hard treatment, is actually a morally appropriate response to our own wrongdoing. I argued in Chapter 4 that when we have sufficiently completed the process of addressing the wrong, self-forgiveness rather than self-condemnation is the morally appropriate response to our own wrongdoing. The process of addressing the wrong includes acknowledging the wrong and taking responsibility for having committed it, understanding why it was wrong, examining and attempting to eradicate the wrongful attitudes and behavior patterns that lead to the offense, and apologizing and making substantive amends to those we have harmed. Although we should be sobered by the fact that we have committed the wrong and should work diligently at the process of addressing it, in the context of the paradigm of forgiveness we do not engage in self-flagellation or self-contempt. Rather, we recognize that in spite of what we have done we still have the valuable capacity for moral growth, choice, and awareness, and we proceed to use that capacity in a constructive manner. It is only when we conflate ourselves with our own wrong actions and attitudes that we will be drawn toward self-contempt and then self-flagellation. If this line of reasoning is correct, then it is not only unjustifiably manipulative but also morally inappropriate to inflict hard treatment on the offender as a kind of secular penance.

Jean Hampton has also proposed a communicative theory of punishment, based on the importance of providing the offender with a moral education. Hampton's theory is explicitly nonretributivist, but it has in common with the retributive theories we are considering an emphasis on communication. Her theory is also interesting in that she seems to accept a central tenet of the paradigm of forgiveness. She notes with approval that both Plato and Jesus reject retributivism "because they insist that the only thing human beings 'deserve' in this life is *good*, that no matter what evil a person has committed, no one is justified in doing further evil to her." Therefore, she holds, we must see punishment as "a good for the wrongdoer" or as "something done *for* [wrongdoers], not to them, something designed to achieve a goal that includes their moral well-being."[31] Specifically, the state punishes the offender "to promote his moral personality ... it punishes him as a way of communicating a moral message to him."[32] Thus, punishment for Hampton is a form of communication with the offender that explains to him that his act was wrong, and why it was wrong. It provides moral education for the offender's benefit, although at the same time society as a whole may receive and benefit from this education as well.

In my judgment, this position starts from the right premise, but then goes badly wrong. Given that Hampton's justification of punishment is goal-oriented, we can and should ask how well the practice of punishment works to achieve the goal of educating the offender and promoting his moral personality. If the practice seldom works as a means to this end, we can legitimately question whether it is justified. But on a more theoretical level, two significant objections can be raised. First, we can make the same point about Hampton's argument that David Dolinko makes about Morris's paternalistic theory of punishment. Dolinko writes that "it is *not*, in general, permissible to confer a benefit on someone against her will. Nor is it ordinarily permissible to treat a person in a manner to which she does not consent, and which would otherwise violate her rights, simply because such treatment will promote her own interests or advance her own good."[33] Further, Dolinko points out that this reasoning holds even when we are dealing with extremely important goods: we hold that in order to respect an individual's autonomy we must even respect her right to reject medical life-saving treatment. It seems, then, that imposing the "benefit" of a moral education by inflicting hard treatment on the offender is also fundamentally incompatible with respecting him as an autonomous moral agent.

Christopher Bennett has developed a second objection to Hampton's line of reasoning. His argument starts from the distinction between an apprentice to a practice and a qualified practitioner of that practice. An apprentice is in the process of learning the practice and is therefore in need of instruction and supervision. On the other hand, Bennett writes, "the qualified member of a practice is one whose participation in the practice is in an important sense self-governing or independent.

---

[31] Jean Hampton, "The Moral Education Theory of Punishment," p. 262.
[32] *Ibid.*, p. 260.
[33] David Dolinko, "Morris on Paternalism and Punishment," p. 354.

The qualified member of the practice knows how to go on in the practice without further intervention or training from supervisors."[34] Just as we would disrespect an experienced teacher who receives poor course evaluations in one course by explaining to her how to teach, "it would be disrespectful of the status of qualified, independent, self-governing moral agents if we were to respond to their wrongs with an attempt at moral education."[35] Thus it seems that Hampton's reasoning leads to the following dilemma: either the offender is a qualified moral agent and it is therefore condescending and inappropriate to impose a moral education on him, or he is not a qualified moral agent and is therefore not properly held responsible (or fully responsible) for his offense.

In light of the difficulties that arise in communicative theories of punishment, Bennett develops a justification of this practice based solely on its expressive function. An interesting feature of Bennett's account is that it is contiguous with and developed from his attitudinal retributivism. Bennett adopts Strawson's position on retributive reactive attitudes. He says that "retributive reactive attitudes are essential to a perspective in which we see people as subject to certain demands: the demands of some interpersonal relationship or moral community. But the retributive attitudes dispose us to a partial and temporary withdrawal of goodwill from the offender – a withdrawal that is bound to cause a certain suffering or to be experienced as hard treatment. Therefore, seeing someone as subject to this withdrawal in the event of his offending is just the same as seeing him as subject to these demands in the first place."[36] Bennett therefore holds that we must adopt retributive reactive attitudes toward unrepentant offenders and at least partially withdraw our goodwill from them if we are to respect them as fully qualified moral agents and members of the moral community. Further, retributive attitudes and withdrawal of goodwill are required if we are to respect morality. Bennett adds that "wrongdoing creates certain responsibilities, and it is a central insight of the retributive tradition that if we are to properly acknowledge the wrong (rather than condoning … it) we ought not deal with wrongdoers on normal terms until they have recognized and taken steps to discharge these obligations."[37]

On the individual level, then, we are responsible for addressing wrongs inflicted on us by withdrawing our goodwill until the offender

---

[34] Christopher Bennett, *The Apology Ritual*, p. 95.
[35] *Ibid.*, p. 97.
[36] *Ibid.*, p. 53.
[37] *Ibid.*, p. 103.

adequately addresses his offense. Collectively, of course, we cannot and should not concern ourselves with every wrong that is committed. But we do have a collective responsibility to condemn some wrongful actions – those that are especially serious or particularly related to the business of the state. According to Bennett, it is a moral fault *not* to condemn wrong acts. Further, verbal condemnation alone is not enough, because it is not "symbolically adequate." On the individual level, he says that "when a person condemns he does not merely *say* that the act was wrong: he shows how the offence *matters* in the way he treats the offender." In the public domain, however, Bennett holds that we should not express our condemnation of wrong acts with moral outrage, anger, or disgust, as this might have a distancing effect on the offender. Instead, he says that "a good way to express how wrong we think an act is would be by making the offender do what we think someone who was sorry enough for their offense would feel it necessary to undertake by way of making amends."[38] Specifically, this would involve apology, restitution, and penance, all of which are proportional to the offense. Bennett believes that it is better to express public condemnation from this perspective, because in doing so we communicate to the offender that after he has completed this work he will be restored to his normal status in the community. It is important to recognize, though, that punishment is not inflicted in order to get the offender to repent or to bring about his reconciliation with the community. Rather, it is inflicted to *express* proportional condemnation of the offender's wrong act.

I want to suggest that serious problems arise in Bennett's defense of attitudinal retributivism and that these same problems undermine his retributive analysis of punishment. Bennett is correct in asserting that "retributive reactive attitudes dispose us to a partial and temporary withdrawal of goodwill from the offender." However, he is mistaken in thinking that "retributive attitudes are *essential* to a perspective in which we see people as subject to certain demands: the demands of some interpersonal relationship or moral community" (my emphasis). He is also mistaken in believing that retributive reactive attitudes are essential if we are to avoid condoning the wrong. Bennett explicitly acknowledges that retributive reactive attitudes embody the perspective of judgment. He writes that "what we do when we have reactive attitudes towards wrongdoers is to *evaluate* those wrongdoers as members of a relationship ..." [39] But if my reasoning in developing the paradigm of forgiveness

---

[38] *Ibid.*, p. 146.
[39] *Ibid.*, p. 61.

has been correct, we should reject the perspective of judgment, which objectifies offenders by conflating them with their actions and attitudes, and instead *identify* with them *as persons*. If we adopt the perspective of identification, we will at all times extend to offenders (and to everyone else) the attitudes of respect, compassion, and real goodwill.

I have argued that by adopting the perspective of identification and extending an attitude of real goodwill toward the offender, we in no way fail to respect him as a moral agent. Rather, we fail to respect the offender as a moral agent when we fail to recognize and respond positively to his moral agency, as distinct from his past record of moral performance. I have also argued that we in no way condone the wrong when we regard the offender with respect, compassion, and real goodwill in spite of his offense. If we do not conflate the offender with the offense, it is certainly possible to condemn the wrong and at the same time extend the attitudes of respect, compassion, and real goodwill toward the offender. Bennett is correct in suggesting that the state is responsible for condemning certain wrong actions, but in order to condemn wrong actions, it need not and should not express hostility or anger toward offenders. Bennett seems to recognize this point when he turns away from a public expression of hostility and anger and proposes instead that the state express its condemnation of the wrong by imposing on the offender the hard treatment that a decent person would undertake as penance for the offense. But as I have just argued, the notion of penance is morally problematic as well. Like the response of hostility or moral anger, it involves us in the moral error of conflating the offender and the offense.

To see this point more clearly, let us examine the passage in which Bennett explains why he believes it is morally appropriate to undertake a penance when one has done wrong: "One sees oneself in the problematic position of having certain responsibilities and hence a certain status (which is normally grounds for self-respect) but having behaved in such a way as no person with this status ought to behave. The way this recognition of one's position is expressed in action is that one puts oneself in a position that would be inconsistent with one's dignity ... That is why penitential behavior can look servile or masochistic: it contravenes one's dignity. But this is precisely the point. It puts into behavior one's recognition that one no longer fully has such dignity..."[40] But this passage commits the error of confusing evaluative self-respect with recognition self-respect. If my reasoning in Chapter 4 was correct, the appropriate basis for one's dignity and one's recognition self-respect is

[40] *Ibid.*, p. 116.

not one's past record of moral performance, but rather one's capacity for moral agency. And an offender who has proper dignity and recognition self-respect will understand that he retains his capacity for moral agency and his basic status as a person in spite of what he has done. In this case he will use his capacities in a dignified, responsible manner, focusing on the positive contributions he can make to his victims and to others. He will not dwell in horror on his past record of moral performance and express self-contempt by undertaking an undignified, humiliating, or masochistic penance. It seems, then, that Bennett fails to provide an adequate justification either for attitudinal retributivism or for retributive punishment.

Margaret Falls also rejects communicative theories and develops an expressive theory of punishment based on the claim that we respect persons as ends in themselves by holding them fully accountable for their wrongful behavior. Punishment, she argues, is the state's way of holding persons accountable for serious wrongs. The state must "express condemnation [of the offense] as well as impress upon the offender why what he did was wrong and how severely wrong it was."[41] Further, hard treatment must be inflicted on the offender in order to make this point. Falls writes that "just as calmly telling a friend she ought not to have lied to us communicates neither the pain she has caused nor our unqualified insistence that we not be so treated, so the state's verbal or written reprimand with attached explanation would be inadequate. It requires a behavioral change on the part of the offended, away from benevolence and toward the infliction of difficult circumstances."[42]

But again, if my arguments in Chapter 3 were correct, we *ought not* move away from an attitude of benevolence toward the offender. It is true that we must express our opposition to wrong acts. It is also true that we must express the idea that certain actions are not acceptable and will not be tolerated. And it is true that we ought to hold offenders accountable for their wrongful behavior. However, we can do these things at the same time that we maintain the attitudes of respect, compassion, and real goodwill toward the offender as a person. If my arguments have been correct, we are simply not justified in adopting an attitude of hostility toward the offender (unless we are the immediate victim of the offense and have not yet completed the process of addressing the wrong).

---

[41] Margaret Falls, "Retribution, Reciprocity, and Respect for Persons," p. 42.
[42] *Ibid.*, pp. 42–43.

While it is important for the state to adopt and express moral standards and appropriate moral attitudes, it must first be sure that these standards and attitudes actually are correct.

Further, even if we were justified in holding an attitude of moral outrage, hostility, or resentment toward the offender, expressing such an attitude through the imposition of hard treatment would be problematic from a moral point of view. While this method of expressing our condemnation of the offender or his offense may be more dramatic and impactful, we are not justified in using the offender as a mere means to the dramatic expression of our beliefs. Our moral beliefs are certainly important, but it is seriously problematic to claim that we must express their importance by imposing years of hard treatment on offenders. To do so is to fail to recognize the intrinsic worth of the offender as a person. We may desire to make an impact on offenders and turn their attention to their moral obligations. But again, we must do so in such a way as to respect their autonomy and moral agency. Although we may legitimately control the behavior of moral agents under certain circumstances to prevent harm to others, a respect for their autonomy requires us to view them as responsible for *their own* inner moral development. They are responsible for authoring their own beliefs and attitudes, and although we may speak to them and reason with them constructively, we cannot legitimately impose hard treatment on them to get them to adopt certain attitudes or endorse certain beliefs.

It seems, therefore, that while expressive theories of punishment may avoid some of the problems that critics have identified in communicative theories of punishment, expressive theories also embody morally inappropriate attitudes toward offenders – attitudes of disrespect, hostility, and withdrawal of goodwill. These are attitudes that we ought not adopt, and particularly that we ought not express through the imposition of hard treatment. Rather, we must have recognition respect for offenders as valuable human beings and as the authors of their own inner moral development. And we must regard them with respect, compassion, and real goodwill.

To summarize, then, none of the central versions of strong retributivism that we have examined seem to provide an adequate justification for the practice of legal punishment. Although strong retributivists have good reason to reject utilitarianism and weak retributivism, they fail to provide adequate support for their claim that it is intrinsically appropriate from a moral point of view for the state to inflict hard treatment on offenders.

RESTITUTION FOR SECONDARY HARM

In the last section I argued that retributivists fail to provide an adequate justification for the practice of legal punishment – the practice that they endorse as the public response to criminal wrongdoing. In particular, strong retributivists fail to justify their claim that punishing offenders is in some way intrinsically appropriate from a moral point of view. In the context of the paradigm of forgiveness, we will reject the claim that it is intrinsically appropriate for the state to inflict hard treatment on criminal offenders. As noted, in the context of this paradigm we will inflict burdens on persons only with reluctance, and only when we must do so to prevent greater or equal harm to others. Therefore the public response to criminal wrongdoing must be derived from our basic principle of justice, which holds that each individual ought to be secured the most fundamental interests in life compatible with like benefits for all, and that no individual ought to be required to sacrifice a significant interest so that others can benefit in less important ways. Some theorists have attempted to derive justifications of punishment from principles of justice that are similar to or compatible with the principle of justice that emerges in the paradigm of forgiveness, and if their arguments were successful, those who endorse this paradigm could accept them. These justice-based analyses of punishment can be divided into two categories: societal defense theories and restitutive theories. I will argue here that we ought to endorse a restitutive analysis of the public response to criminal wrongdoing. To see why this approach is preferable, let us first consider two societal defense theories.

Erin Kelly provides a sketch of a forward-looking societal defense theory in a 2002 article in which she attempts to develop a compatibilist position on response to wrongdoing. With regard to "restraints and penalties," she argues that our central focus should not be on moral desert but rather on causal responsibility. She says that "the guiding principle is simple: we are usually justified in preventing harms by interfering with their causes. An agent's causing harm to others provides us with grounds for restraining her."[43] Kelly argues that this principle allows us to leave aside, for the most part, questions about the origins of antisocial behavior, and more deeply, to leave aside the extremely difficult questions that arise in working out a conception of free will. If we adopt the perspective

---

[43] Erin Kelly, "Doing Without Desert," p. 195.

that she suggests, we need only consider what kind of intervention is needed to prevent significant harm to others.

As Kelly recognizes, this line of reasoning seems to work well in cases of immediate self-defense, and in cases in which we have sufficient evidence to believe that an individual poses a significant risk of harm to others in the future. However, it does not work well for the cases that most commonly occur in our system of criminal law. In the large majority of criminal cases, the offender has committed a past violation that we obviously cannot prevent at this point, and we lack sufficient evidence to justify a claim that he will (or is very likely to) commit another violation in the future. Kelly at least acknowledges that there will be some offenders who do not pose further threats. She argues that they may rightly be penalized in order to promote the ends of deterrence, education about the principles of conduct that we expect citizens to accept, reconciliation of the offender with the community, and solidarity within the moral community, all "by underscoring a collective commitment to bring about a better society."[44] Given that the large majority of criminal cases are cases of this sort, the lion's share of Kelly's justification of punishment rests on the claim that punishment promotes these ends. But in this case, if the proposed justification is to be successful, we need an argument to show that we are not using offenders as mere means to achieve these ends – or in the case of "reconciliation of the offender with the community," an argument to show that we are not violating the offender's autonomy by inflicting hard treatment on him against his will in order to bring about this result for him. Kelly holds that "the content of morality is determined by persons who have some concern for one another's basic needs and would be motivated to reason together as equals to reach an agreement on moral principles to regulate their social interactions."[45] Thus Kelly seems to hold a version of a social contract theory. However, the proposed justification of punishment will not be complete until she can establish which principles governing the public response to wrongdoing would be chosen under the circumstances she outlines, and why. This task remains to be completed, and it seems to be nearly as difficult as the basic task of justifying punishment.

[44] *Ibid.*, p. 194.
[45] *Ibid.*, p. 181. It is also interesting to note that Gary Watson believes that a compatibilist account of this type, in which condemnation and desert drop out of the analysis of response to wrongdoing, applies to blame but not to punishment. See his "The Two Faces of Responsibility."

Phillip Montague has proposed a more fully developed justification of punishment as societal self-defense. He bases his analysis on a moral principle that is fully compatible with, and could be derived from, the principle of justice that emerges in the paradigm of forgiveness. Essentially, this principle is that "when members of a group of individuals are in danger of being harmed through the fault of some, but not all, members of that group; and when some person ... is in a position to determine how the harm is distributed...; then the person has a right ... to distribute the harm among us to those who are at fault."[46] (I have omitted some of Montague's qualifications that need not concern us here.)

Montague acknowledges that although we can use this principle to justify individual instances of self-defense, we cannot use it to justify individual instances of punishment. In individual cases of self-defense, we have reason to believe that harm will unavoidably fall on someone, and we are therefore forced to decide how to allocate that harm. Given that the offender has wrongfully created the situation in which this choice must be made, we are justified in allocating the harm to him. However, in the case of punishment, the offender has *already* inflicted harm on the victim, and we (normally) lack sufficient reason to believe that he will be responsible for any future harm that must be allocated to someone. Therefore we are not in a "forced-choice situation."

But Montague goes on to argue that if we shift our focus from individual instances of punishment to the systemic choices that society must make, a practice of legal punishment *can* be justified as societal-defense. He asks us to imagine a society, S, that includes a subclass of individuals, S1, "who are both strongly inclined and quite able to wrongfully kill or injure innocent members of S and who will do so if not directly prevented from acting."[47] If we assume both that we could deter these individuals by instituting a practice of punishment and that we cannot reduce the risk of harm to innocent citizens without harming offenders, we *are* in a forced-choice situation. We must either allow harm to fall on innocent citizens or allocate harm to offenders through a practice of punishment. Montague also points out that a right to societal-defense has been generally accepted in just-war theory. Many theorists have argued that societies are justified in waging defensive wars if certain conditions are met.

While this argument is ingenious, I think it fails to circumvent the problems that arise in justifying individual instances of punishment.

---

[46] Phillip Montague, *Punishment as Societal-Defense*, p. 42.
[47] *Ibid.*, p. 62.

The problem does not lie in the general notion of societal-defense. Montague is correct in suggesting that if war is ever justified, it will be justified as a form of societal-defense when the relevant conditions are met. Rather, the problem lies in identifying the group of persons, S1, to whom Montague believes we are justified in allocating harm. Recall that the individuals in S1 are those who are strongly inclined and able to harm innocent citizens and who will do so if we do not prevent them from acting. The central problem is that we do not know who these individuals are.

In a defensive war, we know who the enemy combatants are, and we know that they are responsible for creating a situation in which we must harm them or suffer serious harm ourselves. But in the kind of situation we face in justifying punishment, we do not know who is strongly inclined and able to harm innocent persons in the future, and who will do so if we do not intervene. We know only that convicted offenders have harmed innocent citizens in the past. It is not the group of persons who have already harmed others who make it unavoidable that we either harm them now or allow harm to fall on innocent citizens in the future. Rather, it is a group of persons S2 (an unidentified group of persons significantly distinct from convicted offenders), whose future wrong choices will inflict harm on innocent citizens. Therefore we cannot rightly claim that it is that fault of convicted offenders that we must institute a practice of punishment to inflict harm on them now or allow harm to fall on innocent citizens in the future. And in this case, Montague's principle of justice fails to apply. In sum, it seems that if offenders' wrong choices are to be the operative factor in determining their liability to punishment, we cannot base a justification of punishment on an allocation of harm that will result from wrong choices that others will make in the future (or from choices that offenders themselves have not yet made). Instead we would be well-advised to focus on an allocation of harm that results from the wrong choices that offenders have already made – choices for which they can clearly be held responsible.

If so, we have good reason to pursue a restitutive analysis of the public response to criminal wrongdoing. I have already argued here that one component of the public response to wrongdoing in the context of the paradigm of forgiveness is to require the offender to make restitution for the primary harm that he has wrongfully inflicted on others. As I have noted, the practice of requiring persons to make restitution for the harm they wrongfully inflict on others is easily derived from the principle of justice that emerges in the paradigm of forgiveness when we recognize that we all have a fundamental interest in the opportunity to make the most of our own lives through our own choices and efforts. When we require persons to make restitution for the harm they wrongfully inflict on others, we secure for each individual the fundamental benefit of being able to minimize the suffering that she experiences as a result of wrongdoing simply by choosing to comply with her own moral obligations. In this case, requiring restitution is fully compatible with, and in fact emerges from, the basic attitudes of respect, compassion, and real goodwill extended toward all persons equally.

Randy Barnett has proposed that we ought to replace the paradigm of punishment as a response to criminal wrongdoing with a paradigm of restitution.[48] The central problem with his proposal is that his application of this model is incomplete. He believes that offenders should only be held responsible for making restitution for the primary harm that they wrongfully inflict on others, and for paying the process costs associated with this obligation. However, as many authors have noted, criminal violations are, in an important sense, *public* wrongs. When persons commit criminal violations, they inflict not only primary harm on their immediate victims, but also secondary harm on the members of their community. Recall that Bentham defines secondary harm as harm that falls on the members of the offender's community regardless of whether they have any specific connection with the victim.

There has been some disagreement on exactly what secondary harm consists of. Richard Burgh has argued that secondary harm should be understood as a kind of harm that society incurs when its central values are repudiated by intentional violations of the criminal law. He says that "in the sense that society is, in part, constituted by these shared values, it has an interest in these values not being repudiated. Thus a repudiation of these values, constituting an invasion of an interest of society, can be conceived as harming society – the degree of harm being determined by the relative ranking of the valued interest."[49] Criminal offenders then owe society restitution for this secondary harm. Punishment constitutes a means by which society can exact restitution for secondary harm, because it reaffirms these shared values by condemning their violation. He writes that "this condemnation must involve a condemnation of the offender, and punishment, making the offender suffer, is the way

---

[48] See Randy Barnett, "Restitution: A New Paradigm of Criminal Justice."
[49] Richard Burgh, "Do the Guilty Deserve Punishment?," p. 329.

of emphatically expressing this condemnation so that there can be no doubt that it is genuine."[50]

This is an ingenious analysis of secondary harm, but if my reasoning in Chapter 3 was correct, it must be rejected. It is plausible to claim that society is partially constituted by its shared values. However, I argued earlier that in the individual domain, the victim need not devote herself to protesting or repudiating the claim (implicit in the offense perpetrated against her) that she does not warrant a full measure of respect. In fact, she fails to respect herself by engaging in a power struggle with the offender in which she maintains an attitude of resentment toward him in order to protest to him that this implicit claim is false. The victim who truly respects herself and appreciates her own worth as a person will simply recognize the offender's confusion for what it is, put it in proper perspective, and turn her attention to her own positive pursuits. The same point applies in the public domain. If the state has thought carefully about its values and is fully committed to them, it will not be threatened by the simple fact that a small portion of the population repudiates them. For example, if some persons argue against democracy in our society, we need not inflict suffering on them to reaffirm our own values and emphatically express our condemnation of their claims. Instead, we can simply put their disagreement into perspective and go on with the activities that we take to be of value. Therefore it seems that if secondary harm consists of nothing more than a repudiation of society's shared values, then we need not worry about creating a legal apparatus to exact restitution for it.

Unfortunately, however, those who commit criminal violations do inflict a more serious type of secondary harm on the members of their community, and when we understand the full extent of the secondary harm we will see that it is something that we cannot overlook. As I will construe it here, the secondary harm that results from a given type of criminal violation is a kind of harm that is suffered by all the members of the community who are vulnerable to that type of violation. Specifically, criminal offenders harm the members of the community, regardless of

---

[50] *Ibid.*, p. 330. Richard Burgh published this restitutive theory at approximately the same time that I published my restitutive analysis of punishment, "Punishment as Restitution: The Rights of the Community." We arrived at these theories independently. It is interesting to note that whereas the idea of viewing punishment as restitution for secondary harm is the same, the accounts of secondary harm and the analysis of how punishment constitutes restitution for that harm are significantly different.

whether they have a specific connection with the victim, by wrongfully eroding their security with respect to the type of violation in question. When criminal violations of a given sort are committed, the members of the community are wrongfully put in a position in which they have reason to believe that they may become victims of similar violations in the future, and that they should therefore take steps to defend themselves. This type of harm affects us both individually and collectively. Individually we reason that we may become victims of the type of violation in question and that we had better take steps to prevent this from happening. Collectively we reason that our social structures may be weakened by this type of violation and that we will lose the just institutions and law and order that are so necessary to our communal quality of life. Therefore we believe that we must take steps to prevent these occurrences. It is important to notice here that those who simply inform others about offenses that have been committed (citizens who report crimes, police officers who uncover crimes, and journalists who inform the public about crimes) do not wrongfully erode our security. Rather, they give us the facts that we need to make informed, autonomous decisions about our lives.[51]

Perhaps the best way to grasp the nature and extent of the secondary harm is to return to societal defense theories of punishment, or for that matter, to a utilitarian analysis of punishment that is grounded largely on the need for a deterrent against future criminal violations. Whether or not any of these justifications of punishment is successful, it seems undeniable that we do feel a need to protect ourselves against future criminal violations. In fact, we allocate enormous resources to creating such a defense. We build and maintain prisons at great cost to ourselves to create a deterrent to crime and to incapacitate offenders; we finance large police forces; we install locks and alarms on our houses, cars, businesses, and so on, to protect our possessions; we devise and implement cumbersome auditing procedures to ensure that we do not fall prey to financial violations; we sacrifice activities to avoid placing ourselves in situations that might put us at risk for victimization; and so on. And at the national level, we spend hundreds of billions of dollars each year to defend ourselves against potential aggression of other nations.

To understand that secondary harm is a serious and wrongfully inflicted form of harm, we must ask ourselves why we are in a position

---

[51] I thank an anonymous reader from Cambridge University Press for drawing this potential objection to my attention.

in which we feel the need to make these sacrifices and to allocate our resources in this manner. The fact is that we are in this position because persons have chosen to commit criminal violations in the past. We estimate our need for a defense against criminal harm on the basis of our projections of what will happen in the future, and our major basis for making these projections is our observations of what has happened in the past. Of course, we have no way of knowing whether anyone will choose to commit a crime in the future, just as we have no way of knowing that the sun will rise tomorrow, or that any other empirical regularity will continue to obtain. But all rational persons reason inductively about these matters, and arguably we cannot do otherwise. Therefore all rational persons will decide, both collectively and individually, the portion of their resources that they will allocate to defend themselves and their public institutions based on the criminal violations that have been committed in the past. If no criminal violations have ever been committed in a given community, then rational persons in that community will devote very little (if any) of their resources to defending themselves against criminal harm. On the other hand, if frequent and serious violations have recently taken place, the members of the community will be in a very different position. It will be rational for them to sacrifice a far greater portion of their resources to defending themselves against crime. (Notice that this line of reasoning obtains regardless of whether the members of the community are *afraid* of the type of crime in question. For example, business executives may not be frightened by acts of embezzlement, but if they have reason to believe that persons will attempt to commit this offense in the future, they will sacrifice resources to protect their companies from this kind of damage.)

In her book *Moral Repair,* Margaret Urban Walker casts the problem of erosion of our security in terms of trust. She distinguishes between trust and reliance as follows: "The truster relies upon the one trusted not only as one likely to do something, or as one wanting to do something out of positive regard for another or concern for another's reliance, but also as one *responsible* for behaving in the way relied upon."[52] [my emphasis] She goes on to say that "there is a sense in which, in myriad activities of daily life, we trust 'people.' We trust *that* they will behave as they should. Sometimes it seems that what we trust is the reliable good order and safety of the environment. How nice for us the more we can

---

[52] Margaret Urban Walker, *Moral Repair,* p. 83.

do so."[53] This passage, I believe, expresses very well what we lose when offenders fail to meet their responsibilities and commit criminal violations. The quality of life that we all have when people meet their responsibilities, as Walker indicates, is a very fundamental benefit. In fact, it might be argued that the richness of our lives is directly proportional to the extent to which we can reasonably trust people to behave as they should. Further, as Walker points out, they are responsible for doing so. Therefore, when they fail in this regard they wrongfully deprive us of this important benefit.

If this line of reasoning is correct, it follows that those who commit criminal violations collectively inflict a serious form of secondary harm on the members of their community in addition to harming their immediate victims. Specifically, criminal offenders harm the members of their communities by wrongfully putting them in a position in which they have reason to believe that they should sacrifice activities and expend resources to protect themselves and their social institutions from future criminal violations. In a community governed by just laws, all citizens are rightly required to refrain from committing criminal violations. Therefore, in a just community, the secondary harm constitutes a wrongfully inflicted loss. Given that the principle of justice that emerges in the paradigm of forgiveness requires those who wrongfully inflict losses on others to make restitution for those losses, the public response to wrongdoing in the paradigm of forgiveness will include a practice in which those who wrongfully inflict secondary harm on the members of the community are required to make restitution for that harm, as well as for the primary harm that they have inflicted on their immediate victims.

At this point, it is important to establish the fact that each offender contributes to the secondary harm suffered by the community with respect to the type of violation he has committed. Given the nature of inductive reasoning, it seems clear that each person who has committed an offense in a given time period makes an equal contribution in wrongfully providing grounds for rational persons to infer that they need to take steps to protect themselves against this type of violation in the future. However, it might be objected that once a number of violations have been committed, the need for a defense has already been established, and additional offenses make no real difference. There are two points to be made in response to this objection. First, because the seriousness of the secondary harm varies directly with the number of crimes

---

[53] *Ibid.*, p. 84.

that are committed, each additional violation makes the secondary harm that much more serious. Second, if all criminal violations were to cease at this point, our need for a defense against criminal harm would begin to diminish. Therefore each additional violation both strengthens and sustains our need for this type of defense. If so, then each offender contributes to the cumulative secondary harm experienced by the members of his community with respect to the type of violation he committed, and each offender owes restitution for that harm.

In the context of the paradigm of forgiveness, then, the third component of the public response to wrongdoing will be a practice in which criminal offenders are each required to make restitution to the members of the community for wrongfully inflicted secondary harm, to the extent that they are reasonably able to do so, and, as with primary harm, within reasonable limits of sacrifice. It is important to bear in mind here that the paradigm of forgiveness enjoins us to minimize unnecessary suffering and to make everyone's life as rich and rewarding as possible. Once again, our goal in requiring restitution for secondary harm is not to mete out to offenders their just deserts, or to express hostility toward or condemnation of offenders. Rather, our aim is to make good the secondary loss that offenders have wrongfully inflicted on the members of the community. It is to alleviate the suffering of the members of the community rather than to inflict suffering on offenders.

There may well be different ways in which offenders can make restitution to the community for secondary harm. In the context of the paradigm of forgiveness, we will have two desiderata in determining how this restitution is to be made: first, to adequately compensate the community members for the harm that has been wrongfully inflicted on them; second, in doing so, to minimize the burden we place on the offender. Of course, we will be obligated in all cases to treat both offenders and victims with respect, compassion, and real goodwill. In no case may we treat the offender in a manner that is incompatible with a basic respect for him as a moral agent, and in no case may we attempt to compensate immediate victims or members of the community by providing them with some sort of revenge on the offender, as has recently been suggested by David Hershenov.[54] In some situations it may be possible for offenders

---

[54] In his article "Restitution and Revenge," David Hershenov proposes a restitutive theory of punishment and an analysis of secondary harm that is the same as the one I have proposed. Taking a completely different tack, he then argues that "the vindictive satisfaction that comes from 'getting even' should be considered the debt payment that the victim receives from the criminal." (p. 87).

to best compensate the community by doing some form of public service. This option is attractive in that it is likely to minimize the burden placed on the offender, and to be constructive for both the offender and the members of the community. In other cases, however, it may be that a practice of legal punishment will be required in order to approach a state of affairs in which the members of the community are adequately compensated for the secondary harm that has been wrongfully inflicted on them. If a practice of legal punishment functions with a reasonable degree of efficiency to deter future criminal violations, it constitutes a mechanism by which offenders can make restitution to the members of the community for wrongfully inflicted secondary harm. Offenders inflict a loss on the members of their community by wrongfully giving them reason to believe that they need a defense against crime, and a practice of punishment requires offenders to help make this loss good by providing such a defense. By undergoing punishment for their offenses, offenders create a deterrent against future violations.

There are three central questions that must be addressed concerning the way in which a practice of requiring restitution for secondary harm ought to be articulated. These questions concern the determinations of which types of violations are properly considered criminal, which excusing conditions ought to be recognized, and how we are to determine the extent of the restitution owed for secondary harm. Let us consider each of these questions in turn. In the context of the analysis I have presented, the types of transgressions that ought to be classified as criminal violations will be those violations for which we are justified in requiring offenders to make some form of restitution for secondary harm. Three conditions must be met if we are to be justified in classifying a particular type of act as a crime. First, our principle of justice must require that persons refrain from performing the type of act in question. Unless this condition is met, members of the community are not entitled to any assurances that they will not be affected by such acts in the future, and no one will owe them restitution for depriving them of this kind of security. Second, the members of the community must experience a significant amount of secondary harm as a result of the type of violation in question. Third, the costs of enforcing the requirement in question must not impose on persons burdens that are more fundamental than the burdens we aim to relieve by enacting the law in question. Analysis will show that most of the violations that we typically classify as criminal will satisfy these conditions. Most crimes are acts in which the offender inflicts substantial harm on another person in violation of the requirements of justice. In connection with these violations, members of the community have reason to believe that they ought to sacrifice resources in order to protect themselves from future violations, and therefore they suffer significant secondary harm.

Russ Shafer-Landau has pointed out that some of the violations that we classify as crimes do not have immediate victims. For example, tax evasion and driving while intoxicated typically do not result in direct harm to an immediate victim, and yet we still consider these acts properly subject to punishment.[55] On the analysis presented here, these offenses will be classified as crimes. Our principle of justice will certainly prohibit these activities, and they also inflict significant secondary harm on the members of the community. We devote significant resources to defending ourselves against drunk driving, and reasonably so, given that this activity exposes persons to an unreasonable risk of serious harm. We also devote significant resources to attempting to prevent tax evasion, and again, reasonably so. Our public institutions are of great value to us, and they will not last long if we do not take steps to protect them from disintegrating as a result of this offense. These criteria also provide a basis for excluding from the range of criminalization certain acts that may seem to produce some kind of secondary harm but that we would not necessarily want to classify as crimes. For example, selling adulterated milk after having taken every legitimately required precaution to avoid doing so will not be a criminal offense on this analysis even if members of the community experience a feeling of insecurity after such an event. If an individual or corporation is engaging in a legitimate activity and has taken all justly required precautions, members of the community are not entitled to any assurances that they will never be harmed by this activity, and any insecurity they may experience is not wrongfully inflicted secondary harm.

Let us now consider which excusing conditions ought to be recognized in this component of the public response to wrongdoing that emerges in the paradigm of forgiveness. It is important to recall here that in the context of the paradigm of forgiveness, we do not adopt the perspective of judgment and punish persons as retribution for moral culpability. Rather, we punish or exact restitution for wrongfully inflicted secondary harm only because by doing so we secure for each individual the fundamental benefit of being able to make the most of her own life through her own choices and efforts. Therefore our central concern in

[55] See Russ Shafer-Landau, "Retributivism and Desert," p. 193.

determining excusing conditions will not be an assessment of the degree of the offender's moral wickedness. Rather, it will be to secure for each individual the most fundamental interests in life compatible with like benefits for all. In the context of the paradigm of forgiveness, there are two kinds of situations in which we will recognize exculpating excuses for liability for making restitution for secondary harm. First, we will recognize exculpating excuses based on the claim that an individual lacked substantial capacity to conform his conduct to the requirements of law. Because ought implies can, individuals who lack this capacity are not justly required to refrain from performing the act in question, and therefore the members of the community are not entitled to any assurances that they will not be harmed by individuals of this sort. Persons who cannot legitimately be expected to conform to the requirements of law due to physical, cognitive, or conative deficiencies are therefore excluded from criminal liability. Again, the paradigm of forgiveness will rely on empirical research in medicine and psychology to determine which conditions actually render individuals incapable of conforming to the requirements of law.

Second, in the context of this analysis we will recognize exculpating excuses of accident and mistake when the individual in question was engaged in a legitimate activity and has taken all justly required precautions. There are several activities that we find valuable in spite of the fact that they create some risk of harm to others – for example, driving, flying, playing sports, and so on. Certainly we are justly permitted to engage in some of these activities, when they are of significant value and the risk of harm is small. We may be justly required to take certain precautions to avoid an accident or mistake that will produce harm. Whether or not we are required to take such precautions depends on the cost of taking these measures and the benefits that others can be expected to derive if we do so. When an individual has engaged in a legitimate activity and has taken all justly required precautions, he has not violated a requirement of justice. It is still possible that he will bring about harm for others by accident or mistake, but *ex hypothese*, members of the community are not entitled to security from the risk of harm that arises in this way. Thus the person who brings about harm under these circumstances does not owe members of the community restitution for secondary harm and is not properly subject to criminal liability.

Let us now turn to mitigating excuses. Mitigating excuses do not excuse the perpetrator of a harmful act from criminal liability altogether; instead they reduce the extent of that liability. One form of mitigation is incorporated into our current system of criminal law under the doctrine of *mens rea*. When we determine how much punishment ought to be inflicted on an individual who has brought about a certain type of primary harm, we consider his state of mind or the mode of culpability that characterizes his offense. If the offender acted purposefully or knowingly in bringing about the type of harm in question, he is generally punished more severely than if he brought about the harm recklessly, and if he brought about the harm recklessly, he will be punished more severely than if he brought about the harm through negligence. Retributivists may argue that we should take the mode of culpability into account because it bears on our judgment of the offender's moral wickedness. In the context of the paradigm of forgiveness, this perspective is rejected and replaced with an attempt to secure for each individual the most fundamental interests in life compatible with like benefits for all. We will therefore determine whether or not to mitigate the extent of the offender's criminal liability by considering the significant interests that both the members of the community and the offender have at stake in the type of situation in question. More specifically, we will balance the interest that the members of the community have in receiving restitution for secondary harm and the interest that the offender has in being able to recover and to have another chance to fulfill his life plans after having committed the wrong.

Given this framework, we can cite two reasons why we ought to take the mode of culpability into account when we determine the severity of the punishment, or the extent of the restitution for secondary harm that ought to be required. First, the interest that the members of the community have in receiving restitution for the secondary harm varies with the mode of culpability that characterized the offender's violation. When an individual purposefully sets out to harm someone, there is a very good chance that he will succeed. When someone recklessly engages in an activity with no intention of trying to harm someone, there is a much lower probability that harm will result. And the probability of harm is lower still when we shift from recklessness to negligence. Everything else being equal, then, the members of the community have a more substantial interest in defending themselves from intentional wrongdoing than from reckless conduct, and a more substantial interest in defending themselves from reckless conduct than in defending themselves from negligent conduct. Therefore the severity of the punishment will decrease as the mode of culpability becomes less serious. Second, the importance of the interest that we all have in being able to recover if we make a mistake and do wrong increases as the mode of culpability becomes less serious. Most of us can say with some assurance that we will not intentionally harm others. However, we are not as sure that we will never harm another person through reckless behavior, and we are still less certain that we will never harm another as a result of negligence. Therefore it is more important for us to ensure that we have a chance to recover after a negligent violation than after a reckless violation, and more important to ensure that we can recover after a reckless violation than after an intentional offense. Thus, both of these factors combine to reduce the severity of the punishment as the mode of culpability becomes less serious.

It might be objected at this point that although the line of reasoning I have suggested here suffices to explain mitigation for reckless and negligent behavior, it does not suffice to explain the difference between purposeful and knowing conduct. As the likelihood of harm is the same in purposeful and knowing conduct, the community's need for a defense must be the same as well.[56] There are two points to make in response to this line of argument. First, the law does not make extensive use of the distinction between these two modes of culpability. George Dix and Michael Sharlot, authors of a standard text on the criminal law, comment as follows: "In many situations there may be little reason for the criminal law to distinguish between a man who engages in prohibited conduct purposefully and a man who engages in the same conduct not on purpose but knowing that he is doing so. Both are consciously conducting themselves in a way that the law prohibits." They add that "in most cases it will be sufficient for liability that a person engaged in conduct knowingly, whether or not it was his purpose to do so."[57] Second, it is not clear that there is a morally significant difference between the two modes of culpability, such that the position I have developed here can be characterized as distinctly counterintuitive. If an offender knows that his act will produce a specific kind of harm, and he chooses to do it anyway, it seems that he intended to perpetrate this kind of harm whatever his ultimate purpose is, as Sharlot and Dix suggest.

A similar analysis shows that mitigating excuses based on participation of the victim ought to be recognized. This category includes the excusing conditions of provocation, imperfect self-defense, and perhaps

---

[56] Again, I thank an anonymous reader for Cambridge University Press for drawing my attention to this problem.

[57] George E. Dix and M. Michael Sharlot, *Criminal Law: Cases and Materials*, pp. 443–444.

the consent of the victim. The secondary harm that results from violations when provocation is present is not very extensive, because we can avoid becoming the victim of such a crime relatively easily. As long as we require that the provocation be substantial, most of us can avoid provoking another person to the extent that he inflicts harm on us. It is even easier to avoid becoming the victim of a violation involving imperfect self-defense. To do so we need only refrain from attacking other persons. Because the extent of the secondary harm is diminished when these defenses are present, the interest in receiving restitution for that harm becomes less significant, and a reduction in the severity of the punishment or the extent of restitution required is warranted. Further, it is more important to have an opportunity to recover after committing a violation under these circumstances. Again, most of us could say with some assurance that we would not initiate an attempt to deliberately harm another person. But we could not be as sure that we would refrain from harming another person if we were severely provoked or if we were acting under the pressure of trying to defend ourselves against an assault. As before, both of these factors combine to reduce the severity of the punishment or the extent of the restitution required in this category of mitigating excuses.

A third category of mitigating excuses includes duress and diminished capacity.[58] In cases of this sort, the offender is not completely lacking in the capacity to conform to moral requirements, but it is significantly more difficult for him to do so than it is for those of us who operate in the absence of these conditions. When these excusing conditions are present, the extent of the secondary harm may be reduced very little, if at all. We need as much defense against violations that take place when these conditions are present as against violations that take place when they are not. However, the interest that we have in being able to recover when these conditions are present is clearly greater. While we can say with some assurance that we will not harm others under normal conditions, we cannot be as sure that we will refrain from harming others when we are under severe duress, or when our mental health is severely compromised in some way. Therefore this factor serves to reduce the severity of the punishment.

---

[58] Duress, when it is severe enough, becomes necessity and functions as a justification for performing the act in question. For example, if an offender holds a gun on a clerk at a convenience store and threatens to kill her if she does not give him $100 from the till, she is actually justified in giving him the money.

Finally, let us consider how we ought to determine the severity of the punishment or the extent of the restitution required for secondary harm. The first point to notice here is that some punishments or requirements are intrinsically incompatible with the basic attitudes that ground the paradigm of forgiveness. If we have genuine respect, compassion, and real goodwill for offenders, we will abhor capital punishment. We will also abhor punishments that involve torture or unnecessary suffering. We cannot have genuine respect, compassion, and goodwill for a person, and at the same time wish to kill him or to make him suffer. In addition to capital punishment and inhumane punishments, then, punishments or requirements that do not promote concrete human interests will be ruled out. The claim that offenders deserve punishment even when the punishment would do no good must clearly be rejected. If we adopt the perspective of identification as opposed to the perspective of judgment, we will allow a burden to be imposed on an offender only if it is truly necessary to prevent an equal or more serious burden from falling on someone else. Therefore if we have reason to believe that a given punishment or requirement will not be effective in serving the concrete interests of others, we will find another way for the offender to make restitution for the harm he has wrongfully inflicted on the community.

When punishment is to be inflicted in the context of the paradigm of forgiveness, we will determine the severity of the punishment in reference to our principle of justice. Here we must balance the extent of the offender's sacrifice in undergoing punishment (or in making restitution for secondary harm in some other way) against the interest that a representative member of the community has in receiving restitution for the secondary harm that has been inflicted on her with respect to the type of violation in question – a loss over which she had no control. It may be the case that some members of the community are more seriously affected than others by a particular type of secondary harm. For example, if women are more likely to be raped than men, then women may experience more secondary harm in connection with this offense. If we are to ensure that no individual is required to make a disproportionate sacrifice, we must compare the offender's interest with the interests of the members of the community who are most affected by the secondary harm.

The seriousness of the secondary harm clearly depends, in a direct and fundamental manner, on the severity of the primary harm that results from the type of violation in question. Because offenses such as murder, kidnapping, and rape produce very serious kinds of harm, we will reasonably go to great lengths to protect ourselves against these violations. The need for a defense against less serious crimes will clearly be less urgent. As I noted in our discussion of excusing conditions, the seriousness of the secondary harm is reduced when the probability that we will experience harm as a result of a given type of violation is reduced. Further, the seriousness of the secondary harm varies with the cost and difficulty involved in avoiding the type of victimization in question. Therefore, a type of offense that is very difficult to prevent, such as identity theft, may result in more secondary harm than a type of offense that is more easily avoided, such as auto theft. Finally, the seriousness of the secondary harm will vary with the prevalence of the offense. In general terms, the seriousness of the secondary harm will determine significance of the interest that the worst-off representative members of the community have in receiving restitution for the secondary harm they experience as a result of a given type of violation, and the extent of the restitution owed for this harm will vary with this factor.

The severity of the punishment or the extent of the restitution owed for secondary harm also depends on the importance of the interest that the offender has at stake. Because this is the case, we cannot say that a given quantity of punishment or restitution will necessarily be appropriate for every person who commits a particular type of violation. For example, six months of imprisonment will be a much greater sacrifice for an individual who is terminally ill and has only a year to live than it is for an individual who is relatively young and healthy. Thus we must consider the extent of the sacrifice that any given requirement imposes on an individual, and make adjustments in that requirement accordingly.

It is important to notice that this third component of the public response to wrongdoing that emerges in the paradigm of forgiveness also explains some of our moral intuitions in the domain of retributive justice that we commonly express in terms of desert. We commonly say that persons who are guilty deserve punishment. The practice outlined here requires that we impose on the offender the responsibility of making restitution to those who have suffered secondary harm as a result of his violation, although our goal is to alleviate the harm suffered by victims of the offense rather than to make the offender suffer. Restitution to the immediate victim for primary harm is also required. We also say that it is wrong to punish the innocent because they do not deserve punishment. On the analysis presented here, innocent persons have not wrongfully inflicted harm on anyone and have no responsibility to make restitution. We say that persons who have exculpating excuses do not deserve punishment, and that those who have mitigating excuses deserve less punishment than those who do not. Again, the analysis presented here yields these results. Finally, we say that the punishment that the offender deserves is proportional to the gravity of his offense. Again, the analysis presented here requires that the extent of the sacrifice imposed on offenders is generally proportional to the gravity of the offense. Given that this practice is derived from the principle of justice that emerges in the paradigm of forgiveness, we can say that our principle of justice explains, at a preinstitutional level, many of the most significant moral intuitions we have in the domain of retributive justice, including intuitions about the response to criminal wrongdoing. Once again, it is the fundamental interest that we all have in the opportunity to make the most of our own lives through our own choices and efforts that underlies the justification of this social practice.

The response to criminal wrongdoing suggested here clearly diverges from retributive analyses in important respects. At the same time, however, it addresses many of the central concerns that retributivists have raised. I will conclude this section by comparing the analysis of response to criminal wrongdoing that emerges in the paradigm of forgiveness with the types of retributive analyses we have examined. As I do so, I will consider and respond to some of the objections that these theorists might have to the position I have developed. I will also show how the public response to criminal wrongdoing that emerges in the paradigm of forgiveness incorporates some of the central insights of these retributive positions.

First, the restitutive analysis of response to criminal wrongdoing proposed here seems to include the features that are of concern to weak retributivists. H.L.A. Hart clearly thought that if punishment is to be justified, it must provide concrete benefits for the members of the community. In the context of the paradigm of forgiveness, we require punishment or some other form of restitution for secondary harm in order to compensate members of the community for wrongfully inflicted secondary harm, and the members of the community obviously have a concrete human interest in receiving such restitution. Further, the analysis I have suggested clearly incorporates the constraints on punishment that are of interest to weak retributivists. In the context of my analysis, we will never knowingly punish the innocent, as the innocent have not wrongfully inflicted secondary harm on the members of their community. As noted, my analysis will also recognize traditional excusing conditions and generally keep the response to criminal wrongdoing proportional to the offense. Further, because I derived each aspect of our public response to criminal wrongdoing from our basic principle of justice, we have reason to believe that the distribution of burdens and benefits will be fair.

On the other hand, in the context of the paradigm of forgiveness, we can avoid some of the central problems that emerge in weak retributivism. Since both the "general justifying aim" of the practice and the structural features of it are derived from our principle of justice and the basic attitudes that give rise to this principle, we eliminate the problem of potential conflict between the justificatory components of the practice that can occur in a bifurcated approach such as Hart's. Further, having eliminated the utilitarian component of the theory, we can avoid the objection that we are using offenders as mere means to our own ends of obtaining social benefits. On a restitutive analysis of response to criminal wrongdoing, it seems clear that we are not using offenders in this way. Here we only attempt to nullify the harmful effects of the offender's own violation. We do not use him to produce positive social benefits or to achieve ends of our own. In the context of the paradigm of forgiveness, we care as much about the offender as we do about anyone else, and we are always guided by a desire to secure for each individual (offenders included) the most fundamental benefits in life compatible with like benefits for all.

The restitutive analysis of response to criminal wrongdoing differs significantly from simple desert-based retributive theories of punishment. In the context of a desert-based theory of punishment, we adopt the perspective of judgment and assess the offender's wrongful actions and attitudes. We then follow up this judgment by inflicting suffering on the offender in proportion to the gravity of his offense. If we endorse the paradigm of forgiveness, our stance toward the offender will be entirely different. Rather than adopting the perspective of judgment in responding to the offender, we will adopt the perspective of identification. We will have compassion for the offender as a sentient being and respect for him as a valuable human being and moral agent. We will not want him to suffer; nor will we believe that he somehow intrinsically deserves to suffer in light of his offense. Rather, we will want the best for him, and we will be concerned with his personal flourishing and moral development. Here we impose the burden of making restitution for primary and secondary harm on the offender only because we must do so to prevent others from bearing a more fundamental burden.

Nevertheless, the analysis presented here has several characteristics in common with this type of retributive theory. Our analysis entails the notion that there is a price to pay for criminal violations that goes beyond simply making restitution to one's immediate victim for primary harm. When punishment fails to produce any substantial benefit under a particular set of circumstances, some other form of restitution is required. Our analysis requires us to recognize as crimes most of the crimes that are currently recognized in our system of criminal law. And again, it requires that standard excusing conditions must be recognized, that we must never knowingly punish an innocent person, and that the severity of the punishment will generally be proportional to the gravity of the offense.

The one point at which a restitutive theory of punishment diverges significantly from a simple desert-based retributive theory is that on a restitutive theory, the severity of the punishment will vary not only with the gravity of the primary harm that typically results from a given offense, but also with the crime rate with respect to that offense in a given community. Because the members of the community experience a greater need to defend themselves when the crime rate is high, the secondary harm is more extensive and the need for restitution for that harm is more significant. Therefore the severity of the punishment is rightly increased when the frequency of a given offense has become so great that the members of the community experience a significant increase in the secondary harm. For example, suppose that identity theft becomes very prevalent in our society, that we have to take extensive steps to protect ourselves from this offense, and that the normal functioning of our economy is significantly damaged as a result. In this case, the restitutive analysis of punishment endorses an increase in the severity of the punishment for identity theft, provided that such an increase in punishment can be expected to create a stronger deterrent to this kind of activity.

The retributivist might object here that the punishment should always be directly proportional to the gravity of the offense, and that it should not depend on the crime rate. However, there are two points to be made in response to this line of argument. The first concerns the way in which we determine the gravity of the offense. Presumably the gravity of the offense should be measured, at least in part, by the extent of the harm that the given type of act can be expected to inflict on others. Murder is more serious than robbery because the former offense inflicts more harm on the victim than the latter. And murdering five persons is more serious than murdering one person, because more damage is done in the former case than in the latter. If so, then it stands to reason that a type of offense that produces a great deal of secondary harm is more serious than one that does not. Also, we must arguably consider the cumulative damage to those who have been harmed when we determine the gravity of a given offense. For example, tax evasion is a crime with no immediate victim, and the damage that one person alone does by evading his taxes will probably be negligible (assuming that he is not Bill Gates). Nevertheless, tax evasion is not regarded as a completely trivial offense, as it would be if we were to consider only the harm that one offender does individually. As moral agents, we are responsible for considering not only the individual effects of our actions but also their cumulative effects. In determining the gravity of a given offense, then, it would seem to follow that we should consider not only the primary harm of an action that falls on an individual victim, but also the cumulative secondary harm that falls on the members of the community. If we assess the gravity of an offense in terms of both types of harm that it produces, the restitutive analysis may actually perform *better* than desert-based retributivism in terms of matching the severity of the punishment (or the extent of the restitution required) to the gravity of the offense.

Second, we can point out that the victims of criminal violations ought to be considered as well as the offenders. Desert-based retributive theories tend to focus myopically on offenders. However, if we are to respect all persons as ends in themselves, we must also consider the members of the community. If we consider the members of the community and the interest they have in receiving restitution for the secondary harm they have suffered, it seems clear that they should receive more restitution as the secondary harm becomes more extensive. To simply calculate the severity of the punishment in terms of some preconceived, abstract measure of the gravity of the offense is tantamount to claiming that the members of the community should not be compensated when the secondary harm wrongfully inflicted on them increases with an increasing crime rate, and this claim would be difficult to justify. Further, it would conflict with the desert claim cited by Feinberg that persons deserve to be compensated for the harm that has been wrongfully inflicted on them.

The restitutive analysis of response to criminal wrongdoing that emerges in the paradigm of forgiveness also differs significantly from reciprocity or unfair advantage theories of punishment, primarily in that the restitutive analysis is not based on nullifying the supposed unfair advantage that the offender obtains over law-abiding citizens. As noted in the previous section, Russ Shaffer-Landau objects to unfair advantage theories on the grounds that they misrepresent the kind of harm that is involved in criminal violations. The most fundamental wrong involved in a criminal violation is the harm to the victim, and therefore crimes are not adequately characterized as free-riding offenses. Unlike unfair advantage theories, the restitutive analysis of response to wrongdoing that emerges in the paradigm of forgiveness focuses squarely on the harm that the offender inflicts on others – both the primary harm to the victim and the secondary harm to the members of the community. In the context of the paradigm of forgiveness, what is most centrally wrong with a criminal offense is that it inflicts harm on others that they should not have had to bear, and our response to wrongdoing is to require that the offender make restitution for that harm, both to the immediate victim(s) of his offense and to the members of his community.

However, the restitutive analysis of response to criminal wrongdoing that emerges in the paradigm of forgiveness also has some points in common with reciprocity theories. In the context of the paradigm of forgiveness, we will endorse the basic premises that the state is responsible for maintaining a just distribution of burdens and benefits among citizens and that criminal activity disrupts such a distribution. Here we seek to restore a fair distribution of burdens and benefits by requiring those who wrongfully inflict losses on others to make those losses good. Further, on the restitutive analysis, we can make clear sense of Morris's claim that the offender owes a debt to society. The offender has wrongfully inflicted primary harm on his victim(s) and secondary harm on the members of his community, and owes restitution for both forms of harm.

Again, the most interesting comparison may be between the restitutive analysis of public response to criminal wrongdoing and communicative or expressive theories of punishment. As noted, communicative theories seem excessively invasive, and they fail to evince sufficient respect for offenders as autonomous moral agents. Yet advocates of the paradigm of forgiveness have some common ground with these theorists as well. In the context of the paradigm of forgiveness, we can agree that it is a good thing for the offender to understand that his act was wrong, why it was wrong, and how wrong it was. We can agree that it would be desirable for the offender to repent of his wrong, and to reform his wrongful attitudes and behavior patterns. And we can agree that it would be desirable for the offender to make amends for the wrong to the extent that he is able to do so. (In Chapter 8, I will say more about how the state can legitimately help the offender to address these tasks.) However, given that the paradigm of forgiveness incorporates a fundamental respect for the offender as an autonomous moral agent, we cannot impose hard treatment on him against his will in order to manipulate him into accomplishing these aims. Further, as Bennett suggests, we must respect the offender as a fully qualified moral agent. And if we do not recognize him as such, then we are not justified in holding him responsible for his offense

With regard to expressive theories of punishment, in the context of the paradigm of forgiveness we can agree that the state must clearly express its commitment to the moral standards articulated in the criminal law. It must express the importance it attaches to these moral standards, and it must clearly regard its citizens as moral agents who are fully accountable for adhering to them. However, the restitutive analysis of response to criminal wrongdoing that emerges in the paradigm of forgiveness diverges from expressive theories of punishment on two important points. First, in the context of the paradigm of forgiveness we do not consider the desire to express these commitments dramatically or emphatically to constitute sufficient justification for inflicting hard treatment on offenders. Given that we extend the attitudes of respect, compassion, and real goodwill to all persons equally, we will not allow ourselves to use individuals as mere means to this end. In the context of the paradigm of forgiveness, the only way to justify the imposition of a burden on anyone is to show that we are required to do so in order to prevent greater or equal suffering for others.

Second, in the context of the paradigm of forgiveness, we do not endorse any attitude of hostility, contempt, or withdrawal of goodwill toward the offender. Not only must we refrain from direct expressions of hostility, we must also refrain from indirect expressions of contempt by imposing hard treatment as a symbol of the penance that would match the amount of self-contempt that is supposedly deserved for the offense in question. Whereas those who endorse expressive theories of punishment believe that it is morally imperative to respond to moral wrongs with a partial withdrawal of goodwill, in the context of the paradigm of forgiveness it is actually morally inappropriate to do so. In the context of the paradigm of forgiveness, we must not conflate the offender with his wrongful actions and attitudes, and we must not adopt the perspective of judgment. At all times we must recognize the offender as a sentient being and moral agent, and extend to him an attitude of respect, compassion, and real goodwill. (The only exception to these claims is for the victim who has not yet completed the process of addressing the wrong, and who needs to do so.)

Bennett (among others) evinces goodwill toward the offender *after* he has paid the price of the punishment in that he advocates reintegrating the offender into the moral community at that point. In the context of the paradigm of forgiveness, we can applaud the desire to see the offender reintegrated into the community in the long run, but we will hold that he never should have been alienated from the community in the first place. Although we require the offender to take on the burden of making restitution for the losses he has wrongfully inflicted on others, we do not ever withdraw our goodwill from him or regard him as anything less than a full-fledged member of the moral community. At all times we regard him with a full measure of respect, compassion, and real goodwill.

There are two objections to the restitutive analysis of response to criminal wrongdoing that are likely to be raised by those who endorse communicative or expressive theories of punishment. The first of these concerns the fact that on the restitutive analysis of punishment, we see punishment as a means by which offenders can make restitution for secondary harm if it functions reasonably efficiently as a deterrent to future criminal violations. Theorists such as Duff, Hampton, and Bennett hold that inflicting punishment merely as a deterrent is both manipulative and incompatible with respecting the offender as a moral agent who is himself responsible for ensuring that he complies with moral standards. For example, Hampton remarks that "if we aimed to prevent wrongdoing only by deterring its commission, we would be treating human beings in the same way that we treat dogs."[59] She adds that "according to the moral education theory, punishment is not intended as a way of conditioning a human being to do what society wants her to do (in the way that an animal is conditioned by an electric fence to stay within a pasture)...."[60] Rather than viewing punishment as a method for conditioning persons to behave in certain ways, then, we must see it as a method of communicating with persons directly as moral agents.

In the context of the paradigm of forgiveness, we will of course share the aim of respecting persons at all times as autonomous moral agents. We are clearly not justified in adopting Strawson's objective attitude and merely regarding persons as beings to be managed in the same way that we manage animals. Further, we will not be justified in using offenders as mere means to create social benefits, by instituting a practice of punishment simply in order to deter future criminal violations. This is the specific moral requirement that is violated in utilitarian analyses of criminal punishment. If we are to respect persons as ends in themselves,

[59] Jean Hampton, "The Moral Education Theory of Punishment," p. 259.
[60] *Ibid.*, p. 260.

we must recognize that each person has a moral status and intrinsic worth equal to that of every other person, and that no person ought to be regarded as a mere means for pursuing some further goal. In the paradigm of forgiveness, we have respect, compassion, and real goodwill for each person, and we evince these attitudes by adopting our principle of justice that insists that each individual be secured the most fundamental benefits in life compatible with like benefits for all. In this case, no individual is regarded as a mere means to the ends of others. No one is managed or manipulated in such a way as to achieve some further end or goal. Rather, in punishing the offender we are simply requiring him to repair the damage that he has wrongfully inflicted on others. It is important to recognize that even in the ideal case, when full restitution is made to all who have suffered primary and secondary harm, the offender has not been used to *advance* the interests of others. At best, those who have been injured are only as well off as they would have been if the offense had never been committed.

Further, it is clear that we must respect persons' autonomy. Unlike animals, we are autonomous moral agents and must be respected as such. In the context of this paradigm, persons are respected as autonomous moral agents in that we offer them a clear justification for our laws and social practices, especially those that impose burdens on them. And the justification they are offered is one that accords them a status equal to that of every other moral agent. The practice of punishment, when it is justified, is no exception to this rule. We do not merely punish offenders to condition them into doing what we want them to do. Rather, we explain to offenders that they have wrongfully inflicted secondary harm on the members of the community, and that although we have respect, compassion, and real goodwill for them, we regretfully impose punishment on them in order to provide the members of the community with restitution for this harm. We further respect persons' autonomy by honoring their right to make their own choices, insofar as we can do so without making others worse off in this regard. And perhaps most importantly, we honor them as autonomous moral agents by recognizing them as the authors of their own inner moral development.

Finally, it is important to recognize that if we were to regard the use of deterrents and incentives as in some sense intrinsically incompatible with respect for persons as autonomous moral agents, we would have to make radical changes in most areas of our lives. We use deterrents and incentives extensively in our educational systems, our businesses, our tax codes, our athletic competitions at all levels, our free-market economy, and in many other areas.

A second objection that might be raised by those who endorse communicative or expressive theories of punishment is developed very clearly by Thaddeus Metz in his interesting article "Censure Theory and Intuitions about Punishment." Metz argues that many people have the intuition that the state has a *pro tanto* obligation to punish all those who are guilty of criminal violations, and to do so in proportion to their guilt. Further, he argues that a censure or expressive theory of punishment explains this intuition more adequately than any other moral analysis of punishment. If we hold that the state is responsible for censuring criminal violations in proportion to the degree of their wrongfulness, and that punishment is justified on these grounds, then proportional punishment is, *a fortiori*, a *pro tanto* requirement in response to criminal wrongdoing. On the other hand, a restitutive theory of punishment will sanction punishment only if it is an effective means of deterring future violations, and only if there is no other means of exacting restitution for the members of the community that is more beneficial to them and no more costly to the offender.[61]

I believe that Metz is correct in believing that a censure theory of punishment best explains the intuition he has cited, and it may be that many people hold this intuition. However, there are two responses to this line of argument. First, the restitutive analysis of punishment comes closer to explaining this intuition than Metz has recognized because, on the restitutive analysis of response to criminal wrongdoing, when punishment is not required of those who commit criminal violations without justification or excuse, the offender is responsible for making restitution in some other manner. Further, the extent of this restitution is proportional to the extent of the secondary harm that the members of the community have suffered. Thus the offender who is (reasonably) able to make some kind of restitution for the secondary harm he has inflicted is, *pro tanto*, always required to do so.

Second, the cases in which punishment is not required will be cases in which some other form of restitution is more beneficial for the community and within the limits of sacrifice justly required of the offender. In cases of this sort, we have a strong, principled reason for abandoning punishment and imposing instead the requirement that is more mutually beneficial. If we extend an attitude of respect, compassion, and real

---

[61] See Thaddeus Metz, "Censure Theory and Intuitions about Punishment," p. 502.

goodwill to all persons equally, we will have both reason and motive to make each person's life as good as it can be, compatible with like benefits for all. We will therefore always be motivated to minimize the burdens we inflict on persons when we are able to do so without unfairly burdening others. Therefore we have strong reason to believe that the intuitive belief that Metz uses as the basis for his argument should be revised in this manner.

Finally, one who endorses a retributive theory of any kind may object to the analysis presented here by arguing that someone other than the offender could make restitution for him. An anonymous reader for Cambridge University Press clearly articulates this kind of objection as follows: "The logic of restitution does not require the one who has wrongfully harmed others to pay the restitution; his rich uncle may do it for him instead. So even if one is liable, by the logic of restitution theory, to go to jail, it would in principle be permissible for someone other than the offender to do it on his behalf." In response to this line of argument, it is important to recognize that in the context of the paradigm of forgiveness, the point of sending someone to jail (when this response is justified) is to provide protection for the members of the community against future criminal violations, in compensation for the secondary harm they have suffered. It is not clear that any general deterrence would be produced if we sent other persons to jail for offenders, assuming that such volunteers would be forthcoming. And more importantly, it seems clear that no special deterrence would be produced in this manner. Finally, it is clear that the members of the community would not be protected by incapacitating the offender if someone else went to prison in his stead. Therefore it seems very unlikely that this situation will arise in connection with a practice of punishment.

But the objection raised here is correct with regard to forms of restitution that do not involve preventing future violations through incapacitation or deterrence. In the context of the paradigm of forgiveness, our goal is not to make the offender suffer, but rather to alleviate for the victim the suffering that was wrongfully inflicted on her. If someone other than the offender wishes to make restitution to those who were harmed by the offense, this end will be accomplished. In the context of the paradigm of forgiveness, our only worry about the kind of scenario described here will be that the offender may experience more moral growth if he makes the restitution himself. Given that we hold an attitude of respect, compassion, and real goodwill toward the offender, we will not want him to suffer, but we will sincerely care about his moral and personal development. If the rich uncle adopts the attitudes of respect, compassion, and real goodwill toward the offender, he will take the offender's moral growth into account when he decides whether he will provide restitution for the victims. However, regardless of the rich uncle's decision here, and regardless of how we would like the offender's inner development to proceed, respect for the autonomy of moral agents precludes us from using the coercive apparatus of the law in an attempt to force inner moral development on the offender.

My discussion of the basic laws and social practices that emerge in the paradigm of forgiveness as the public response to wrongdoing is now complete. I have argued that the public response to wrongdoing has three components: prevention of wrongdoing, restitution for wrongfully inflicted primary harm, and restitution for wrongfully inflicted secondary harm. The requirement of making restitution for wrongfully inflicted secondary harm, like the first two components of the public response to wrongdoing, strengthens the response to Kekes' worry that we will not be able to respond adequately to the evil we find in the world if we adopt a version of choice-morality. With all three of these components combined, I believe that in the context of the paradigm of forgiveness, we will be able to do an adequate job of protecting our citizens (and other beings or objects that we value) from unnecessary harm. It is worth noting that the fact that our response to criminal wrongdoing is tailored to the extent of the secondary harm suffered by the members of the community strengthens our position in responding to Kekes' concern about protecting innocent citizens. As our need for protection against a certain type of crime increases, the secondary harm is more extensive and we are warranted in increasing the punishment (or other kind of restitution for secondary harm) for this type of offense. Further, I would suggest that the emphasis on prevention in the paradigm of forgiveness as well as our consistent attitudes of respect, compassion, and real goodwill for offenders will enhance our ability to prevent unnecessary harm. Not only do these features of the paradigm of forgiveness eliminate the unnecessary suffering imposed by retributive attitudes of hostility and contempt, they should also be effective in motivating persons to deal with wrongdoing in an open and constructive manner. Thus we might expect that the paradigm of forgiveness will perform at least as well as, if not better than, retributive positions in this regard. I will now turn to some refinements of the practices I have suggested.

8

Restorative Justice: The Public Response to Wrongdoing and the Process of Addressing the Wrong

A discussion of the paradigm of forgiveness would not be complete without addressing the restorative justice movement, nor would it be complete without some indication of how the public response to wrongdoing ought to be implemented. The restorative justice movement has received substantial attention in recent literature, and it is becoming increasingly well-developed. It is also making inroads into the practice of criminal justice in many jurisdictions around the world. It is important to recognize that there is some variation in the proposals advanced by those who identify themselves with this position.[1] I will not attempt to canvas the different (and sometimes conflicting) versions of restorative justice here. For our purposes it will suffice to explain how the paradigm of forgiveness incorporates some of the central tenets of this movement, although some qualification of some of the tenets may be required. A discussion of these matters will also provide us with an opportunity to consider in more detail how the public response to wrongdoing ought to be implemented in the context of the paradigm of forgiveness. The refinements of the public response to wrongdoing explained here will be derived in part from the processes of addressing the wrong described in Chapters 3 and 4, and in part from the basic attitudes that ground the paradigm of forgiveness.

It has generally been assumed that when an individual commits a crime, he should be tried in a criminal court and then punished if convicted. Advocates of restorative justice tend to believe that this manner of proceeding is indirect, overly formal, and counterproductive. Rather

---

[1] See Gerry Johnstone, *Restorative Justice: Ideas, Values, Debates*, p. 11.

than a formal criminal trial followed by some impersonal form of punishment, advocates of restorative justice propose an informal face-to-face meeting between the offender and the victim, and perhaps between the offender and representative members of the community who were significantly affected by the violation. Public officials are to be present at these meetings, but only as facilitators. Ideally, in these meetings the offender will accept responsibility for his offense, explain to the victim what was going on for him when he committed it, and apologize sincerely for having wrongfully harmed the victim. He will also offer to make restitution for the harm he has inflicted. Further, the victim will explain to the offender in some depth how she has been affected by his violation, and what her perspective is on the question of restitution for the wrong. The parties to the discussion will then mutually agree upon the steps that the offender can take to make substantive amends for the harm he has done. The same type of communication can take place between the offender and the members of the community. Some advocates of restorative justice believe that this kind of informal, personal procedure should largely replace our current system of criminal justice. Others believe that it should merely supplement our current system in cases in which it seems most promising and appropriate.

More specifically, Christopher Bennett summarizes the tenets of the restorative justice movement as follows: "(a) criminal justice should be more focused on the needs of victims than it presently is; (b) criminal justice should be more focused than it presently is on the needs of offenders to gain reacceptance or reintegration into the community; (c) offenders have a responsibility to make reparations to victims; and (d) these aims can best be met when matters of justice are left as far as possible for citizens to sort out for themselves."[2] To this list we will add a fifth central tenet of the restorative justice movement: (e) the state should get out of the business of pain delivery and attempt to facilitate resolutions of crimes that are more constructive for all involved than our traditional forms of punishment.

THE NEEDS OF THE VICTIM

It should be apparent by now that the paradigm of forgiveness incorporates important elements of each of these claims. The first claim is that the criminal justice system should be more focused than it presently is

---

[2] Christopher Bennett, *The Apology Ritual*, p. 21.

on the needs of the victim. The paradigm of forgiveness clearly yields this result. It is interesting to note that both retributive reactive attitudes and retributive theories of punishment are often focused primarily on the offender. An attitude of resentment focuses on the fact that the offender did something wrong, and that as a moral agent he could have and should have done otherwise. And some retributive theories of punishment focus on the fact that the criminal has done wrong and deserves to suffer accordingly. Arguably, the focus on the offender has led to the neglect of the victim in our criminal justice system. In contrast, our attitudes toward both offenders and victims in the context of the paradigm of forgiveness are the consistently positive attitudes of respect, compassion, and real goodwill. We are therefore concerned to benefit both victims and offenders to the extent that we are able to do so consistent with securing the most fundamental interests in life for everyone. The only requirement we impose on offenders in the context of the paradigm of forgiveness is to make restitution for the harm they have wrongfully inflicted on others, and we impose this requirement specifically for the sake of those who have been adversely affected by such acts. Thus our public response to wrongdoing is strongly focused on the victims of criminal violations.

In fact, all three components of the public response to wrongdoing in the paradigm of forgiveness are oriented toward victims or potential victims of wrongs. The first component of the public response to wrongdoing, which is strongly emphasized in the paradigm of forgiveness, is prevention. This component serves the needs of those who would otherwise become the victims of wrongdoing. One of the most important things we can do for persons is to try to prevent situations in which they will be victimized. The point of prevention is to protect persons from harm that they should not have to suffer (as well as to spare potential offenders, whenever possible, the agony of wrongdoing and its attendant difficulties). The second component of the public response to wrongdoing is also clearly directed toward the needs of the victim. The offender is required to make restitution to the victim for wrongfully inflicted primary harm. The victim should not have had to suffer the loss that the offender inflicted on her, and the offender is responsible for making the loss good. Likewise the third component of the public response to wrongdoing is directed toward the victims of wrongdoing – in this case, the members of the community. Our intention in requiring the offender to make restitution for the secondary harm that he has wrongfully inflicted on the members of the community is not to mete out to him some kind of suffering we believe he deserves. Rather, it is simply to mitigate *for those who have suffered secondary harm* a loss they should not have had to suffer.

Authors in the restorative justice movement have pointed out (again correctly) that we do the immediate victim of a crime a real disservice when we respond to the criminal violation in a manner that makes it unlikely that she will receive restitution for her primary loss. The paradigm of forgiveness also yields this result. The state must not overlook the victim's need for restitution for primary harm as it pursues restitution for secondary harm for the members of the community. Our basic principle of justice dictates that an individual ought not to be required to sacrifice an important interest so that others can benefit in less important ways. Therefore, when the immediate victim's need for restitution for the primary harm she has suffered is more fundamental than the community's need for restitution for secondary harm, as will often be the case, the state must give priority to securing restitution for the immediate victim of the crime.

In connection with this point, restorative justice advocates have also argued that the victim of a crime should be accorded a status that is more significant than a mere witness to the offense. Again, the paradigm of forgiveness incorporates this point. In the context of the public response to wrongdoing that emerges in the paradigm of forgiveness, the immediate victim is not merely a witness to the offense; she is owed restitution for the primary loss she has suffered. Therefore the state must ensure that the nature of her primary loss is fully explored, and that she is asked what would be most beneficial to her as restitution for this loss. Further, the state must see to it that the offender actually follows through and makes this restitution to the victim, within the limits of sacrifice that can reasonably be expected of him.

Authors in the restorative justice movement have further indicated that we ought to treat victims of crime in a much more respectful manner than we have in the past. Those who have been injured by criminal violations are sometimes treated in such a disrespectful manner that they feel just as victimized by the criminal proceedings as they did by the original offense. Again, the paradigm of forgiveness will endorse this extremely important point. The paradigm of forgiveness clearly requires that the attitudes of respect, compassion, and real goodwill be extended to the victims of crime (as well as to offenders) in all facets of the public response to wrongdoing. If we are to regard the victim with respect, compassion, and real goodwill, we must remember that, depending on the type of violation committed against her, she may well have suffered significant trauma and require special forms of help at this time. We must also remember that she is likely to be suffering from emotional distress, insecurity, and low self-esteem as a result of the violation. It is important, therefore, that she be offered the help she needs, and that all those involved in any aspect of the proceedings treat her in a respectful and compassionate manner that reflects a genuine concern for her welfare, recognition of her worth as a person, and respect for her autonomy.

Finally, Margaret Urban Walker has pointed out that communities have an important role to play in meeting the needs of victims, especially when offenders fail to do so. She says that "when those who are most clearly responsible for harm are absent, unavailable, or unresponsive … then communities must by default take up some of the efforts to provide, at least, acknowledgement, validation, and reassurance to victims of wrongs."[3] If the community has respect, compassion, and real goodwill for the victims of wrongdoing, it will clearly recognize their needs and respond to them in the way Walker suggests.

THE NEEDS OF THE OFFENDER TO GAIN REACCEPTANCE INTO THE COMMUNITY

The second central tenet of the restorative justice movement is that criminal justice should be more focused than it currently is on the needs of the offender to gain reacceptance or reintegration into the community. Advocates of the paradigm of forgiveness will strongly endorse this claim as well. In the context of the paradigm of forgiveness, retributive reactive attitudes are rejected. Although we have recognized that those who are personally wronged in a nontrivial manner are likely to experience an initial attitude of resentment and may need to work through a process of addressing the wrong, we have argued that it is ultimately appropriate and desirable from a moral point of view for them to adopt an attitude of unconditional genuine forgiveness toward the offender. Further, it is morally appropriate for those who are not personally affected by the crime to regard the offender continuously with respect, compassion, and real goodwill. As I have noted, if all persons held the attitudes endorsed in the paradigm of forgiveness, there would be no need for the offender to be "reintegrated" into the community, as he never would have been alienated from it in the first place.

[3] Margaret Urban Walker, *Moral Repair*, p. 222.

While some individuals may not respond to the offender in this ideal manner, the state can and should make sure that *its own* attitudes toward the offender are morally appropriate. Not only must his rights be respected; all those involved in the criminal justice system should also consistently regard the offender with respect, compassion, and real goodwill. They should show genuine concern and respect for the offender as a person, and attempt to make his life as good as possible within the limits of the requirements of justice. By adopting morally appropriate attitudes toward the offender themselves, those involved in the criminal justice system will set a good example for others to follow. Further, if the state does regard the offender with real goodwill, it will clearly be motivated to do what it can, within the limits of its resources, to facilitate the offender's reintegration into the community. As I will soon argue, the state can go some distance toward facilitating reacceptance of the offender by those who were affected by the crime with the type of face-to-face meetings proposed by advocates of restorative justice.

THE OFFENDER'S RESPONSIBILITY TO HIS VICTIMS

The third central claim advocated by those in the restorative justice movement is that offenders have a responsibility to make reparations to victims. This claim is clearly and centrally incorporated in the paradigm of forgiveness, as the second two components of the public response to wrongdoing are based entirely on this premise. In the context of the paradigm of forgiveness, we do not impose any negative consequences on offenders other than requiring them to fulfill their responsibility to make restitution for the harm they have wrongfully inflicted on others. But this much *is* required of them, in order to secure a fundamental benefit for everyone: the opportunity to make the most of our own lives through our own choices and efforts.

LEAVING MATTERS OF JUSTICE FOR CITIZENS TO SORT OUT FOR THEMSELVES

The fourth central tenet of the restorative justice movement – that matters of justice should be left as far as possible for citizens to sort out for themselves – is the tenet that will require the most qualification if we accept the paradigm of forgiveness. Much has been written about this claim, and I will not undertake a full discussion of it here. For our purposes it will be enough to note the aspects of this claim that we can accept and the aspects that require qualification if we accept the paradigm of forgiveness. Some of the authors in the restorative justice movement may accept what is said here, while others will not. There is certainly some room for the type of personal resolution of crimes proposed by advocates of restorative justice in the context of the paradigm of forgiveness, but let us begin by examining some of the aspects of this fourth tenet that require qualification.

The first point to notice here is that in the context of the paradigm of forgiveness, we must respect the autonomy of both the offender and the victim. Whereas retributive reactive attitudes incorporate a demand that the offender acknowledge his wrong and repent, and enforce this demand with at least a partial and temporary withdrawal of goodwill, in the context of the paradigm of forgiveness we consistently regard the offender with respect, compassion, and real goodwill. Although we recognize that the offender ought to repent and apologize, we also respect him as the author of his own attitudes. We do not try to force or manipulate him into an attitude of repentance. Therefore we cannot rightly require or pressure the offender to participate in the kind of direct, face-to-face communications envisioned by advocates of restorative justice. If, as a result of a fair trial, we determine that he owes restitution to others for primary and/or secondary harm, we can require him to make that restitution within reasonable limits of sacrifice. But his attitudes are his own to determine.

Likewise, although we have argued that it is appropriate and desirable for the victim to work through the process of addressing the wrong and reach a state of unconditional genuine forgiveness, respect for the victim's autonomy requires that we not force or pressure her to do so. Because we must respect her right to determine her own attitudes, and because, as I argued in Chapter 3, it may be detrimental for the victim to attempt to forgive the offender before she is ready to do so, we must allow the victims of wrongdoing to freely determine their own stance toward the offender at any given time. In light of these points, if direct meetings between offenders and those they have harmed are to take place, they must be fully voluntary. A formal criminal trial in which we fairly determine how much restitution (if any) is owed should be the default position when one or more of the parties involved does not wish to engage in the kind of informal, direct communications proposed by advocates of restorative justice.

Second, we must revert to formal criminal procedures if the kind of direct meeting proposed by advocates of restorative justice results in (or is likely to result in) disagreement between the parties involved and/or failure to follow through on an agreement that has been reached. In the context of a face-to-face meeting between the offender and those he has harmed, there may be disagreement between the participants about whether the offender was responsible for the offense, and if so, to what extent. There may also be disagreement as to how much harm the immediate victim and the members of the community have suffered, or as to how much restitution is owed. And even when there is agreement on all these points, the offender may fail to follow through in making the amends that have been agreed upon.

It is also important to notice that even when there is *initial* agreement on these points, either the offender or those whom he has injured may have second thoughts about them as they work through the process of addressing the wrong. At the time of the initial communication, the offender may not yet recognize the full extent of the harm he has imposed on others. Conversely, he may feel overly guilty and exaggerate the extent of his wrongdoing. He may also be too anxious to please the offender, or to secure her forgiveness. As he works through the process of addressing the wrong, he may gain a more realistic understanding of what he has done and what he actually owes by way of amends for his violation.

Likewise, the victim may have second thoughts as she works through the process of addressing the wrong. She may initially be overly resentful toward the offender or have an exaggerated view of how extensively she was harmed by the offense. Conversely, she may be inclined to engage in premature forgiveness, in the manner described in Chapter 3. She may be suffering from low self-esteem, fail to realize that she was actually wronged, or fail to recognize that she is now owed compensation for the loss. She may feel that her needs and feelings are not as important as the offender's. Or she may feel that she has a "duty" to forgive, and believe, mistakenly, that forgiveness entails a willingness to forgo restitution.[4] In cases of this sort, the victim may wish to modify what she has said in her initial communication with the offender as she works through the process of addressing the wrong. The same line of reasoning applies to members of the community who suffer secondary harm as a result of the violation.

---

[4] As we have seen, even an accomplished philosopher such as Claudia Card may believe that forgiveness entails a willingness to forego restitution. See Claudia Card, "The Atrocity Paradigm Revisited," p. 211.

To accommodate these possibilities, it is advisable to allow some waiting time between the initial communication between the offender and victim and the time that the agreement between them is finalized, to ensure that the parties involved remain in agreement as to the nature of the wrong and its proper resolution. When disagreement arises between the parties, or when the offender fails to follow through in making restitution after a clear agreement has been reached, the state has an obligation to step in and resolve the dispute with traditional legal proceedings.

Finally, because of the complications that can occur, it is essential for all parties to be advised of their procedural rights before the initial communication takes place. They should know that participation in this process is strictly voluntary and that they can withdraw from it at any point. They should be informed of their right to a criminal trial and to legal counsel throughout all proceedings. They should suffer no adverse consequences if they do choose to revert to a criminal trial. And they should be informed in advance of the nature of the informal procedure and of its possible results.

This much said, however, the paradigm of forgiveness will clearly endorse the kind of informal face-to-face meetings advocated in the restorative justice movement under many circumstances. Let us consider in turn meetings of this sort as they pertain to the resolution of primary and secondary harm. It is certainly possible that direct, interpersonal communications between the offender and his immediate victim will work out well. Both parties may well agree on the nature of the offense, on the extent of the primary harm, and on a fair amount of restitution, and the offender may follow through in making the restitution that has been agreed upon. When a meeting between the offender and victim could reasonably be expected to proceed in this manner, the type of direct interpersonal communication proposed by advocates of restorative justice seems clearly preferable to a formal trial. In addition to providing a just resolution of the primary harm that was wrongfully inflicted on the victim, a meeting of this sort provides both the offender and the victim with important opportunities. It provides the offender with an opportunity to express his sincere remorse to the victim, to learn how she was affected by his violation, and to learn what she would like as substantive amends for the primary harm she has suffered. It provides the victim with an opportunity to explain to the offender how she was affected by the crime, to learn what was going on for him when he committed it, and to let him know her current needs and feelings about the situation. Finally, a meeting of this sort provides an opportunity for a good relationship to form between the victim and the offender – a relationship characterized by mutual respect, compassion, and real goodwill.

In special cases it is also possible that the victim who has worked through the process of addressing the wrong will choose, in an informed, clear-headed, and emotionally mature manner, to forgo some or all of the restitution that she is owed for primary harm. A person who adopts an attitude of unconditional genuine forgiveness toward her offender may wish to engage in a merciful act of this sort, or she may wish to receive full restitution for her loss. Each course of action is fully compatible with an attitude of unconditional genuine forgiveness, and the victim's decision is likely to depend on her perception of the relative importance of the interests that both she and the offender have at stake. In any case, clear-headed, emotionally mature acts of mercy are admirable, and they exemplify to a strong degree the basic attitudes of respect, compassion, and real goodwill that ground the paradigm of forgiveness. And when they are undertaken in the context of direct interpersonal communication between the offender and the victim, arguably they will be especially beneficial to both parties. Each party may experience significant personal growth as a result of this kind of interaction.

Let us now consider the resolution of the secondary harm. Here the situation is more complex. If our analysis of secondary harm is correct, criminal offenders inflict harm on the community as a whole in addition to harming the immediate victims of their crimes. In order to ensure that citizens are not unfairly burdened by having to absorb the secondary losses that were unjustly inflicted on them, the state must require the offender to make restitution for secondary harm, to the extent that he is able to do so and within the limit of sacrifice that can reasonably be required of him. And while individual victims of criminal violations may mercifully choose to forgo the restitution they are owed for the primary harm, given the number of individuals who suffer secondary harm it seems unlikely that they will all agree to forgo the restitution they are owed for secondary harm.

Nevertheless, the paradigm of forgiveness provides moral space for the informal handling of crimes proposed by advocates of restorative justice. As we have noted, in the context of the paradigm of forgiveness the only reason we will ever impose a negative consequence on an offender in addressing the secondary harm he has wrongfully inflicted on others is to provide some kind of benefit for the members of the community to compensate them for the secondary loss that they should not have to absorb. Therefore, in order to determine the appropriate public response to a criminal offense, we must address an important empirical question: we must determine which method of responding to a given offender will produce the most good for the members of the community, within the limits of sacrifice that we can legitimately require of that offender. Economists, criminologists, and sociologists will be the ones to provide us with our best answers to this kind of question, and again the full development of the paradigm of forgiveness will rely heavily on the empirical sciences at this point. Suffice it to say here that the kind of informal procedures proposed by advocates of restorative justice will be endorsed in the context of the paradigm of forgiveness whenever they constitute the most effective method available for producing lasting benefits for the members of the community as restitution for secondary harm within the limits of sacrifice that are properly required of the offender.

It seems reasonable to believe that the procedures suggested by advocates of restorative justice will meet these conditions when we are addressing certain groups of offenders – for example, juvenile offenders, or those who commit less serious offenses for the first time and then show genuine remorse. In some cases, the community may derive more lasting benefit if the only requirement for the offender is to meet face-to-face with the immediate victim of his crime and make amends to her. If simply making direct amends to the victim is the procedure that is most likely to make the offender a productive, law-abiding citizen in the future, perhaps the community will benefit maximally by adopting this approach. In other cases more benefit may be derived for the community as a whole if the offender meets face-to-face with some representative members of the community as well as the victim, or, when the victim is unwilling or unable to participate, if the offender meets with these community members alone. In cases of this sort, it is again possible that the informal procedure is most likely to make the offender a contributive, law-abiding citizen in the future, and that this result will be maximally beneficial for the community. Both the immediate victim of the crime and the members of the community may also benefit significantly from the enhanced understanding of the motive for the crime and from the renewed sense of confidence in the offender that may result from these meetings.

But regardless of whether a criminal case should be addressed by the kind of face-to-face meetings endorsed in the restorative justice movement or by a formal criminal trial followed by sentencing, advocates of the restorative justice movement make an extremely important point in suggesting that the process of addressing criminal wrongs is not best conceived as a wholly formal, bureaucratic process in which the offender and victim play only passive roles. This point will be endorsed in the paradigm of forgiveness as well. As I have argued in Chapter 4, the offender, as a moral agent, is responsible for undertaking a process of addressing his wrong. Whether the informal meetings envisioned in the restorative justice movement take place in lieu of a criminal trial, or after a criminal trial has been completed and a requirement set for the offender, they are likely to play an important role in this process. They may also provide other significant benefits for the offender in his development as a person and as a moral agent. Further, meetings of this sort are likely to play an important role for those who have been injured (both immediate victims and community members) as they work through the process of addressing the wrong, and to provide additional benefits for these persons as well. Let us consider in turn the potential benefits of these meetings for the offender, the immediate victim, and the members of the community.

Given that as a moral agent the offender is responsible for undertaking the process of addressing his wrong, and given that the state is obligated to respect the offender as a moral agent, it follows that the state should do its best (within the limits of available resources) to provide the offender with the opportunity to complete this process. Again, in order to respect the offender as an autonomous moral agent, we must recognize him as the author of his own moral development. We should therefore not require him to undertake this process, except as it involves making restitution for the harm he has wrongfully inflicted on others, nor should we impose hard treatment or other kinds of pressures that are designed to manipulate him into doing so. But it is important that we provide all offenders with the *opportunity* to fulfill their responsibilities as moral agents and therefore that we support them in completing the process of addressing their wrongs if they wish to do so. To review, in order to responsibly address the offense, the offender must first acknowledge the offense and take full responsibility for having committed it. He must also come to understand why it was wrong and to recognize and appreciate the victim's status as a person. He must allow himself to experience the emotions that arise for him in connection with the wrong, such as intense grief and remorse for having committed it. He must then identify the problematic attitudes and behavior problems that led him to commit the wrong, and attempt to eradicate them. Finally, he must approach the victims of his offense to make a sincere and thorough apology and to offer restitution for the wrong, unless such a course of action would do the injured persons more harm than good.

In order to support this process for criminal offenders, the state will ideally offer counseling sessions to offenders to help them look honestly at the offense, work through their emotional responses, identify their problematic attitudes and behavior patterns, and find techniques to eradicate them. Ideally, the state will also make available to offenders a variety of programs of personal and spiritual growth to choose from that will support and enhance their efforts to reform their attitudes and behavior patterns. And ideally, the state will facilitate meetings between offenders and victims in which offenders can offer direct and sincere apology to their victims and offer to make substantive amends for the harm they have inflicted. Advocates of restorative justice have made great strides here in describing the structure of meetings that can facilitate this latter part of the process.

Other significant benefits are likely to result for the offender from the type of meeting under consideration. I argued in Chapter 4 that the offender is ultimately responsible for forgiving himself independently of his victim's forgiveness. Whether or not she forgives him, it is important for him to respect himself as a valuable human being with the capacity for moral choice, growth, and awareness. He is also responsible for transcending the focus on himself and his past record of moral performance, and for using his moral capacities responsibly by directing them toward positive pursuits. This much said, however, it will certainly be a fulfilling experience for the offender to be forgiven by the victim of his offense. We all seek to be understood by others and to feel some kind of positive connection with them. If a meeting with the victim can result in genuine forgiveness, it will certainly be valuable for the offender.

In addition to providing him with the fulfilling experience of having been forgiven, a meeting of the sort described by advocates of restorative justice may well have a positive effect in inspiring the offender to work harder to reform his attitudes and behavior patterns. Arguably we can all make more progress in improving our moral character in an atmosphere of acceptance and support than we can in an atmosphere of hostility and rejection. If the offender is forgiven by his victim, he may feel as if he has a new lease on life, or a second chance to be a decent, contributive member of society. Further, we have argued that persons should always regard the offender with respect, compassion, and real goodwill regardless of what he has done, but unfortunately, many people may adopt retributive reactive attitudes toward the offender instead. In this case, the forgiveness of his victim may benefit the offender in another important respect. If others see that the victim has forgiven the offender, then they may be more likely to accept him as well, and to extend toward him the morally appropriate attitudes of respect, compassion, and real goodwill. Thus a meeting between the victim and the offender, when it goes well, can lead to an upward spiral in the offender's life that makes a significant contribution to his happiness, moral growth, and personal fulfillment. Again, it is important to stress that the offender may derive these benefits from a face-to-face meeting with the victim regardless of whether it occurs in lieu of a criminal trial or after a criminal trial has taken place and legal requirements for the offender have been set.

Let us now consider the benefits that the immediate victim may derive from a face-to-face meeting with the offender. The process that the victim must typically work through in addressing the wrong was described in Chapter 3. In this process, the victim of a serious wrong must typically establish for herself that she is a valuable person with a moral status equal to that of everyone else, and that the act perpetrated against her was wrong. As noted, the offense carries an implicit message that the victim does not warrant a full measure of respect. The victim who has not yet completed the process of addressing the wrong is likely to be struggling with that message. It is at this stage of the process that the victim can benefit significantly from the type of interaction between victim and offender that is advocated in the restorative justice movement.

In a personal conversation between the victim and the offender, the victim has an opportunity to ask the offender why he did what he did. If he answers this question honestly, the offender will explain that he was reacting to various pressures in his own life. As the victim listens to the offender, she will ideally come to realize that the wrong has nothing to do with her own lack of worth, but rather with the offender's own needs, which he unjustifiably chose to pursue by victimizing her. For example, arguably the offender who commits a rape responds not to the victim's lack of worth, but rather to his own need to feel some kind of dominance, control, or power – perhaps as a way of coping with past abuse or humiliation that was inflicted on him. And arguably the offender who burglarizes the victim's home responds not to her lack of moral status, but rather to his own need for money or possessions, and his own lack of self-respect as a person who can effectively make his own way in the world. As the victim comes to understand why the offender committed the offense, she is likely to be aided in her own task of recovering her self-esteem. She may come to see the offender as a person who is separable from his offense – a person who suffers from various needs, pressures, and confusions, just as she does. To the extent that she can identify with the offender and see him as a person, she will be aided in reaching a state of genuine forgiveness.

If the offender sincerely apologizes to her and offers to make amends for the offense, the victim's self-esteem will be bolstered further. I have argued that the victim is ultimately responsible for recognizing her own worth, and it is important for her well-being that she finds a way to do so. But having her offender sincerely apologize to her for the wrong may be very helpful to her in reaching the point at which she can recognize her own worth for herself. Therefore, a meeting between the victim and the offender in which the offender sincerely apologizes for the wrong act and offers restitution for it may be very beneficial to the victim in healing from the offense.

The victim may also be able to complete some of the remaining steps she needs to take in addressing the wrong as she meets with the offender. She may be able to express her feelings about the incident to him, and tell him that it is not acceptable for her to be treated in this manner. Further, she may be able to explain to him the kind of harm she has incurred as a result of his violation, and to ask him for the kind of restitution she would like to have for that harm.

As was the case for the offender, a meeting of this sort can also lead to a positive spiral for the victim. If the victim is able to successfully complete the process of addressing the wrong and manages to forgive her offender, she will benefit in significant ways. If my arguments in Chapter 3 were correct, she will reach a morally appropriate attitude toward the offender. Further, she will achieve the peace of mind that accompanies a state of unconditional genuine forgiveness. Her mind will no longer be focused on the incident of wrongdoing and the moral faults of her offender, and she will be free of the corrosive anger that accompanies an attitude of resentment. As she lets go of the incident of wrongdoing, she will be able instead to focus her attention on her own positive pursuits. And as she does so, her self-esteem will be enhanced even further. In the context of the paradigm of forgiveness, we will certainly have reason and motive to secure these important benefits for victims whenever we can do so without violating the autonomy of either the victim or the offender. As before, it is important to recognize that these benefits can be obtained regardless of whether the meeting between the victim and offender occurs in lieu of a criminal trial or after a criminal trial has taken place and a requirement set for the offender.

Finally, the kind of meetings that have been proposed by advocates of the restorative justice movement can also produce significant benefits for the members of the offender's community, and the paradigm of forgiveness will enjoin us to secure these benefits when we can do so without violating other moral requirements. If my reasoning has been correct, the immediate victim and those with a personal connection with her are not the only ones who are seriously harmed by criminal violations. The members of the community are wrongfully burdened with secondary harm as well. To the extent that members of the community harbor personal resentment for this wrong, they may need to undertake a process of addressing the wrong that is very similar to the process faced by the immediate victim. And regardless of whether they develop any resentment, the members of the community face the task of seeking restitution for the secondary harm they have suffered. Thus, a face-to face meeting with the offender may assist the members of the community in working through the process of addressing the wrong in much the same way that this type of meeting assists the immediate victim in doing so.

Further, it is important to recognize that the effects of secondary harm can at times be very local. In addition to responding to our knowledge of the general crime rate as we determine what steps we will take to protect ourselves from victimization, we often respond to immediate local conditions. If a particularly disturbing crime (or series of crimes) has been committed in our neighborhood, it is likely that we will sacrifice more activities and resources to protect ourselves than we otherwise would. Walter Dickey describes a meeting between an offender and victim that served to significantly reduce the kind of secondary harm just described.[5] The meeting was between the offender, Johnny Singleton, and the pastor of the church he burglarized, Reverend Harry Davis. The offense took place in a neighborhood where a shooting had recently taken place in another church, resulting in the death of one of the parishioners. As a result of this crime and then the burglary of their own church, many of the church members were feeling quite apprehensive about continuing to attend. In the meeting between the reverend and Singleton, Singleton explained that he had been involved with drugs at the time and that he had not realized that the building was a church. He also expressed his sincere remorse for the crime and offered to speak to the whole congregation in order to apologize and explain the situation. Further, he offered to make restitution to the congregation by doing yard work for

[5] Walter Dickey, "Forgiveness and Crime," pp. 108–109.

the church or by working on its renovation project. By responding in this manner, the offender was able to reduce the secondary harm that the members of the congregation experienced as a result of his offense.

Once again, it is important to note that a positive spiral can result from interactions of this kind. Not only did the members of the community have their secondary harm reduced as a result of this interaction, they also learned more about how such offenses originate and therefore about how they might be prevented. Further, by forgiving Singleton and incorporating him into their workforce, they benefited from his company and from the positive attitudes of compassion and respect that replaced their attitudes of fear and resentment. It is also possible that other drug addicts in the community will see the kind reception that Singleton is receiving, and that they will ask for help and start participating in the church as well. This, in turn, may make the community stronger and safer. As before, given that the paradigm of forgiveness is based on the attitudes of respect, compassion, and real goodwill extended to all persons equally, it will clearly endorse this kind of interaction for the benefit of offenders and community members alike.

Finally, as advocates of restorative justice have pointed out, those involved in a criminal violation are empowered when they have a significant personal role in resolving the situation. Rather than passively waiting to see what results will emerge from the procedures undertaken by the state, they are actively involved in working through the offense and the needs and feelings it has generated in them. Considerable personal and moral growth can take place for those involved when they participate actively in resolving the crime.

CONSTRUCTIVE SOLUTIONS TO CRIMES

The fifth central tenet of the restorative justice movement, and the last claim we will consider here, is that the state should get out of the business of pain delivery and attempt to facilitate resolutions of crimes that are more constructive for all involved than our traditional forms of punishment. The paradigm of forgiveness will clearly endorse this claim as well. First, it is important to recognize that in the context of the paradigm of forgiveness, inflicting pain will never be a legitimate, primary purpose of any public or private response to wrongdoing. Those who endorse retributive reactive attitudes and retributive theories of punishment may consider inflicting pain to be an intrinsically fitting response to wrongdoing, and therefore a primary purpose of a practice of punishment, but advocates of the paradigm of forgiveness do not. Although the paradigm of forgiveness may endorse legal punishment as a response to criminal wrongdoing under certain circumstances, the sole purpose of any requirement imposed on the offender in the context of the paradigm of forgiveness is to make good the losses that have been wrongfully inflicted on those who have been injured. At a greater level of abstraction, the sole purpose of each of the components of the public response to wrongdoing is to ensure that each individual is secured the most fundamental interests in life compatible with like benefits for all.[6]

In the context of the paradigm of forgiveness, we will strongly encourage creative thought about the resolution of crimes. We should certainly not assume that our traditional forms of punishment are maximally beneficial, either for those who have suffered harm as a result of the criminal violation or for the offender. Creative experimentation and empirical analysis should be undertaken to determine which means of making restitution are actually most beneficial for those who have been wrongfully harmed. Further, given that we consistently regard the offender with respect, compassion, and real goodwill, we will want his situation to be as good as it can be, compatible with the requirements of justice. If we can think of a response to wrongdoing that actually benefits the offender overall, at the same time that he makes full restitution to those he has wrongfully harmed, this will be the preferred response. The second best response is one in which the offender can make full restitution to those he has harmed without suffering any pain himself. It is only when neither of these options is available that we will resort to responses that impose some kind of loss or pain on the offender. And when a response that requires loss or pain of the offender is indicated, everything else being equal, we will always prefer the response that minimizes his loss or pain. Again, creative experimentation and

---

[6] This is a point that David Boonin finds to be contradictory. On p. 233 of *The Problem of Punishment* he refers to my restitutive theory of punishment and writes: "But this is a mistake, and an important one. Not every legally imposed restriction on a person's freedom of movement is punishment. It is punishment only if it is done with the aim of making the offender suffer for his offense." However, I find no contradiction in saying that we impose punishment, which involves some hardship for the offender, not because we ultimately desire to make him suffer, but rather because we want members of the community to receive restitution for the secondary harm they have suffered. Likewise we may send a child to his room, which will involve some suffering, not for the primary purpose of making him suffer, but for the purpose of making him a well-behaved and viable member of the family. Still, we might call this action "punishment."

empirical research are called for to make these determinations. In the context of the paradigm of forgiveness, then, the state is not in the business of inflicting pain; rather, it is in the business of ensuring that those who have been wrongfully harmed are offered restitution for their losses, and of ensuring that all citizens are secured the highly significant benefit of being able to make the most of their own lives through their own choices and efforts.

To summarize. In the context of the paradigm of forgiveness we will want to incorporate many of the suggestions made in the restorative justice movement. The public response to wrongdoing must include state oversight of the processes of requiring restitution for both primary and secondary harm to ensure that immediate victims and community members are not unfairly disadvantaged by offenders and likewise that offenders are not unfairly disadvantaged by those they have harmed. But our public response to wrongdoing must also be flexible enough to facilitate the kinds of processes described by advocates of restorative justice, in order to help offenders, victims, and community members work through the process of addressing the wrong when they wish to do so, and to ensure that the needs of these parties are met in the most effective way possible given the resources that are available. At times, judgment will be required to determine which of the available responses to wrongdoing should take priority. For example, we may wonder whether to incarcerate the man who burglarizes the church to compensate community members for secondary harm by creating a deterrent to future burglaries, or to allow him to make restitution to the church congregation through apology and work on their renovation project. To resolve these conflicts, we can appeal to our principle of justice, which enjoins us to secure the most fundamental interests for each person compatible with like interests for all. If we cultivate within ourselves the morally integrated attitudes of respect, compassion, and real goodwill for all persons, and extend them equally to everyone, we should be well able to make these judgments as required in particular cases, given the relevant empirical data.

Finally, it is worth reemphasizing that in the context of the paradigm of forgiveness, whatever specific actions we undertake as a public response to wrongdoing should be implemented with the attitudes of respect, compassion, and real goodwill for all concerned. Clearly, victims should always be treated with respect, compassion, and a genuine concern for their welfare by any officials with whom they have contact. And, importantly, offenders should always be treated in this manner as well. Eric Reitan beautifully describes the appropriate attitude to adopt toward criminal offenders with regard to punishment in the following passage: "The punishment must be inflicted without righteousness or malice, but instead in such a way that it is clear to the recipient of punishment that those who impose the punishment share at least vicariously in the suffering of the one punished."[7] In the context of the paradigm of forgiveness, this is the attitude we should adopt toward any offender on whom we are required to impose a requirement that causes him pain or loss. All officials involved in the criminal justice system should attempt to cultivate in themselves morally integrated attitudes of respect, compassion, and real goodwill for the offender, and should consistently interact with him in a manner that evinces these attitudes.

In sum, it seems that the paradigm of forgiveness and the restorative justice movement are based on very similar moral ideals. Therefore the paradigm of forgiveness may be considered as a possible theoretical framework to ground the restorative justice movement.

CONCLUSION

In this book I have developed an outline of the paradigm of forgiveness as a broadly coherent response to wrongdoing. I have also argued that the paradigm of forgiveness is preferable to prominent versions of both attitudinal retributivism and retributive theories of punishment. Attitudinal retributivism respects offenders as autonomous moral agents in some respects, but ultimately fails in this regard because it objectifies the offender by conflating him with his wrongful actions and attitudes. This position goes further astray by adopting the perspective of judgment, and then by reacting with hostility or partial withdrawal of goodwill toward the conglomerate of the offender and his wrongful actions and attitudes. If we are to fully respect the offender as a moral agent and sentient being, we must clearly separate the offender from his wrongful actions and attitudes. We must reject the perspective of judgment, adopt the perspective of identification, and relate to the offender as a person. In this case, we will extend to him an attitude of respect, compassion, and real goodwill, regardless of what he has done or suffered and regardless of whether he repents.

---

[7] Eric Reitan, "Punishment and Community: The Reintegrative Theory of Punishment," p. 76.

I have also argued that an attitude of unconditional genuine forgiveness is grounded in defensible philosophical analyses of the nature of persons. I argued that the paradigm of forgiveness rests on a plausible analysis of human worth and moral status, that it is compatible with a persuasive position on personal identity, and that it incorporates a robust and defensible position on moral responsibility. On the other hand, I suggested that attitudinal retributivism may be problematic in each of these respects. I then argued that the basic attitudes embedded in the paradigm of forgiveness will lead to a justice-based moral theory, and that a justice-based moral theory can be more easily defended than the kind of desert-based moral theory generally endorsed by some retributivists. Finally, I have derived the three components of a public response to wrongdoing from this justice-based moral theory and the attitudes from which it emerges, and I have argued that the reasons for endorsing this public response to wrongdoing are more defensible than the arguments that retributivists have offered to justify a practice of punishment. And I have argued that the public response to wrongdoing advocated in the paradigm of forgiveness underwrites the central tenets of the restorative justice movement. If my arguments have been successful, we can now attempt to purge our attitudes toward wrongdoers of resentment, judgment, and self-righteousness. Rather than conflating offenders with their wrongful actions and attitudes and responding to them with hostility or a partial withdrawal of goodwill, we can consistently regard all persons with respect, compassion, and real goodwill.

We are now at a point at which we can assess the virtue-ethical approach to response to wrongdoing that I have pursued in this book. I began by arguing that the basic attitudes of unconditional genuine forgiveness and genuine self-forgiveness are always appropriate and desirable from a moral point of view for those who have sufficiently completed the process of addressing the wrong. In other words, these attitudes are virtuous, and worthy of cultivating in ourselves as character traits, or regular responses to wrongdoing. I then argued that these attitudes, when extended to all persons equally, will lead us to adopt a justice-based moral theory that enjoins us to secure the most fundamental interests in life compatible with like benefits for all. From there, I derived a fairly detailed outline of a morally appropriate public response to wrongdoing. If my arguments have been correct, I have derived from the moral attitudes that are fundamental to virtue ethics an integrated set of conclusions about what we ought to do in responding to wrongs. In this case, I have provided at least some response to critics who claim that virtue ethics fails to provide us with sufficient guidance as to what we ought to do. I have also provided some support for His Holiness the Fourteenth Dalai Lama's claim that if our overall state of heart and mind is wholesome, then the rest of our moral deliberation and decision-making will be wholesome as well.

Works Cited

Adams, Marilyn McCord. "Forgiveness: A Christian Model." *Faith and Philosophy* 8 (1991): 277–304.

Allais, Lucy. "Wiping the Slate Clean: The Heart of Forgiveness." *Philosophy and Public Affairs* 36/1 (2008): 33–68.

Aristotle, *Nichomachean Ethics*. Trans. Sir David Ross. London: Oxford University Press, 1954.

Barnett, Randy. "Restitution: A New Paradigm of Criminal Justice." *Ethics* 87 (1977): 279–301.

Benjabi, Hagit, and David Heyd. "The Charitable Perspective: Forgiveness and Toleration as Supererogatory." *Canadian Journal of Philosophy* 31/4 (December 2001): 567–586.

Bennett, Christopher. *The Apology Ritual: A Philosophical Theory of Punishment*. New York: Cambridge University Press, 2008.

———. "The Varieties of Retributive Experience." *Philosophical Quarterly* 52 (2002): 145–163.

Bentham, Jeremy. *Introduction to the Principles of Morals and Legislation*, eds. J.H. Burns and H.L.A. Hart. London: University of London and Athlone Press, 1970.

Blum, Lawrence. "Compassion." In *Explaining Emotions*, ed. Amelie O. Rorty, pp. 507–518. Berkeley: University of California Press, 1980.

Boonin, David. *The Problem of Punishment*. Cambridge: Cambridge University Press, 2008.

Boss, Judith A. "Throwing Pearls to Swine: Women, Forgiveness, and the Unrepentant Abuser." In *Philosophical Perspectives on Power and Domination: Theories and Practices*, eds. Laura Duhan Kaplan and Laurence F. Bove, pp. 235–247. Atlanta, GA: Rodopi, 1997.

Brandt, Richard B. *Ethical Theory*. Englewood Cliffs, NJ: Prentice-Hall, 1959.

Brison, Susan J. *Aftermath: Violence and the Remaking of a Self*. Princeton, NJ: Princeton University Press, 2002.

Burgh, Richard W. "Do the Guilty Deserve Punishment?" *The Journal of Philosophy* 79 (1982): 193–210.

Calhoun, Cheshire. "Changing One's Heart." *Ethics* 103 (October 1992): 76–96.

Card, Claudia. *The Atrocity Paradigm: A Theory of Evil*. New York: Oxford University Press, 2002.

———. "The Atrocity Paradigm Revisited." *Hypatia* 19/4 (Fall 2004): 210–220.

Casarjian, Robin. *Forgiveness*. New York: Bantam Books, 1992.

Chang, Victor, and His Holiness the Dalai Lama. *The Wisdom of Forgiveness: Intimate Conversations and Journeys*. New York: Riverhead Books, 2004.

Coleman, Jules. "Theories of Tort Law." *The Stanford Encyclopedia of Philosophy* (Fall 2008 Edition), Edward N. Zalta (ed.). URL=http://plato. stanford.edu/archives/fall2008/entries/tort-theories/>.

Daniels, Norman. "Wide Reflective Equilibrium and Theory Acceptance in Ethics." *The Journal of Philosophy* 76 (1979): 256–282.

Darwall, Stephen L. "Two Kinds of Respect." *Ethics* 88 (1977): 34–49.

Davis, Michael. "Criminal Desert and Unfair Advantage: What's the Connection?" *Law and Philosophy* 12 (1993): 133–156.

———. "How to Make the Punishment Fit the Crime." *Ethics* 93 (1983): 726–752.

———. *To Make the Punishment Fit the Crime*. Boulder, CO: Westview Press, 1992.

Dickey, Walter. "Forgiveness and Crime: The Possibilities of Restorative Justice." In *Exploring Forgiveness*, eds. Robert D. Enright and Joanna North, pp. 106–120. Madison, WI: University of Wisconsin Press, 1998.

Dillon, Robin. "Self-Forgiveness and Self-Respect." *Ethics* 112 (October 2001): 53–83.

———. "Self-Respect: Moral, Emotional, Political." *Ethics* 107 (January 1997): 226–249.

Dix, George E., and M. Michael Sharlot. *Criminal Law: Cases and Materials*. St. Paul, MN: West Publishing Company, 1973.

Dolinko, David. "Morris on Paternalism and Punishment." *Law and Philosophy* 18 (1999): 345–361.

———. "Some Thoughts about Retributivism." *Ethics* 101 (April 1991): 537–559.

Duff, R.A. "Legal Punishment." *The Stanford Encyclopedia of Philosophy* (Fall 2008 Edition), Edward N. Zalta (ed.). URL=http://plato.stanford.edu/ archives/fall2008/entries/legal-punishment/>.

———. *Punishment, Communication and the Community*, Oxford: Oxford University Press, 2001.

———. *Trials and Punishment*, Cambridge: Cambridge University Press, 1986.

Dzur, Albert, and Alan Wertheimer. "Forgiveness and Public Deliberation: The Practice of Restorative Justice." *Criminal Justice Ethics* (Winter/Spring 2002): 3–20.

Ellis, Anthony. "Critical Study: Recent Work on Punishment." *The Philosophical Quarterly* 45/19 (April 1995): 225–233.

Enright, Robert D. "Counseling within the Forgiveness Triad: On Forgiving, Receiving Forgiveness, and Self-Forgiveness." *Counseling and Values* 40/2 (January 1996): 107–126.

Enright, Robert D., and Richard P. Fitzgibbons. *Helping Clients to Forgive.* Washington, DC: American Psychological Association, 2000.

Falls, Margaret. "Retribution, Reciprocity, and Respect for Persons." *Law and Philosophy* 6 (1987): 25–51.

Fitzgibbons, Richard P., and Robert D. Enright. *Helping Clients to Forgive.* Washington, DC: American Psychological Association, 2000.

Feinberg, Joel. *Doing and Deserving.* London: Princeton University Press, 1970.

Fortune, Maria M. "Justice-Making in the Aftermath of Woman-Battering," in *Domestic Violence on Trial*, ed. Daniel Jay Sonkin. New York: Springer Publishing Co., 1987.

French, Peter A. *The Virtues of Vengeance.* Lawrence, KS: University Press of Kansas, 2001.

Garrard, Eve, and David McNaughton. "In Defense of Unconditional Forgiveness." *Proceedings of the Aristotelian Society* 103 (2003): 39–60.

Glynn, Patrick. "Towards a Politics of Forgiveness." *The American Enterprise* (September/October 1994): 50–54.

Govier, Trudy. *Forgiveness and Revenge.* London: Routledge, 2002.

Govier, Trudy, and Colin Hirano. "A Conception of Invitational Forgiveness." *Journal of Social Philosophy*, 39/3 (Fall 2008): 429–444.

Griswold, Charles. *Forgiveness: A Philosophical Exploration.* New York: Cambridge University Press, 2007.

Haber, Joram Graf. *Forgiveness.* Lanham, MD: Rowman and Littlefield, 1991.

Hampton, Jean. "The Moral Education Theory of Punishment." *Philosophy and Public Affairs* 13 (1984): 208–238.

Hampton, Jean, and Jeffrie G. Murphy. *Forgiveness and Mercy.* Cambridge: Cambridge University Press, 1988.

Harman, Gilbert. "Is There a Single True Morality?" In *Morality, Reason and Truth*, eds. David Copp and Michael Zimmerman. Totowa, NJ: Rowman & Allanheld, 1985, pp. 27–48.

——. "Moral Philosophy Meets Social Psychology: Virtue Ethics and the Fundamental Attribution Error." *Proceedings of the Aristotelian Society* (1999): 315–331.

——. "Three Trends in Moral and Political Philosophy." *The Journal of Value Inquiry* 37/3 (2003):415–425.

Harris, George W. *Dignity and Vulnerability: Strength and Dignity of Character.* Berkeley, CA: University of California Press, 1997.

Hart, H.L.A. *Punishment and Responsibility.* Oxford: Oxford University Press, 1968.

Hershenov, David. "Restitution and Revenge." *The Journal of Philosophy* (1999): 79–94.

Heyd, David, and Hagit Benjabi. "The Charitable Perspective: Forgiveness and Toleration as Supererogatory." *Canadian Journal of Philosophy* 31/4 (December 2001): 567–586.

Hieronymi, Pamela. "Articulating an Uncompromising Forgiveness." *Philosophy and Phenomenological Research* 62/3 (May 2001): 529–555.

His Holiness the Fourteenth Dalai Lama. *Ethics for a New Millennium.* New York: Riverhead Books, 1999.

His Holiness the Fourteenth Dalai Lama and Victor Chang. *The Wisdom of Forgiveness: Intimate Conversations and Journeys*. New York: Riverhead Books, 2004.

Holmgren, Margaret R. "Forgiveness and the Intrinsic Value of Persons," *American Philosophical Quarterly* 30 (1993): 341–352.

———. "Forgiveness and Self-Forgiveness in Psychotherapy." In *Before Forgiving: Cautionary Views of Forgiveness in Psychotherapy*, eds. Sharon Lamb and Jeffrie G. Murphy, 112–135. New York: Oxford University Press, 2002.

———. "Justifying Desert Claims: Desert and Opportunity." *The Journal of Value Inquiry* 20 (1986): 265–278.

———. "Punishment as Restitution: The Rights of the Community." *Criminal Justice Ethics* 2/1 (Winter/Spring 1983): 36–49.

———. "Self-Forgiveness and Responsible Moral Agency." *The Journal of Value Inquiry* 32 (1998): 75–91.

———. "The Wide and Narrow of Reflective Equilibrium." *Canadian Journal of Philosophy* 19/1 (March 1989): 43–60.

Horsburgh, H.N.J. "Forgiveness." *Canadian Journal of Philosophy* 4/2 (December 1974): 269–282.

Jacoby, Susan. *Wild Justice: The Evolution of Revenge*. New York: Harper, 1983.

Johnstone, Gerry. *Restorative Justice: Ideas, Values, Debates*. Portland, OR: Willan Publishing, 2002.

Kant, Immanuel. *Groundwork of the Metaphysic of Morals*. Transl. H.J. Paton. New York: Harper Torchbooks, 1964.

Kekes, John. *Facing Evil*. Princeton, NJ: Princeton University Press, 1990.

———. "Pluralism and the Value of Life," in *Cultural Pluralism and Moral Knowledge*, eds. Ellen Frankel Paul, Fred D. Miller, and Jeffrey Paul. Cambridge: Cambridge University Press, 1994, pp. 44–60.

Kelly, Erin. "Doing Without Desert." *Pacific Philosophical Quarterly* 83 (2002): 180–205.

Kleinig, John. *Punishment and Desert*. The Hague: Martinus Nijhoff, 1973.

Korsgaard, Christine. "Personal Identity and the Unity of Agency: A Kantian Response to Parfit." In *Creating the Kingdom of Ends*, ed. Christine Korsgaard, pp. 363–397. New York: Cambridge University Press, 1996.

Lamb, Sharon, and Jeffrie G. Murphy, eds. *Before Forgiving: Cautionary Views on Forgiveness and Psychotherapy*. New York: Oxford University Press, 2002.

Luskin, Frederic. *Forgive for Good: A Proven Prescription for Health and Happiness*. San Francisco, CA: Harper San Francisco, 2002.

MacIntyre, Alastair. *After Virtue: A Study in Moral Theory*. Notre Dame, IN: University of Notre Dame Press, 1981.

Mackie, J.L. "Morality and the Retributive Emotions," *Criminal Justice Ethics* 1(1982): 3–9.

McDowell, John. "Virtue and Reason." *Monist* 62 (1979): 331–350.

McNaughton, David, and Eve Garrard. "In Defense of Unconditional Forgiveness." *Proceedings of the Aristotelian Society* 103 (2003): 39–60.

Metz, Thaddeus. "Censure Theory and Intuitions about Punishment." *Law and Philosophy* 19 (2000): 491–512.

———. "Judging Because Understanding: A Defence of Retributive Censure." In *Judging and Understanding: Essays on Free Will, Narrative, Meaning and the Ethical Limits of Condemnation*, ed. Pedro Alexis Tabensky. Burlington, VT: Ashgate Publishing Company, 2006.

Mill, John Stuart. *On Liberty*. In *Essays on Politics and Society*, ed. J.M. Robson, *Collected Works*, vol. XVIII, 213–310. Toronto: University of Toronto Press, 1969.

———. *Utilitarianism*. In *Essays on Ethics, Religion and Society*, ed. J.M. Robson, *Collected Works*, vol. X, pp. 203–259. Toronto: University of Toronto Press, 1969.

Minas, Anne. "God and Forgiveness." *Philosophical Quarterly* 25 (1975): 138–150.

Montague, Phillip. *Punishment as Societal-Defense*. Lanham, MD: Rowman & Littlefield Publishers, Inc., 1995.

Moore, Eric. "Desert, Virtue, and Justice." *Social Theory and Practice* 26/3 (Fall 2000): 417–442.

Moore, Michael. "The Moral Worth of Retribution." In *Responsibility, Character, and the Emotions*, ed. Ferdinand Schoeman, pp. 179–219. Cambridge: Cambridge University Press, 1987.

Morris, Herbert. "Persons and Punishment," *Monist* 52 (1968), pp. 475–501.

Murphy, Jeffrie G. *Getting Even: Forgiveness and Its Limits*. New York: Oxford University Press, 2003.

———. "Forgiveness in Counseling." In *Before Forgiving: Cautionary Views on Forgiveness and Psychotherapy*, eds. Sharon Lamb and Jeffrie G. Murphy, pp. 41–53. New York: Oxford University Press, 2002.

———. "Mercy and Justice." In Murphy and Hampton (1988): 162–186.

Murphy, Jeffrie G., and Jean Hampton. *Forgiveness and Mercy*. Cambridge: Cambridge University Press, 1988.

Neblett, William R. "Forgiveness and Ideals." *Mind* 83 (1974): 269–275.

Nielsen, Kai. "On Not Needing to Justify Equality," *International Studies in Philosophy* 20/3 (1988): 55–71.

Nietzsche, Friedrich. *On the Genealogy of Morals*, trans. W. Kaufman and R.J. Hollingdale. New York: Random House, 1967.

Norlock, Kathryn. *Forgiveness from a Feminist Perspective*. Lanham, MD: Lexington Books, 2009.

North, Joanna. "The 'Ideal' of Forgiveness: A Philosopher's Exploration." In *Exploring Forgiveness*, eds. Robert D. Enright and Joanna North, pp. 15–35. Madison: University of Wisconsin Press, 1998.

Novitz, David. "Forgiveness and Self-Respect." *Philosophy and Phenomenological Research* 58/2 (1998): 299–315.

Nozick, Robert. *Philosophical Explanations*. Cambridge, MA: Belknap Press, 1981.

Oldenquist, Andrew. "An Explanation of Retribution." *The Journal of Philosophy* (1988): 464–478.

Parfit, Derek. *Reasons and Persons.* Oxford: Oxford University Press, 1984.

Pelke, Bill. *Journey of Hope: From Violence to Healing.* Bloomington, IN: Xlibris Corporation, 2003.

Pincoffs, Edmund L. "Are Questions of Desert Decidable?" In *Justice and Punishment,* eds. J.B. Cederblom and William L. Blizek. Cambridge, MA: Ballinger Publishing Co., 1977.

——. "Does Responsibility Have a Future?" In *Law and the Future of Society,* eds. F.C. Hytley, Eugene Kamenka, and Alice Erh-soon Tay. Wiesbaden: Steiner Verlag, 1979.

——. *The Rationale of Legal Punishment.* New York: Humanities Press, 1966.

Pojman, Louis. "Are Human Rights Based on Equal Human Worth?" *Philosophy and Phenomenological Research* 52/3 (September 1992): 605–622.

Quinn, Carol. "On the Virtue of Not Forgiving: When Withholding Forgiveness is Morally Praiseworthy." *International Journal of Applied Philosophy* 18/2 (2004): 219–229.

Rawls, John. *Political Liberalism.* New York: Columbia University Press, 1993.

——. *A Theory of Justice.* Cambridge, MA: Harvard University Press, 1971.

——. "Two Concepts of Rules," *Philosophical Review* 64 (1955): 3–13.

Reitan, Eric. "Punishment and Community: The Reintegrative Theory of Punishment." *Canadian Journal of Philosophy* 26/1 (March 1996): 57–82.

Richards, Norvin. "Forgiveness," *Ethics* 99 (October 1988): 77–97.

Roberts, Robert C. "Forgiveness." *American Philosophical Quarterly* 32/4 (October 1995): 289–306.

Sandel, Michael. *Liberalism and the Limits of Justice,* 2nd ed. New York: Cambridge University Press, 1998.

Sayre-McCord, Geoff. "Metaethics," *The Stanford Encyclopedia of Philosophy* (Fall 2008 Edition), Edward N. Zalta (ed.), URL = <http://plato.stanford.edu/archives/fall2008/entries/metaethics/>.

Scarre, Geoffrey. *After Evil: Responding to Wrongdoing.* Burlington, VT: Ashgate, 2004.

Scheffler, Samuel. "Responsibility, Reactive Attitudes, and Liberalism in Philosophy and Politics." *Philosophy and Public Affairs* 21/4 (2002): 299–323.

Schmidtz, David. *Elements of Justice.* Cambridge: Cambridge University Press, 2006.

Shafer-Landau, Russ. "Retributivism and Desert." *Pacific Philosophical Quarterly* 81 (2000): 189–214.

Sher, George. *Desert.* Princeton, NJ: Princeton University Press, 1987.

Smith, Nick. *I Was Wrong: The Meaning of Apologies.* Cambridge: Cambridge University Press, 2008.

Smith, Tara. "Tolerance and Forgiveness: Virtues or Vices?" *Journal of Applied Philosophy* 14/1 (1997): 31–41.

Snow, Nancy E. "Self-Forgiveness." *The Journal of Value Inquiry* 28 (1994): 75–80.

Solomon, Robert. "Justice v. Vengeance: On Law and the Satisfaction of Emotion." In *The Passions of Law*, ed. Susan Bandes. New York: New York University Press, 1999.

Stocker, Michael. "The Schizophrenia of Modern Ethical Theories." *The Journal of Philosophy* 73/14 (August 12, 1976): 453–466.

Strawson, P.F. "Freedom and Resentment." In Strawson, Peter, *Freedom and Resentment and Other Essays*, pp. 1–25. London: Methuen, 1974.

Swinburne, Richard. *Responsibility and Atonement*. Oxford: Clarendon Press, 1985.

Tutu, Desmond. *No Future without Forgiveness*. New York: Doubleday, 1999.

Von Hirsch, A. "Punishment, Penance and the State: A Reply to Duff." In *Punishment and Political Theory*, ed. M. Matravers. Oxford: Hart, 1999, pp. 69–82.

Walker, Margaret Urban. *Moral Repair: Reconstructing Moral Relations after Wrongdoing*. New York: Cambridge University Press, 2006.

Watson, Gary. "The Two Faces of Responsibility." *Philosophical Topics* 24 (1996): 227–248.

Wertheimer, Alan, and Albert Dzur. "Forgiveness and Public Deliberation: The Practice of Restorative Justice." *Criminal Justice Ethics* (Winter/Spring 2002): 3–20.

Wiesenthal, Simon. *The Sunflower*. New York: Schocken Books, 1969.

Williams, Bernard. "The Idea of Equality." In Williams, Bernard, *Problems of the Self*, pp. 230–249. London: Cambridge University Press, 1973.

Wolfendale, Jessica. "The Hardened Heart: The Moral Dangers of Not Forgiving." *Journal of Social Philosophy* 36/3 (Fall 2005): 344–363.

Yongey Mingyur, Rinpoche, with Eric Swanson. *Joyful Wisdom: Embracing Change and Finding Freedom*. New York: Harmony Books, 2009.

Index

on strong retributivism, 212
on weak retributivism, 211
duress, 243
duty-based approach to analysis of
    forgiveness, 52–53
Dzur, Albert, 44

egalitarianism. *See also* paradigm
    of forgiveness, and equal moral
    status of persons
    and distinction between self and its
    qualities, 141–42
    and morally arbitrary qualities,
    142–44
    and potential for evil, 144–45
Ellis, Anthony, n. 13, 211
Enright, Robert D., 58, 115, 120
Enright, Robert D., and Richard
    Fitzgibbons, *Helping Clients
    to Forgive*, 59
ethics
    naturalistic approach to, 19–20
    objectivity in, 19–21
    two approaches to study of,
    18–20
evaluation of offender.
    See perspective of judgment
evaluative respect, 93–94, 98–99
exculpating excuses. *See* restitutive
    theory of punishment, and
    exculpating excuses
explanatory power, and pluralistic
    analyses of desert, 173

Falls, Margaret
    expressive theory of
    punishment, 226
    on reciprocity theories of
    punishment, 216
Feinberg, Joel, 175, 207
Fitzgibbons, Richard, 59
forgiveness. *See also* self-forgiveness;
    separating offender from
    offense
    affective component of, 34
    on behalf of another, 36–38
    bilateral, 65–66
    cognitive component of, 33–34

and condoning wrong, 75–76
as corrective attitude, 32
defined, 32–35
defined as response to
    wrongdoing, 34
and forgetting, 40–41
genuine forgiveness defined, 63
of groups, 45–47
groups as forgivers, 47–50
invitational, 65–66
and making ourselves feel
    better, 57
motivational component of, 34
motive for, 38–40
and passivity, 74
rational consistency as grounds for,
    96–97
and reconciliation, 41–42
and respect for morality, 84
and respecting one's own needs,
    73–74
and self-respect, 66–75
and speech acts, 43–45
solidarity as grounds for, 95–96
unilateral, 65–66
as unnecessary for some, 32
as virtue, 26
Fortune, Maria, 31
fragmented attitude. *See* attitudes,
    fragmented
French, Peter, 6, 76, 90
fundamental attribution
    error, 28

Gandhi, Mahatma, 70, 153
Garrard, Eve, 57, 93, 95
genuine forgiveness defined, 63
genuine self-forgiveness defined,
    110–11
Glynn, Patrick, n. 45, 50
goodwill, 96
Govier, Trudy, n. 18, 65
    on being conditionally
    unforgivable, 77
    on forgiveness of groups, 46
    on groups as forgivers, 47–50
    on types of victims, 36
    on vindication of victim, 70–71

Stocker, Michael, 97
  disharmony between reasons and
    motives, 2, 54
  "The Schizophrenia of Modern
    Ethical Theories," 2
Strawson, P.F.
  on distinction between reactive
    participant and objective
    attitudes, 6–7
  on objective attitude, 84, 101
  on resentment, 31
  on retributive reactive
    attitudes, 84
strict liability in law of torts, 209
strong retributivism. *See* retributive
  theories of punishment
Swinburne, Richard, 112

theories of punishment. *See* restitutive
  theory of punishment; justice-
  based theories of punishment;
  retributive theories of
  punishment
TRC. *See* Truth and Reconciliation
  Committee
trust and forgiveness, 41–42, 61,
  73–74, 98–99
Truth and Reconciliation Committee,
  47–50
Tutu, Desmond, 70, 81.
  See also Truth and
    Reconciliation Committee
  No Future without Forgiveness, 47

unfair advantage theories of
  punishment. *See* retributive
  theories of punishment,
  reciprocity theories
unnecessary harm defined, 197
utilitarianism
  and accounting for desert, 183

analysis of punishment, 5–7,
  211, 212
approach to analysis of forgiveness,
  53–55
as compatibilist position, 157
and important objection to
  retributivism, 183–84
structural virtues of, 183

value pluralism, 186
victims, types of, 36
vindication of victim, 70–71
virtue ethical approach to analysis of
  forgiveness, objections to, 55–58
virtue ethics, 3–4
  and focus on interests of others,
    55–57
  objection to, 3–4
virtue-ethical approach to analysis of
  response to wrongdoing, 168–70,
  277–78
virtues
  defined, 26
  possession of, 27–28
  ranking of, n. 18, 178
Von Hirsch, Andrew, 219

Walker, Margaret Urban, 261
  Moral Repair, 235–36
Watson, Gary, n. 45, 229
weak retributivism. *See* retributive
  theories of punishment, weak
  retributivism
Wertheimer, Alan, 44
wide reflective equilibrium, 2, 17–18
Wiesenthal, Simon, *The Sunflower*,
  116–17
Williams, Bernard
  and human point of view, 137
  "The Idea of Equality," 137
Wolfendale, Jessica, 32, n. 55, 87